DO IT LIKE A WOMAN

CAROLINE CRIADO-PEREZ is the author of *Invisible Women: Exposing Data Bias in a World Designed for Men* (2019). She is a British journalist and feminist activist whose work has appeared in *The Times*, the *Telegraph*, the *Guardian*, the *Independent* and the *New Statesman*. In 2013, she won the Liberty Human Rights Campaigner of the Year Award and was named one of the *Guardian*'s People of the Year, and in 2015 she was awarded an OBE in the Queen's Birthday Honours. She tweets @CCriadoPerez.

From the reviews of *Do It Like a Woman*:

'Striking... It is refreshing to read a feminist work informed by lives far removed from that of the author... Like any woman who is vocal in the public sphere, Criado-Perez has been obsessively threatened. She doesn't dwell on the experience, instead using her platform to shed light on the lives of others. There is bravery in that, too' *Guardian*

'If all the campaigning rhetoric has left you cold, you can relight the radical fire in your soul with this blisteringly essential manifesto. Eminently readable and deeply inspiring' Editor's Choice, *Bookseller*

'Compelling... a book full of fascinating stories and facts' *Prospect*

'Well researched and packs a punch' *Sunday Herald*

'A powerful and inspiring read' *Manchester Evening News*

Do It Like a Woman

... and Change the World

CAROLINE CRIADO-PEREZ

GRANTA

Granta Publications, 12 Addison Avenue, London W11 4QR

First published by Portobello Books,
an imprint of Granta Publications, in 2015

This paperback edition published by Granta Books in 2019

A CIP catalogue record for this book
is available from the British Library

2 4 6 8 9 7 5 3

ISBN 978 1 84627 581 4
eISBN 978 1 84627 580 7

www.granta.com

Typeset in Bembo by Patty Rennie
Printed and bound by CPI Group (UK) Ltd,
Croydon, CR0 4YY

This book is for my mother:
my inspiration and my holdfast

Feminism is like a tapestry; every woman brings her own thread.

LIZ KELLY

Women have been taught that, for us, the earth is flat, and that if we venture out, we will fall off the edge. Some of us have ventured out nevertheless, and so far we have not fallen off. It is my faith, my feminist faith, that we will not.

ANDREA DWORKIN

Contents

Foreword

Darling Caroline,

I don't suppose you'll hear about this during the day and worry, but it is already on the BBC website and it may be on the news tonight. So just to let you know I am, of course, fine: I'm in Bangui and this was in Boguila, in the north-east of the country.

'This' being the killing of about 20 people, including 3 of our national staff, inside the hospital run by MSF. It was armed militia looting, looking for money. Local leaders were having a meeting at the hospital and nobody knows yet what caused the shooting.

It's hard to explain the mixture of pride and misgiving that greets each announcement from my mother about which new crisis she will be attending in her work as a nurse for Médecins Sans Frontières (a non-governmental organisation that provides humanitarian aid in crisis zones). On the day I got this email, from the moment I saw the word 'worry', misgiving took over and my eyes leapt from the first line to the next paragraph. My mother is always telling me not to worry. I didn't want to read any more of her hedging and placating. I wanted to know what, this time, she was telling me not to worry *about*.

'Shooting', I read. 'Inside the hospital run by MSF'. 'Killing'. '3 of our national staff'. I wasn't worried. I was terrified.

It wasn't till later, after I'd scoured every news website for what little detail they revealed, and fired off an email full of unrepeatable language asking why on earth she wasn't being evacuated and sent home, that I read the crucial sentence. This shooting, although it had taken place in an MSF hospital, was not in her hospital. It was 400 kilometres to the north of where she was.

I was able to dispense with the images of my mother taking cover as pitiless militias roamed the corridors of her workplace. But I couldn't let go of the worry. The last time my mother told me not to worry, she was about to sail on a boat into Misrata harbour, under shelling from Gadaffi's troops, to evacuate war-wounded from Libya. I've learnt to take my mother's exhortations not to worry with a pinch of salt. In fact, it's when she tells me not to worry that I start worrying in earnest.

I try to keep the panic in check when it comes to Mum. No one wants her mother to keep heading off into danger; but I can't help feeling my desire to keep her here, and safe, is selfish. It's selfish because she could be helping people who in practical terms need her far more than I do. And it's selfish because I know how happy, how fulfilled, her work makes her. I also know that that feeling is gold dust, especially for women. Especially for women my mother's age. Especially for my mother.

Mum's story follows the lines of those of many intelligent women of her generation. Bright enough to be pushed a year ahead at school, but born too early for university to be an automatic destination. A decade or so of throwing herself into the religion of the time: free love, free travel and hippy experimentation. And then, love, marriage, three children, and putting her life on hold to raise those children and support her husband's career.

I didn't know much – or, in fact, anything – about feminism

growing up, but one thing I became increasingly aware of was a sense of my mother's dissatisfaction. We moved from country to country, following my father's work. Each new country meant a new language, a new culture, and, for my mother, finding a new way to give her life some meaning beyond home and family. Just as she got her teeth into something, Dad would announce he was being sent somewhere new. She would have to give it up and start again. She did it willingly – but that didn't make it any easier to handle.

But then, in her fifties, divorce. These things happen, of course, and no one should stay in a marriage that makes them unhappy, but it hadn't been what she wanted. To us, as children, it didn't come as much of a surprise, but to my mother it seemed like the end of times. I remember watching with helpless teenage horror as she withdrew into herself, becoming a desperate, suicidal stranger. She had nothing, she said, and no one. Having spent her life following someone else around the world, she didn't know who she was any more.

But slowly, step by step, she started to wonder whether this personal tragedy might be a chance for yet another new life, this time of her own choosing. She had always wanted to work with Médecins Sans Frontières, ever since she first heard about them in the 1970s when she was a nurse in London. But back then, she'd never had a chance to do more than dream, to wonder 'what if?'

Apprehensive but ever practical, she figured out what steps she needed to take to be in a position to apply for a job with them. And then she started taking the steps, one by one, until there were no steps left. Stepped out of excuses, she applied for a job. And she got it.

Since then, my mother has emailed me from the Central

African Republic, Libya, Tunisia, the Democratic Republic of Congo, Turkey, Colombia, Uganda, Nigeria... the list goes on. After a while, the missions blur into each other, apart from the moments of terror that stick out, when I can't concentrate on anything other than the latest news update. All I'm left with is that indefinable mix of pride and misgiving, misgiving and pride that this woman, my mother, didn't let life defeat her. She didn't listen to a society that told her that a woman's life ends when the wrinkles appear and the children leave. She proved that, in fact, the end of one phase of a woman's life could mark the beginning of a whole new one.

While the media is awash with venerable old men, it would have us believe that all women over fifty have retreated to the nuclear bunker built to protect us from the horror of a woman beyond the first blush of youth. There is a very simple explanation for this discrepancy. Men are fully human individuals. Women, in the words of Virginia Woolf, 'have served all these centuries as looking-glasses possessing the magic and delicious power of reflecting the figure of man at twice its natural size'. Rather than being human ourselves, we are a foil to male humanity. And who wants a wrinkly foil?

Do It Like A Woman is an antidote to a prevailing culture that tells women that they can only aspire to remain a foil for as long as their body allows – longer if they can afford Botox and eventually a good surgeon. It is an antidote to Woman as imagined by a sexist culture and propagated in books, films, television shows and magazines, where women are wives, sisters, girlfriends, crazed ex-girlfriends, victims, but rarely at the heart of the action. The famous Bechdel test for gender representation in fiction, films and TV is set at the absurdly low bar of having two named female characters talk to each other about something other than men, and even so it is rare to find a film that meets these criteria.

How, when and whether we represent women matters. Negative representations instil women with 'stereotype threat', which means they perform badly in contexts where they are stereotyped as incompetent – not because they *are* incompetent, but because a portion of their brain is given over to the desire to disprove that stereotype, rather than to focusing solely on the task at hand. Simply reminding women of their gender has been shown to impair their performance in maths tests. Likewise, 'impostor syndrome' has affected every successful woman I've met or read about: a woman can never quite believe her achievements are deserved. That she belongs at the top. That she can do it. On the positive side, the burgeoning field of role-model research demonstrates the palpable impact role models can have on a woman. They can influence her academic course choices; they can radically alter her knowledge of political candidates, and her likelihood of voting; they can transform her public-speaking ability, enabling her to speak better, and for longer; and they can even change her test scores, causing her to score higher than men who beat her in a test where she had no female role model, or a bad one. By denying women access to the achievements of women who have gone before them, we are condemning them to keep having to leap over the same hurdles, while men perfect their hundred-metre sprint to the finish line of full humanity.

This misrepresentation has to stop. We have to stop ignoring real-life women or reducing them to demeaning, inaccurate two-dimensional stereotypes. There are women from our past whose achievements need resurrecting – but that task is for another book. And there are women in our present whom we must not ignore or allow to be forgotten. This book is about those women, what they do and how they do it. It is about how being a woman in a sexist society affects what they do and how they do it. It is about keeping going in the face of hearing 'no' a thousand times, both culturally and legislatively. It is a book written in awe of and in gratitude to brave women who refuse to accept living life as a stereotype.

At the heart of this book lies the question of what it means to do anything *like* a woman – and, because you can't answer any question without first defining terms, what it means to *be* a woman. Do we have to accept the hierarchised boundaries imposed on one person because they were born with a penis, and on another because they were born with a vagina? If we don't, does it follow that everything that has traditionally been ascribed to me is worthless? If we were to accept, for the sake of argument, that women *are* more emotional than men (they aren't; we just don't count, for example, male anger as an emotion), should this be considered less valuable than the 'rationality' men are supposed to embody? These are difficult questions, because much of what we think we know about gender is tied up with value judgements to which we never consented. It's difficult to know where our socialised bias ends, and where reality begins. We will never really know the answer until we live in a utopia where being born with a vagina doesn't mark you out as an inferior being with an inexplicable liking for pink, and being born with a penis doesn't magically infuse you with the leader gene, a penchant for violence, and an inability to iron.

We don't live in that utopia yet – but the women in this book give us an inkling of what an answer to these questions might look like. They show us that women are not the deficient creatures we have been taught they are, and that perhaps we are wrong to reject so quickly everything we have been told belongs to women. They show us that we don't need to become more like men in order to succeed, to lead meaningful, fulfilling lives, or to be whole humans. They force us to question our preconceptions about what women can do, what it is that we value in humanity, and why.

This is why the book opens with a woman who not only pushes at the boundaries of what it means to be a woman, but who specifically pushes at the boundaries of what a human body is capable of – and cries while she does it.

Emotion is a curiously gendered trait: big boys don't cry, we are told. This is often positioned as one of the many ways in which 'gender hurts men too', and it is, of course. But we rarely think about the other side of that; or if we do, it is to point out that girls *can* cry. Girls can indeed cry, but it's not as simple as that. Girls can cry, are often expected to cry, are in many ways socially conditioned to cry – but, in the usual double-bind of being a good girl and conforming with femininity, when girls cry, this immediately confirms their weakness, their irrationality, their emotional incontinence. (We always knew girls were rubbish!) So when we tell boys not to cry, it's not because the act of letting salt water fall out of our eyes and sobs out of our throat is bad in itself. It is because crying is associated with the feminine. To cry is to be emasculated, to 'do it like a woman'. So, is crying bad because it's been gendered feminine? Or is it gendered feminine because it's bad?

It is questions like these that the women in my first chapter struggle with as they navigate life in various male-dominated environments. If these women were to 'do it' as women, would that mean to do it inadequately? Must they then become stereotypical men? Must they aim to help everyone forget that they are women? Or does their perspective actually offer something valuable? Can we break the mould of what it means to be a man and what it means to be a woman? Can we rebalance the hierarchy of stereotypes?

An eloquent woman is never chaste. This proverb comes from Renaissance England, but it is rare to find a moment in history or a language in the world that doesn't parade its own version of this adage. Chapter two examines the women who reject this feminine virtue of silence, and the price they are supposed to pay for rejecting it. It traces the connection often made, implicitly or explicitly, between loose lips on the face and loose lips between the legs – as if a woman's sexual desire is inherently bad and shameful. It ponders the power of a woman's voice, the fear it engenders in its listeners, and the importance of women continuing to speak up and speak out.

The inspiration for chapter three came from one of my favourite cartoons. A table is surrounded by men and one woman. All the men are turned to this lone interloper. The caption reads: 'Well, you're the only one who thinks we're a sexist organisation'. This Grizelda cartoon is funny because it taps into a truth about perspective: that the world looks very different when it has been designed around you and your needs. There's a great anecdote about this in *Lean In* by Sheryl Sandberg (the Chief Operating Officer of Facebook): when she gets pregnant, she finds it increasingly difficult to walk across the car park to her office, and because she is in a sufficiently senior position, she demands parking by the front of the building for pregnant women. She says in the book that she feels ashamed that she had never even considered this issue until she herself was pregnant – but if it hadn't occurred to her, what chance was there of it occurring to her male colleagues? Some feminists are critical of what Sarah Jaffe has called 'trickle-down feminism' that centres on the concerns of an 'elite' minority of women, and they are right that we would do women a disservice if we only focused on women who 'have it all'. But we also do women a disservice if we fail to celebrate the achievements of the women who are using their position at the top to offer a fresh angle and change the prevailing view, because in the world order as it stands, those with power affect all our lives, for better or worse. I would rather that the people making decisions about my life were people who had experienced the world from my perspective. And no matter how rich or privileged a woman is, she still has a woman's body, she is still treated as a woman by those around her: she is still at risk of being patronised, of being paid less, of being raped. Her perspective as a woman matters. Sandberg's change is a small one. But then the world is rarely transformed by seismic shifts: it's all the little individual changes we barely notice that make the difference.

In 2006, Catharine MacKinnon, the famous feminist lawyer, argued that rape law is written from the point of view of rapists. 'The most obvious sense is that most rapists are men and most legislators are men and most judges are men and the law of rape was created when women weren't even allowed to vote. So that means not that all the people who wrote it were rapists, but that they are a member of the group who do [rape]'. This might seem to be a tall claim, but the stories in this book, about justice denied, about women wrongly prosecuted after having been raped, must make us seriously question how gender neutral our justice systems are. Around the world, women are seen to be worth less than men – indeed, in some countries their lives are worth precisely half what their brothers', fathers' and sons' lives are worth. In chapter four, I focus on the women who, in their various roles – some as leaders, some as grassroots activists, some as victims – fight for justice in a system that is designed without them in mind, and who fight for that system to be changed.

In my final chapter, I address women's choices. 'Feminism is about choice' is a popular cry among modern feminists. I beg to differ – at least, I beg to differ while we retain such a simplistic understanding of what we mean by choice. Giving women choice is not about congratulating every woman for every supposed choice she makes simply because she made it while being female. That is not only patronising, it is a guaranteed method of making sure everyone feels better about nothing much changing. What giving women choices actually means is removing the barriers (legislative, cultural, internal) that prevent women from being free. In this chapter, I meet women who push against the limitations imposed upon them and others. These are women whose driving force is not to make women feel better by convincing them that they have chosen their chains, but to open their eyes and set them free to forge their truly chosen path through life.

Do It Like a Woman is a book that could have been written a million times with a million different women. I am not claiming that these are the definitive women of our time – another woman would have come up with a completely different list. But these are some of the women who are changing what it means to be a woman in the twenty-first century. They are women whose names deserve to be known. They deserve to be celebrated and remembered. More than this, *we* deserve to know about them. We deserve to know about the women who show us what can be done and how to do it. We deserve to know how brilliant, how game-changing, how inspirational it can be to Do It Like a Woman.

I

Doing It Like a Woman

It was the crevasses Felicity Aston couldn't stop thinking about. She tells me about her vivid daydream of falling into one. 'Usually if that happens, you're so badly injured on the way down that there's no way you're going to come back up.' Crevasses narrow sharply, Felicity tells me, so if you fall, you tend to get wedged in ice. 'And so you're pressed up against two ice walls, and probably you've broken some ribs, you've broken some limbs, you might have bashed your head. You won't have a first aid kit, you won't have any food or drink with you, you won't even have much clothing on. When I'm skiing, I have a thermal layer and then a windproof over the top and that's about it. So you're pressed against cold ice walls, seriously injured on the outside, maybe bleeding internally, but there's absolutely no way...' When she pauses to take a breath I realise I've been holding my own in claustrophobic horror.

'... no way you can get yourself out of there. You don't have to go very deep into a crevasse before there's no chance of any kind of satellite signal. *That's* if you've got your satellite phone within reach. So then you're just relying on this protocol to be rescued.' Felicity had to make a call to base camp every twenty-four hours. If she missed a call they would wait until the end of the twenty-four-hour period before coming out to look for her, starting at her last known position and moving out in ever-larger spirals to find her.

'So, there I am, down a crevasse… and I've got to wait potentially twenty-four hours, maybe more, before they even *start* looking for me.' And being found is by no means guaranteed: 'If you've fallen into a crevasse, you've probably left a little hole, but that's it. So you're almost totally invisible from the surface. And this is a deserted continent twice the size of Australia. When you start thinking about the realities like that, you ask yourself, "What on earth am I doing?"'

The orderly precision with which Felicity runs over the details of her potential death adds horror to her description. But this shrewd attitude to her own demise is, to Felicity, one factor among many that ensured her survival as she became the first woman to cross Antarctica alone – and the first person to cross it using nothing but the power of her own aching muscles.

'It sounds really obvious, but you don't go out there intending to die,' Felicity says. 'You have to be really methodical, you have to be a bit of a pedantic nit-picker to make sure that you've got all the details in place, otherwise it just wouldn't work. Even really basic stuff, like if you have to stop to redo a ski binding, you don't just stop and do up a ski binding. Once you've stopped, you have to take off your gloves and secure them. You have to have some kind of thin layer on your hands so that the skin doesn't freeze to the metal part on your binding. You've got to do something with your ski poles. Then you have to redo your binding and then put your gloves back on and pick up your poles. If you do it without thinking, your gloves will blow away, you'll get too cold, you'll lose stuff because the snow's always blowing and everything gets covered really quickly. And before you know it, you'll be in real trouble.'

It's the same with safety, Felicity says. 'You go out there feeling fairly confident that you've minimised the risks to an acceptable level, but you still can't shake the *fear* of dying. And that's what makes me keep my skis on, even though I'm sometimes really desperate to take them off: it's the thought of the increased risk of you going into a crevasse if you cross one, the thought of the serious consequences, the thought of death. It stops you taking shortcuts.'

Felicity ended up as an explorer almost by accident. She studied astrophysics at university, but having realised that she 'just wasn't in that top per cent to get one of the very few jobs available in astronomy', she switched to meteorology for her master's. A newly discovered interest in palaeoclimatology led to a dissertation on Antarctica, which in turn led to a stint working as a meteorologist for the British Antarctic Survey. Twenty-three when she first arrived in Antarctica, by the time Felicity left again, she was twenty-six. Many of her thirty-six months there had been spent without seeing the sun.

She was hooked. 'Once I'd spent that time in Antarctica there was no going back,' she says. She landed a job with the Royal Geographical Society in London, organising expeditions with sixteen-to-twenty-four-year-olds, and even got to go on some of them. But it wasn't enough. 'In retrospect,' she laughs, 'the RGS was a terrible place to work, after being in Antarctica, because everyone you bumped into at lunch, or in the lift, or in the tea room had just come back from somewhere exciting or was just about to go off and do something exciting.' She lasted about three months before leaving to start organising her own expeditions.

She wanted to explore Greenland, the Poles, Siberia, but a trip through Antarctica costs around £40,000, so for her the best way to do it was to take part in a ski expedition. 'Endurance sport has always been a means to an end for me,' Felicity says. And when she started out, that end was no more than discovering far-flung parts of the world. But, like many women who push at the boundaries of what it means to be a woman, on entering this male-dominated scene, Felicity started to encounter the word 'no'. Women can't. Women don't. And, slowly, her exploring became about more than discovering new places. It became about refusing to be told who she was.

It was Felicity's second winter stationed at the meteorology outpost in Antarctica, when she had been one of two women out of a crew of twenty. The outpost was about two hours' flight south from Rothera, the main base. Since she had closed it down for the winter season, the convention was that she would open it up again, as she would know where everything was. But, Felicity tells me, 'in his wisdom the manager sent a guy, a junior meteorologist, to open it up. His reason was that there was a lot of digging to be done. The outpost doubled as a refuelling point for the planes, so you had something like two hundred barrels of fuel that you had to dig out and have ready when the planes came in to refuel for the winter season.'

'I was flabbergasted. This guy was skinny, short, looked about twelve years old, and the thought that he could dig harder or more than I could was ridiculous! You know, I'm quite a large lady, tall and pretty strong, and it was just ridiculous, but it was this kind of ingrained mindset that, oh, if you need someone to do digging, you need to send some lads along, not Felicity. I'd dug out more oil barrels than anybody else I think, but that went unnoticed. Little things like that that would drive me absolutely bonkers.'

Another example of this ingrained sexist mindset tumbles

out. This time there were more serious consequences for the hapless men who'd been considered more adept than Felicity at slinging up a rope suspension bridge. 'I was the most experienced polar traveller there, and none of the guys on that particular team had any experience of doing anything like that.' But still her male manager put her on registration detail, rather than letting her carry out the task. The men ended up getting frostbite. 'So, you know, I think it was quite clear that the wrong decision was made,' Felicity concludes drily.

Then there were the all-male groups she had to train – particularly, Felicity tells me, the military ones, who found it 'very difficult to have a girl in her twenties as an instructor'. This manifested itself in not accepting her instructions until her junior male colleague backed her up, or in going and checking with one of her male colleagues that Felicity's advice had been sound. 'I'd be thinking: so, you're asking a man who's doing his first season in the Arctic, rather than taking it from me, who's now on my seventh?'

It took Felicity a while to recognise this behaviour as sexism. At first, she just assumed there was something wrong with her. 'Having been to a single-sex school, it had never really occurred to me that there was something I couldn't do, because we were never taught that way. Gender never came into it.' Her treatment in her new male-dominated environment came, therefore, as an extra shock. 'Once I'd realised what was happening, it made me furious.'

I always think of patriarchy as something like the film *The Matrix*. You are living in it every day, but you don't see it. Indeed, it is *because* you are living in it that you don't notice it: it's everywhere, in everything. How can you know, when you don't know any different? But then something happens to make you see the world in all its carefully organised inequality, all the hundreds, thousands of strands that make it up – and suddenly you can't stop seeing it. And the more you look, the more you see. It's inescapable. It can make you desperate, and it can make you angry. That's how it was for me, anyway; and it's how it seems to have been for Felicity.

'I suddenly saw just how limited the majority of women are,' she says. 'And it made me really angry, you know, just livid. And I was almost incredulous that I lived in a world where the majority of women aren't able to make their own choices in life. It makes me mad.' More than feeling mad, she felt responsible. 'I felt that I should be *doing* something to change this crazy situation. But what do you do about it?'

She decided that she needed to turn to what she was good at. 'The only thing I was good at was organising expeditions,' she says, so she set about organising an all-female expedition to the South Pole. 'Skiing to the South Pole is seen as a male thing, undertaken by explorers with beards with ice in them.' She tried to put together a team of as many women as possible from countries where they wouldn't just be the first woman, they'd be the first *person* to ski to the South Pole. In 2009, seven women, who came from New Zealand to India, Cyprus to Brunei, ended up joining Felicity on the groundbreaking trek.

The trip provided Felicity with a sharp lesson in just how quickly things could go wrong. She had been travelling at the back, as she usually did, when her sledge caught on a block of ice. Her team carried on, trudging inexorably away from her, forgetting the protocol of periodically turning round to check behind. She tried calling out, but the wind blew her voice away, and no one turned back. 'They got so small so quickly,' Felicity says. 'My biggest worry was that I was going to fall down a crevasse so that by the time they turned round to find me, I would no longer be there to be seen.' She eventually managed to heave her sledge off the ice through sheer strength, summoned up by her fight-response adrenalin, and rushed to catch up with her team, reaching them just as they finally remembered to look round.

But for all the horror she had felt at being left behind by her team, nothing could have prepared Felicity for being left alone on the edge of a vast icy desert three years later, at the beginning of her first solo trip across Antarctica: 'I remember being on the plane and it felt like there was a lead weight in my stomach, pinning me to the ground,' Felicity says of her flight to the start line. 'I was practically shaking when that plane first left me: that was one of the hardest parts of the whole expedition, the first ten minutes of it, just watching that plane disappear. My heart was racing, I was short of breath, my hands were shaking, and I didn't at first connect the two things. I was thinking, what's wrong with me, what's going on? Then I realised, gosh, this is what it feels like to be terrified. I was absolutely terrified.'

The terror did not overwhelm her. As she stood shaking in the impenetrable whiteness that enveloped her, 'this real sense of being where I was supposed to be came over me. I wanted to be there,' she tells me. 'I could see the landscape and I just wanted to be striding out across it, and I wanted to be out there by myself.' This whole trip was about testing her limits – both her physical and psychological limits, and the limits others imposed on her as a woman. 'There was something about crossing an entire continent, of finding out if I *could* do it. It sounds silly, but it felt almost like a sort of pilgrimage.'

She strode off, not thinking about the end, only the mental milestones she had marked out for herself. The Transantarctic

Mountains. The Pole. The Thiel Mountains. As she made her way across 1,744 miles, in temperatures ranging from −5°C to −20°C, and battling katabatic winds so strong they have been known to scour away whole valleys of snow, there were many times when she felt she couldn't keep going. But during those moments, she told the *Guardian*, 'the most powerful motivator was thinking of all those people who had underestimated me or put me down − I didn't want them to be right, *I* wanted to be right. And so I'd get the strength to carry on, to get up and go.'

It was a race against time: the last plane was due out of Antarctica on 26 January, and there came a point when Felicity didn't see how she'd ever make it in time. 'To reach the South Pole, I had done six hundred kilometres in twenty-six days, and now I had something like thirty-five days left in the season in which to get to the other coast. But I had twice as far to go.' The maths just didn't add up. 'I remember thinking: I *cannot* go twice as fast as I've been going when I've already been going maximum speed. There just wasn't enough time.' She left the South Pole convinced she wouldn't make it, that she was now 'just going for the experience, just to see how far I could get'.

It was only when the Ellsworth Mountains came into view on day 56 that Felicity let herself contemplate the fact that she might actually finish. And she did. 'I did speeds that I would never have predicted for myself.' She gives me various explanations: the wind being 'mostly' at her back; the fact that Antarctica is a dome, so she had done the uphill part and now she was going (slightly) downhill; 'I was getting fitter, my routines were getting slicker' − 'and,' she laughs, 'maybe I was getting a little bit more desperate'. Whatever it was, her daily distance increased from an average of about twenty-five kilometres a day to forty-seven on her 'biggest' day. 'I didn't quite go twice as fast,' she concludes, 'but almost.'

And this despite the bouts of terror brought on by the isolation of Antarctica. 'People tend to think of the Arctic and Antarctica as just two big white frozen places, but they're actually very different in geography.' While the Arctic is ice over water, Antarctica is over land, so dry that 'it's officially a desert'. This makes all the difference. 'When you're in the Arctic you're never far from life. There's always polar bears, or seals, or lemmings. There are islands where you don't have to scratch very far through the snow before you find grass and moss and little bugs and flies.' In Antarctica, she says, 'there is just nothing and it's one of the things that is just so different about it... there is *nothing*'. The desolation defies description. 'Nothing' just doesn't cut it when describing a landscape devoid not only of animal life, but also of plant life, and even, once you get a little bit further inland, of rocks. 'It's just ice and snow and sky.'

Although she prefers Antarctica to the Arctic (the humidity of the latter results in cold and wet clothes and equipment, and, she says, it 'is *miserable*'), Felicity acknowledges that 'at least in the Arctic you never get the same sense of having fallen off the edge of existence'. What you experience in Antarctica is a level of isolation that those of us who live in cities struggle to imagine. Felicity tells me about an exchange with a researcher. 'She was organising the logistics for a film crew that we were looking after and she said to me, "Once they get to the South Pole we'll just get them a hire car and they can drive themselves back."' Felicity laughs. 'I didn't quite know where to start.' She tried to gently explain that not only was there no car hire, there were also no roads, but she was met with brisk disbelief:

'"Oh, surely there's like a Hertz, or a… you know, we'll find something."'

I don't feel smug at the researcher's expense for long. My own ignorance is exposed when I ask Felicity about the psychological difficulty of a there-and-back expedition, rather than crossing from A to B as she did. The thought of turning round and going back across the same hundreds of miles you've just trudged sounded, to me, horrific. Felicity smiles wryly. 'I think the advantage that you have in the polar environment is that everything looks exactly the same.' She laughs before going on, 'In fact, this would happen to me a lot. I would stop to pitch my tent and the sastrugi, which are the formations of the snow around me, would look so similar to exactly where I'd camped the night before that I'd have a *whoa* moment, wondering have I come round on myself and is this actually exactly the same spot? And I'd have to work hard to tell myself, Felicity, don't be so ridiculous, you can see on your GPS that you're here rather than where you were last night, you know you have moved. But the landscape is so similar, particularly in Antarctica, that if you didn't have a GPS you'd have no way of knowing that you were actually moving anywhere at all, you could just be going round and round on yourself.'

The isolation and desolation-induced mind-trickery led Felicity to a 'wacky moment where I ended up running outside my tent'. She was looking for some tracks she'd seen earlier that day, and which she had followed briefly before they trailed off. 'Because I was worrying about crevasses, I put unnecessary importance on these tracks. I mean, it's the first rule: if you see tracks in Antarctica, which doesn't happen very often, the last thing you want to do is follow them, because you don't know how old they are and you don't know where they're going. You absolutely don't follow them. But, I'd seen these tracks and I *clung* to them. They made me feel some vague kind of safety.' But then they disappeared.

'I carried on for a bit, and then I ended up pitching my tent, and I got myself in such a state about the thought of these crevasses that, in my head, it was a *certainty* that I was going to fall down a crevasse and that I was going to end up in this horrible situation *unless* I could find those tracks again, so I rushed outside my tent, and I was in nothing but my booties and a thin layer, and I was rushing about searching for any sign of these tracks, and when I turned round my tent was just this tiny little blob in the distance.' The weather was bad, the tent was coming in and out of visibility. She had no way of getting back to the tent if she lost sight of it – 'and then I remembered that I'd left my stove on inside my tent'.

Felicity went on: 'I have no idea what came over me. The thought of going down a crevasse had just loomed so large in my mind that it had turned me a bit doolally. I ran straight back to my tent, and everything was fine, but it scared me, because it just showed how you can push yourself to a point where you can't rely on your own common sense any more, on the fact that you're making good decisions. And that's really scary. I mean, you tend to think that the base line of any situation is that you can rely on your own brain, and yet, sometimes you can't. People get driven mad by cold, or isolation, or just by the pure pressure of something, or mental and physical exhaustion. Your brain's not infallible.'

The isolation affected Felicity's mind in other ways. 'Being alone I found very difficult and unsettling. I became emotional and I cried a lot,' she says. 'When you're surrounded by a group of people, you suppress that, particularly if you're in a leadership role, as I have been most often. You know, you can't suddenly burst into tears or have a tantrum, because everybody else is drawing a lot of their own emotional equilibrium from you.' But on her own in Antarctica, her emotions found their way to the surface much more quickly. 'I found that anything that I felt on the inside very quickly manifested itself either in getting very angry, shouting or having a tantrum, or I'd get really upset and I'd cry.'

Felicity wrote about her experience as honestly as she could in her book *Alone in Antarctica*. Somewhat inevitably, this honesty inspired a rash of articles of the 'incontinently over-emotional woman' variety, my favourite being a *Daily Mail* piece entitled 'Weeping Her Way Across Antarctica'. 'It surprised me a bit,' says Felicity. 'It's slightly frustrating that out of all the subjects and issues raised in what I was writing about, they decided to focus on "she cried a lot".' She acknowledges that perhaps she should have expected this reaction, but says that to have cut out the emotion 'just wouldn't be a realistic representation of being out there. You're pushing yourself to mental and emotional limits and it's a very natural release.' Why, she asks, should she be ashamed of it? 'Everyone can relate to getting to that point where your automatic reaction is to burst into tears. It doesn't mean that we're weaker people, it doesn't mean that we're incapable, it just means that it's a coping strategy.' As Adrienne Rich had it, 'There must be those among whom we can sit down and weep, and still be counted as warriors.'

Part of Felicity's irritation seems to be a sense that she is being painted as a 'typical' woman. She's been asked why men don't cry. 'But I've had men who've not stopped crying the entire time we were out there. One time, a man became so overwrought and hypersensitive about everything, I actually had to say, "John [not his real name], you know, the crying, you need to rein it in a bit."' She laughs. 'We'd reached the point where we needed to get past it somehow.'

'People tend to think that women are more touchy-feely and supportive, but I've also worked with women who've been absolutely horrendous and real hard work,' Felicity points out. On the other hand, she tells me about past female explorers who have particularly inspired her. Women like Lady Anne Blunt, the Victorian equestrienne and breeder of Arabian horses who, after a long and miserable marriage, eventually left her philandering poet husband and became the only woman to ride with the Egyptian sheikhs. Or Margaret Fountaine, a lepidopterist whose quest for rare butterflies took her to Damascus, where she embarked on a love affair with her Egyptian guide, fifteen years her junior, with whom she would spend the next twenty-seven years making trips around the world, from Algeria to Australia, via the Caribbean, Central America, the Far East and Africa. In her diaries, she writes about falling in love in 'a very female way', Felicity says. 'It made me identify with her in a way that I can't with the stories of Scott and Shackleton because they're men who are writing in a very different mindset, men who would never conceive of a woman going to Antarctica to ski across it by herself. They wouldn't even think women would want to!'

Of the combination of fearless endeavour with romance, Felicity says, 'I think it's very woman.' And this is important to her. 'I hate seeing women who are obviously very capable but feel that the only way they can survive in their world is to effectively turn themselves into men. I've seen this happen, but I don't think that's the way forward. It's certainly not what I want to do. Why shouldn't you admit that you've got a softness for romance, or that you go weak at the knees when a man does something lovely for you? Why should I deny that that happens? And, in the same way, why should I deny that I have a good cry when I feel scared and upset? That's just a coping strategy. I think becoming equal is only possible if you're able to go about things in the way that's best for you and not feel that you have to do it in a way that's prescribed by a different gender.' And this is the crux of the issue. There is nothing inherently 'female' about going 'weak at the knees' – but similarly, there is nothing wrong with it. The only reason that we think there *is* something wrong with it is because of the admirably circular logic of sexism that declares it feminine because it is bad, and bad because it is feminine.

It's a perennial problem for feminism: you don't want to just accept that doing it 'like a dude' is inherently better – after all, that would be to reify traditional ideas of male superiority and dominance. But you also don't want to be forced to do it like a stereotypically defined woman, when that generally means doing it in an inferior or mediocre way – or, in some cases, not doing it at all. It's a fine line to tread – and one that London-based graffiti artist Amy Ash, spray-name Candie, struggles with.

'People used to paint on trains because you could get your name out there: it would run across the city, like a billboard with your name on it. And it's advertising your own self,' Candie tells me. Your own self. Not just any self. Not the outer self, the one that's owned by those you meet, you work with, you pass in the street. Not even the people who love you. This is a deeper, truer self, and this self belongs to you. And you're putting it out there to run across the urban landscape. You are shouting out, screaming in block letters with drop shadows: 'This is me.' The real me: Candie, rather than Amy.

I'm curious about Candie's choice of name to proclaim her 'own self'. Candie is, as she herself says, 'a very obviously girly name' – and if there's one thing she makes clear to me, it's that she does not want to be defined by her gender. When I ask her if women tend to be known as *female* graffiti artists rather than simply graffiti artists, she immediately says, 'Definitely, yeah,' before launching into a long account of her crew, Girls on Top, and the week-long celebration of women in graffiti they're taking part in, called Femme Fierce.

'I love the all-girl crew that we're in. At first I was a little bit like, I don't think that's cool, but actually it's just so much fun. There's nine of us and we're like best friends. We hang out, have a laugh together. When we go out painting, we're all a bit naughty and egg each other on. In terms of that, it's brilliant, I love it.' It sounds similar to the 'special energy' Felicity felt in her all-female trek. But as for Femme Fierce, Candie says, 'I don't really know how I feel about it. I'm along for the ride because it's fun, because all my girls are doing it and it's just kind of *joke*, but there's something about it that doesn't quite sit right with me, because I don't want to be celebrated as a woman in street art.'

Which brings me back to the choice of name. Why Candie? 'At the beginning I wanted people to know I was a girl, because there's so few people doing it. But my attitude has changed now.' She hesitates. 'Because… I guess… because I believe in my art now.'

In an odd way, choosing a 'girly name' when she was first putting her art out there seems to have been something of an act of pre-emptive self-sabotage for Candie. In a scene with such a clear hierarchy between 'graffiti artists' and 'female graffiti artists', to mark yourself as female is to relegate yourself. But it also offers a kind of protection. As Candie puts it, 'People can be like, oh it's a bit shit, but it's all right for a girl.' She laughs. 'Now I know I'm better than a lot of the boys, so I don't really need that safety net.' Her voice rises at the end of her sentence slightly questioningly, as if she's unsure. 'But,' she pauses, 'I haven't really thought about it.'

While she might not have been thinking about it consciously, it seems to me that this question of how women are perceived – whether she wants to paint with a group of women or men, whether she wants to be a woman or just one of the boys – is one that occupies a central position at the heart of her identity. An identity represented by a girly name.

Candie has been spraying her name on walls since she was about fourteen. As a bored teenager in Brentford, west London, she started 'urban exploring' in the wasteland of derelict warehouses and factories. 'There were offices with all of the papers still in the drawers, you know, it looked like people had suddenly left.

'I was climbing up onto a roof once, walking along, and my foot just went through. I was fine, but I remember seeing this hole and there was probably a three- or four-storey drop below and I had a moment of thinking, had I fallen, no one would find me. I suddenly realised it was a really stupid thing to be doing. But when you're a kid you just don't really care, do you? You're just there for a bit of an adventure.

'I'd take cans of paint with me and it wasn't like anyone would see it, so I could just practise on the wall.' The invisibility of her art is another contradiction: a desire to both stand out and disappear as Candie, 'some girl that no one knows'.

But Candie no longer wants to be invisible. Her dream is 'to be doing graffiti, doing my designs, and for someone to pay me, not only for me to put it up, but for it to stay, for everyone to see'. She has a love–hate relationship with London's most famous legal wall, in Leake Street: 'It's good that you can go down there and paint a piece, and have a lot of people walk past and see your work, but it will only last a day. And that's quite a lot of effort and time gone into something that only lasts a day. But I guess it's all about the photo anyway.'

At the time she was putting her foot through roofs in Brentford, Candie was also spending a lot of her time as part of the skateboarding crew in the Southbank. 'That's really where I started graffiti. Skating and graffiti are always more or less synonymous.' The skateboarding scene was another male-dominated arena – and it throws up another contradiction. Candie says it 'never really bothered' her, yet she tells me that whenever she came across one of her fellow female oddities, she found herself thinking: 'Oh, OK, we're going be friends because we're both girls.'

Although Candie 'never grew up thinking that as a girl I couldn't do what the boys could do' and felt accepted by the male skaters, it soon became clear that there was a difference: 'In the evening, they'd go off, but they wouldn't really invite me, because I guess they didn't want to chaperone a girl. And I always felt pushed out by that – especially when I was younger it used to get to me a bit how the boys would have their own little thing going on and although we were really good friends in the daytime, when it came to socialising, it made me feel like I wasn't really welcome in that context. But, you know, that's sort of just as it is.'

'That's sort of just as it is.' It's a phrase Candie echoes later on when I ask her if Femme Fierce is being put on because women don't tend to be included in the mainstream shows. 'If there's a group show it tends to be all boys. If they're in a crew, they tend to be all male but that's because they're all buddies. It's not because they're excluding women, it's just because that's how it is.'

Although she presents a convincing front of nonchalance, Candie admits that she *was* gradually demoralised by the loneliness and, for a time, defeated by being continually left out: 'When I was about seventeen, I stopped graff for years and years because I didn't really have anyone to do it with, but again, it's just…' She trails off.

It may just be how it is. But I can't help feeling glad that she's involved in an all-female collective, whatever her misgivings. Because otherwise Candie may never have got to the stage she is at today with her graffiti, precisely because of 'how it is'. And when I suggest to her that role models are a positive thing for young girls she immediately agrees. 'As much as I wasn't bothered to be the only girl, I want a younger generation to be able to look up to me and She [another graffiti artist] and the other girls I write with and see it as something that they can get into. Because, for us, there wasn't really anyone like that.'

The importance of having a mentor, someone to show you what it's all about – particularly in such an inward, secret-code society like graffiti – becomes clear when we start talking about the shadowy side of the scene. 'I'm sort of a legal artist,' Candie announces. Sort of – has she always been legal? 'Ye…' She stops and clears her throat. 'Sort of,' she says, again.

I try a different tack. Is there a stigma against people who operate legally? 'Yes, absolutely,' she says. 'I didn't realise that at first. When I started, I just liked graffiti. I liked to practise it and I liked to spend time doing it, rather than doing something quickly in case you get caught. Also I'm not really into vandalising someone's property,' she adds, and laughs.

And yet, a few years later, the illegal side of graffiti proved to be Candie's way back into it. When a friend of hers started dating a train-writer, Candie started train-writing too. 'That's when I really learnt what graffiti is, because I hadn't really had that experience of meeting other people who went and did it "properly", and to get a rep or to be taken seriously, you do have to do that.' And then she drops another of her contradictions: 'And I think, being a girl and being quite competitive as well, I felt that that was something I needed to do, for someone to be like, "Oh actually, she knows what she's talking about, she's not just a girl who's just having a go."'

Just a girl. Running through Candie's narrative is an almost unacknowledged sense that, as a woman, there's an extra wall you have to cover. Where a man can go out and create billboards for his own self and be respected for that, a woman has to first prove herself worthy of transcending her femaleness. Candie talks a lot about the 'positive discrimination' she could use to her advantage when she was starting out, and she tells me that one of the pluses is that 'boys *like* girls that do graff'. And yet, her desire not to be seen as a *female* graffiti artist, not to have her worked judged in the context of her gender, not to be patronised on the basis that she's a girl who doesn't know 'what she's talking about' suggests that, deep down, Candie realises that this supposed positive discrimination is something of an insult. An expectation of inferiority. And that, while it could personally work in her favour as a confidence-builder when she was starting out, in the end, it does her and her girls no favours. Instead, it points to the fact that men are still holding the overall power in this scene, even if only through sheer numbers.

This awareness comes into sharper clarity when Candie tells me about the emerging trend for 'girls and vandals' Instagram feeds (Instagram is a picture-sharing website). You can immediately see the problem from the name: the opposition between girls and vandals implicitly genders vandals as male. I think about how Candie at one point identifies herself as 'a part-time vandal' and realise that, for her, given how integral identity is to the graffiti world, this opposition must sting.

'With the rise of legal walls, there's more and more women getting into graffiti,' Candie says. 'And because it's always been such a boys' club, a lot of the boys, the majority of the scene I should say, don't take too kindly to all these girls coming along.' I wonder how this squares with Candie's earlier insistence that 'boys *like* girls that do graff'. They like a few, but not too many, perhaps?

But Candie doesn't like them either. 'A lot of these girls haven't paid their dues. They just come to it. They think they're graffiti artists because they're going down to legal walls and they use a bit of a spray can. Suddenly there are all these girls who have photos of themselves up ladders with little short skirts on, using their sexuality to flaunt their art and selling canvases and getting lots of recognition from it.'

It's not the recognition that bothers her, not really. She has a full-time job and doesn't need to sell her art for a living. But, she explains, 'there's a few very specific cases of girls getting into our scene,' – and she seemingly involuntarily presses both her hands hard against her heart – 'that we feel that we've worked so hard to earn a name for and to be taken seriously as a girl in this male-dominated scene. For them to come along and to not be able to paint properly or work seriously at it, but just know that they can become popular by pretending that they're doing what we do. That's not on.'

But it goes deeper than the sense of injustice at these girls not having 'paid their dues'. 'I think the thing that annoys us,' Candie continues, 'is the way that it undermines what we do and what we've achieved. That's the crux of it really. They're perpetuating the idea that it's all women are good for.' And, I silently add, perpetuating it to the men who think 'it's shit, but all right for a girl', the men who are still running the show – and, as it happens, running the Instagram feeds to which the new girls on the block submit their photos. But can Candie really blame these women for doing an admittedly more overt version of what she did when she first started out, and making use of that so-called positive discrimination when she chose her 'girly' name?

And of course, her name is part of this. 'If my alias came up in passing, someone who didn't know my work would assume that I was that type of girl, when actually I'd prefer to be taken seriously as a real girl writer who has been doing it for years.' This sub-genre of girls who aren't 'real' writers, who aren't vandals, is an assault on Candie's name, and so on her public identity. Her hard-won 'own self'.

There's little doubt that this is down to the male-dominated nature of graffiti – and Candie admits that, despite her reluctance to be party to anything like what she calls 'man-bashing'. These women can hardly be blamed for recognising where the power lies in the scene and doing what they feel they have to to get noticed and get ahead. The 'blame', if that is the right word, should lie surely with the men before whom the girls feel they must parade. But this makes the whole assault especially hard for Candie to bear, because there's little doubt that it was this very feature of the graffiti scene, the fact that it is so male-dominated, that first attracted her. 'It gives it an appeal to me. I'm saying I can do what you do. Like, your gender doesn't come into art really, you can be as good as a man doing art.' Like Felicity, part of Candie's identity was about proving that she could be a woman, but as good as a man. And to have that identity stolen away from her, and at the hands of the men with whom she tried to fit in, whom she looked on as her peers – that must feel disorientating. An unwelcome reminder that, no matter how much she may fight against it, no matter how much she proves herself and proclaims her own self on illegal walls, for some of the men – perhaps many of them, given the popularity of these feeds – women are ultimately best deployed as 'tits and ass'. No wonder she fights against it.

For women, legality seems to be a particularly double-edged sword. It's enabled them to join the scene in increasing numbers, but without the need for anonymity, the photos of girls doing graffiti are drawing more attention than the graffiti itself. This shift in emphasis might appear to lose some of the ground that women like Candie have fought so hard to claim as their own, but she holds firm. 'Girls who do graff don't have to be good-looking, they just have to be good at what they do and love it and have a passion for it and that's enough. You don't also have to be sexy with it. That's just selling out. Anyone can sell sex. But we're not selling our bodies; we're selling our art.'

Given how often the distinction between artistic talent and sexual availability is elided in male-dominated scenes, Candie's insistence that she is selling her art, not her body, is poignant. She may want to sell only her art, but she's not dictating who's buying. And that material reality cannot be changed simply by wishing it away.

The first time a man came up to Dana McKeon after she had finished performing a beatbox set, ostensibly to congratulate her, he looked at her mouth and asked, 'What else can you do with that?' Dana felt shocked and demeaned – as no doubt she was meant to. The message was clear: you might be a talented beatboxer, love, but don't forget I still see you as sexually subservient to me. Like Candie, Dana wanted to sell her art, not her body.

The issue for both these women is a clash of identities. Dana and Candie wish to assume for themselves the identity of artist, performer, human. But they are fighting against a prevailing culture where to be a woman is to be the subject of a gaze that strips her of interiority, and reduces her to what this external gaze can see and lust after – or find wanting. Such a being cannot be a fully independent human because its identity is reliant upon the perception of others. Such a being cannot have a stable identity, because no matter how strongly it may protest that it is who it feels it is, it is fighting against a thousand magazine covers, a million social media feeds, a stable of music video channels that market women as existing almost purely for the visual stimulation of others. Such a being's identity can only ever be a negotiation between a woman who insists she is a human, a performer, with an identity that is wholly unconnected to an external gaze, and the weight of the expectation that for a woman to perform, she is willingly giving herself up to that gaze and becoming one with it. This dynamic is at work when Dana finishes furiously working her mouth to produce a dizzying exhibition of clicks, snares, beats and song and the men in her audience believe (however subconsciously – which, after all, is how marketing works) that her performance was a pronouncement about her sexual availability.

But it's not just about sex. In fact, it's not even mainly about sex. In many ways, the reduction of women to the sum of their bodily parts is no more than a symptom of the trivialising of women and all they do. In a 2014 interview with the *Guardian* to mark the release of her new album, the pop-country recording artist Taylor Swift said, 'I really resent the idea that if a woman writes about her feelings, she has too many feelings,' adding, 'And I really resent the "Be careful, buddy, she's going to write a song about you" angle, because it trivialises what I do. It makes it seem like creating art is something you do as a cheap weapon rather than an artistic process.' There is a connection between the sexualising of women performers and calling their music too over-emotional or too personal to be art. (Ironically, Beyoncé has been criticised by a male commentator for being 'Living art, but art that says nothing', which goes to prove that as a woman you can't win.) Society cannot conceive of women as being serious artists with full access to the manly realm of the mind. They are too trivial, too occupied with personal private details, too rooted in the body to make art with a capital A, because that must address the 'male', public domain. It is exactly the same dynamic that is at play in criticism of Jane Austen for writing about such trivial matters as the coercion of women within the nineteenth-century marriage market, when she should have been writing about the Napoleonic Wars. In this context, then, the sexualisation of female performers is an issue not so much because of the nudity or sexiness per se, but rather because of the message it transmits about women's triviality, women's unmanliness in so far as manliness means access to the rational mind.

When Dana started out, she tells me, she used to get really offended at the constant implications that because she was performing in public, she should be available for private add-ons. But after a while she grew more used to it, which is tragic in its own way, although of course more convenient for her, given her belief that it's 'always going to be there'. The technique she has now developed is one of non-engagement. 'The second I notice someone is going to come up with that kind of comment, I tend to just walk away or shut them off. There is no point in arguing with every person who says it.'

But, like Candie, Dana turns the automatic assumption that her femaleness renders her incapable of running with the men to her advantage. 'You always have to prove yourself,' she tells me. 'There is always a barrier and they're going to think, "Oh she's a girl, she's going to be really bad." I remember once overhearing a guy in the audience saying, "*She* is the beatboxer you brought?"' 'But,' Dana says, grinning, 'by the end he was clapping and dancing along.'

Dana clearly takes a lot of pleasure in the volte-face she invariably conjures in her audiences. 'First of all,' she says, 'I'm Maltese, so being a foreigner from a tiny island, people are already thinking, "Why is she here?" And then, being a girl, "She probably doesn't even know what to do." But I love getting up there and looking at people's faces – and when you start to perform, you see their faces change from being judgemental to, "Oh, I wasn't expecting this." It's great to be showing people that you can't judge a book by its cover and to know that lots of people need to eat their words. It's the best feeling you can get on stage.'

Five years ago, Dana didn't even know beatboxing existed. Like the original beatboxers must have done, she discovered her instrument simply by inventing it. 'I hurt my thumbs playing basketball, so when I couldn't do that, I used to release my frustration by creating a beat while studying. And I tried doing this with my mouth and I suddenly started going...' She breaks into beat.

'There are two different ways of doing it,' Dana tells me. 'You can either breathe in between each beat so you put down a beat and take a quick breath in and continue, or there's something called circular breathing. It's similar to what didgeridoo players use. Basically, you can breathe in and out through your nose and push breath in and out of your mouth simultaneously, but at different rates.' Some sounds are also made on an intake of breath, like the snare sound Dana demonstrates for me, 'so you can catch your breath using one of those noises quickly', before blowing out with another sound. It all sounds horribly complicated, but beatboxing is about creating sounds, not thinking your way through the theory. For Dana, the circular breathing 'just came naturally'.

Excited by her discovery, she boasted to her friends, 'Guys, guys, look what I invented! I came up with this new thing!' Unimpressed, her friends informed her that her invention had, in fact, already been invented, and pointed her towards YouTube. Although slightly deflated at her demotion from inventor to beginner, Dana was soon making the most of an already existent and burgeoning scene. 'On YouTube, I came across an organisation called Beatbox Battle. It's the largest worldwide beatbox community.'

Except it wasn't quite worldwide: like Dana, most people in Malta had never even heard of beatboxing, let alone started organising their own inter-country World Championship qualifying battles. Not one to be put off by such trifling details, Dana called the organisers and asked how she could get involved. They invited her to Berlin 2010. By then, she had been beatboxing, mainly alone in her room, for just a year.

Dana had been prepared to be in the minority when she showed up in Berlin; she knew enough about the scene to know that it was male-dominated. But despite this, she was under-standably thrown by the 40:1 male-to-female ratio when she got there. 'I was very nervous about it,' she tells me. 'It was the first time I was travelling alone and it was the middle of my annuals at university, so it was a stressful time. But if there is a challenge, I've always been the kind of person to take it up. I also grew up with two brothers, and I'm used to holding my ground in an environment where there are more boys than girls. So although I was intimidated, I was also determined to just go out there and to say, "Hey, this is me and I can do what you do."' Shades of Candie.

'The first few hours were a bit awkward,' Dana continues, 'because everyone knew each other and they were wondering, "What's this girl doing here?"' She laughs. But once she got on stage and beat the first man she battled, the crowd became more receptive. 'I could see them thinking, "Oh, OK, she's actually not that bad." People started talking to me and I ended up making lots of friends. It turned out to be a really good experience.'

But Dana didn't only make friends in Berlin – she also qual-ified for the World Championships, where she placed fifth in the female category. It was, she says, 'a good start, I think'. Given that most of the other people there had been beatboxing for between eight and ten years, and had received at least some training, Dana's evaluation of her first foray into competitive beatboxing, only a year after having discovered it by accident, is something of an understatement.

Dana now teaches beatboxing, as well as performing full time (with 'a bit of physiotherapy on the side'). She tells me that it is still harder for women to get booked: 'When a promoter is looking for a beatboxer, they automatically think: I need a man. They find it hard to trust the suggestion of a woman.' But as each performance goes by and she becomes more established in the scene, there are fewer promoters who share that default assumption. The audiences can still be difficult too, she says. 'You do tend to get hate from guys who think that girls don't belong on stage and that this is a man thing, so why are you intruding?' And, of course, the online contingent are ever ready with their suggestions that she get back to the kitchen and make them a sandwich. But they are little more than evidence of how threatened some men feel when a woman achieves success in any sphere they consider to be theirs, and in any case, their jibes fall on deaf ears, as Dana continues to beatbox her naysayers into submission.

There are other ways of beating the odds and breaking down cultural barriers. In Afghanistan, they say that 'steel gets harder with hammering' – and Latifa Nabizada has been hammered more than most. Her journey to becoming Afghanistan's first female military helicopter pilot has been a turbulent one. But she believes her achievements have been worth it: 'You don't get your wish if you don't take the risk.' She is, she says, 'in love with the sky', and the closer she gets to it, the happier she feels.

As a child, Latifa and her sister, Laliuma, grew up looking at the sky. 'We loved playing outside in the open field.' She used to ask her mother to let them 'sleep outside in the open, to see the skies and the stars'. When she saw the birds flying, she says, 'it was a dream for me. I wondered if it was also possible for me to fly some day'. Together with her sister, she used to climb onto the water butts that lay dotted around near their home: 'I used to… imagine that they are helicopters and I'm flying on them and talking to stars in the sky. Me and my sister, we always talked about the stars and the universe, we spoke about how the aeroplanes were made and how it feels to be a pilot.'

After graduating from school with the kind of grades that would have enabled them to go on to study medicine or engineering, the sisters were determined to turn their childhood play into reality. They informed their surprised parents that they wished to be pilots, and convinced them to allow the sisters to apply to Afghanistan's military flight school. The military flight school was less easy to convince: the army doctor delivered the first hammer blow to their steel, as he conjured up non-existent heart and hearing problems, and failed them on their medical examinations three times. Eventually, a civilian doctor certified them fit, and in 1989, they became the first women to train in the flight school.

Their fellow students continued to wield the hammer. 'We were the only girls in that class and there were seventy-two boys. We were very scared,' says Latifa. 'The other students threw stones at us. We used to leave the classroom in protest – then our teachers would come out and apologise and we would go back in.' She is, however, surprisingly upbeat about this treatment. 'We were all so young and such things happened at that time.' Her phrasing reminds me of Candie's 'that's just as it is' and Dana's 'it's always going to be there': resignation seems to be a common coping mechanism for women who stray into male-dominated territory. 'Considering the social conditions,' Latifa says, 'people were quite positive about it.' And in any case, it didn't hinder the sisters' progression through the academy. 'We worked really hard and our exam results were quite good,' she says. Too good: unable to believe that the girls could really have scored higher than the boys, the school subjected Latifa and her sister to more rigorous testing than the boys had faced. They ended up being assessed by an entire committee instead of simply their own teachers.

Like Felicity, like Dana and Candie, Latifa saw her and her sister's eventual triumph not only as a personal achievement, but as public proof that women are as capable as men. She describes the day she was finally allowed to graduate as, 'a landmark day in my country where women are still oppressed and seen as less than men'. A day when she 'showed the authority of Afghan women'. A day when she 'hoped all [her] difficulties had ended'.

For a while, it seemed as if they might have. Latifa flew around Afghanistan performing her duties as the first female fighter pilot. On her safer journeys she would land in villages and find herself surrounded by Afghan women, fascinated by this outlandish, inspiring flying woman. 'These village women showed an incredible interest in me and my success,' she says. 'I hope I encouraged them to follow their own dreams.'

But the two sisters had qualified just at the time the Taliban was in its ascendancy. In 1998, Latifa was nearly captured as she delivered ammunition and other supplies to the front line. Villagers who ran to meet her as she landed told her the Taliban had just taken the area. Gathering up as many villagers as she could, she took off and made her escape under heavy fire. The situation continued to deteriorate, and Latifa, Laliuma and their family were forced into the north of the country, where they went into hiding. Before long, the Taliban was on their trail. A former colleague defected and delivered a letter to their new hiding place: it was a warning to leave within twenty-four hours, or be killed. There would be no refuge in Afghanistan for women who so flagrantly defied the norms of acceptable womanhood.

It was no idle threat, Latifa knew; they packed up what they could carry and climbed across the mountains into Pakistan. Their life as refugees began, and Latifa found work sewing carpets all day and into the night for just a handful of rupees. It was, she told a reporter for Australia's ABC News, 'painful and discouraging to fall from the high-ranking job of being a pilot to working as an ordinary, uneducated woman'. But she had 'no other option and no hope'.

And still they hounded her. 'The Taliban hated the fact that I was a female pilot,' she told the US news website *Daily Beast*. 'Their mentality was "How does this woman dare fly – and for enemy forces?"' They captured her brothers and tried to torture them into revealing where the women were hiding. The brothers courageously resisted and did not disclose their sisters' location. Someone else did though. Talking to the BBC, Latifa explained how 'one day we saw a newspaper that had a story about us, saying that a couple of Afghan women pilots had sought refuge in Pakistan'. It was a shock, she says, 'that made us scared to hell'. Nowhere was safe. These troubling women who resisted the earthbound box of femininity would be hunted to the ends of the earth. They must be made an example of, to remind other women of their place.

But eventually word came that the Taliban was being pushed back. It was, Latifa says, both joyous and unbelievable news. But she was ready to believe it. Rushing home to Kabul, she arrived at night, but went straight to the military base and announced, 'I am back and I want to start my work.' A few days later, she was once more in the air. 'It was beautiful.'

In 2006, in a fitting continuation of their parallel lives, Latifa and Laliuma became pregnant within weeks of each other and the next steeling began, with another episode that highlighted the difficulty of being a woman in an environment designed with men in mind. Knowing that their military superiors would baulk at the idea of pregnant women flying (the hormones! the horror!), she and her sister agreed to hide their pregnancies for as long as possible. '[T]here was a need for us to fly,' Latifa says, matter-of-factly. And so 'we kept flying' – and they did so until they gave birth.

Childbirth was the last thing Laliuma and Latifa would do together. '[M]y sister was going through labour, and at that time we thought it was a simple operation.' But it wasn't. '[S]he had a difficulty and she bled so very much.' So much that she was asked, 'Do you want us to save your baby or yourself?' Laliuma chose her baby. The next day, she was dead. 'That was a big defeat in life for me. All our life we flew together. Always we were together, we played together. She was my strength and I was hers.' Latifa took in Laliuma's child. 'I cannot tell you how it feels bringing up her kid,' she says. 'I cannot tell you enough how it feels every day without her.'

Latifa was back at work within two months of giving birth. 'I was very sad. Every day when I went to the office, I had to sign an attendance book. Her name was above mine. Whenever I saw her name, I would feel like fainting.' And there was the small matter of who would look after the baby while she was flying, as there were no childcare facilities – another relic of a previously all-male environment. But for a woman who had been so determined that she had even made her own flying outfits (there were no uniforms for female pilots, so she sewed herself tunics and trousers – an issue that also affects women in the US military, who only had uniforms designed for their bodies in 2014), there was no way a trifling detail like the lack of a kindergarten was going to prevent her from being airborne. Latifa simply made a bed in the cockpit and flew her missions with her baby alongside her. Her daughter, Malalai, is now five years old, and, Latifa reveals, while the usual custom in Afghanistan is for a child to give their father's name when they are questioned on whose child they are, Malalai always says, 'I am the daughter of Pilot Latifa.' 'She is immensely proud – and so am I.'

While there is little excuse for the Afghan military's continuing refusal to provide childcare now that Latifa has brought the issue to its attention, its initial oversight, together with the failure of the Afghan and US military to provide female troops with uniforms designed for their bodies, highlights an issue that is not often discussed. A lot of sexism is not so much deliberate and malicious as it is a problem of perspective – and an inability to be able to conceive that the world could be anything other than 'just how it is'. As if 'just how it is' is innate, or natural, rather than constructed by a society with only half of humanity in mind – in large part because the other half weren't allowed a voice.

Men are not from Mars and women are not from Venus. We are not two alien species. But there is little point in denying that there are differences in the ways we live our lives. These differences are partly as a result of our physical bodies not being identical – for example, women tend to menstruate and have wombs; men tend to have testes and produce sperm. The impact of these differences does not need to be particularly significant – but they have been greatly exacerbated by our living in a world that has been historically designed around the male body and the male experience. As a result, relatively minor differences in biology have resulted in ever-widening differences in experience and perspective. Those differences now need to be accounted for and correctives need to be applied if we are to have any hope of creating a society in which having a female reproductive system means exactly that, no more and no less. We must account for the perspectives and the bodies of those humans who have never been considered the default in arenas as relatively trivial as clothing, and as potentially life-threatening as drugs testing. We must challenge the concept that 'one-size-fits-all', when in fact it fits only men.

When she formed part of the six-woman Greenpeace team that was the first to climb the London skyscraper the Shard (at the time, the tallest building in the European Union) as a protest against Shell's drilling in the Arctic, Victoria Henry was surprised to discover the difference a woman's perspective can make. Rather like Felicity and Candie, it wasn't until Victoria had the chance to work with an all-women team that she became aware of the accommodations she'd routinely been making: 'All of a sudden I found myself experiencing a lot of things that I didn't realise I'd been missing before.'

It's a problem that is not specific to the world of activism, Victoria is quick to point out. 'If you walk into a room in *any* circumstance and there's ten dudes laughing and shouting, of course it's going to feel a bit…' She trails off. '… alienating?' I finish for her. I'm reminded of Felicity Aston's summing up of the main conversation topics in Antarctica: 'porn and poo'.

'I think a lot of women can end up feeling like they need to compete on those terms,' Victoria goes on. 'Or they at least need to relate to people on those terms, so if the vibe is really macho with lots of back-slapping and shouting, then that's the vibe that they feel that they need to fit into.' The one-size-fits-all vibe that fits women only if they, in Felicity's terms, 'turn themselves into men' – or at least the stereotype of what a man is. We clearly need more sizes.

Victoria's recognition of the male bias on campaigns was

sparked by the question of how the women would urinate. 'When you go on long-term actions where you're going to be stuck somewhere for ten hours, if you're doing it with a group of men, the whole question of what to do about having to go to the bathroom or being on your period is not even considered, right? A guy can just kind of whip it out and go at the side, women are left thinking: er, what am I meant to do?' In the midst of a 'macho vibe', women will often remain silent out of embarrassment, and even if these concerns are voiced, they tend to be given short shrift: 'Guys will say, well just piss over the side of the boat, but I just don't feel comfortable doing that. And, on this particular action – where we were going to be locked halfway up a skyscraper – well, you can't take your trousers down in a climbing harness, you have to take the whole harness off, so it was like: what are we going to do?'

But being with a group of women in the planned action at the Shard meant that her body was no longer deviant. 'We spent loads of time talking to each other, all like,' she shifts into a conspiratorial undertone, 'OK, what are you gonna do? I think my period's due, but I could just extend my birth control by a few days, or, you can take this hormone pill if you want, or how long do you think you should leave a tampon in for?' She grins as she tells me about the concern of the man who was helping them prepare for their climb. 'One or two of the women said they were going to be on their periods the day when the climb was meant to happen, and he went, "Oh well… well maybe we should delay it then?"' She burst into laughter. 'You do the math, right? There's six of us, twenty-eight-day cycle… it's gonna be a problem for someone!'

Victoria has been trying to get Greenpeace to customise its wetsuits for women: 'If you look at the wetsuits in the warehouse, they have a little flap for guys' – of little use to a woman trying to use a Shewee urinating device. 'So, you need to get a few where you've got a hole cut in the bottom,' Victoria says, laughing again, 'but it's not even considered.' On this action, however, like Latifa and Laliuma, Victoria and her fellow climbers took matters into their own hands: 'We got together and modified our clothes with Velcro and stuff,' she says, explaining that they also practised beforehand using Shewees.

Victoria recognises that this lack of consideration of female needs is a legacy of the traditional gender divide in the environmental movement. In the past, she says, women were assigned the 'Mother Earth role, while the men go out and save the planet. I think in particular with direct action environmentalism, women have been relegated to the sidelines as the helpers and the preparers of tea and the makers of meals and the cleaners of toilets.' While that kind of archaic thinking and the language that accompanies it does still crop up, she tells me that in recent years there has been a real focus on 'diversifying what kind of people get to participate in direct action'.

'It's partly that women are now putting themselves forward and demanding to be a part of direct actions,' Victoria says. 'Partly, it's that women have always been involved, but our contributions haven't been as widely celebrated – which is changing. And of course organisations know that their supporters are not just beardy, shouty men and that, rather than seeing someone who is a big strong hero do a big scary stunt, it can be more interesting and inspiring to see a normal person like you or me do something brave.'

But the balance between men and women in the movement and the kind of actions they are practically able to join nevertheless remains an issue. 'Think about the thirty people who went to jail in Russia [for protesting on Gazprom's oil rig against drilling in the Arctic]: they were a mix of men and women. Some of them had kids – but only the men. None of the women. Zero. The fact that the men had children but were still able to go on a two-month voyage through the Arctic certainly says something, doesn't it?' It does, although to be fair to Greenpeace, it doesn't only say something about them: it says something about society at large and the unequal sharing of care work between men and women.

There are two complementary ways in which we can address this issue. Organisations like Greenpeace (not to mention all workplaces) must stop conducting their business on the basis of a mythical workforce made up of atomised individuals who are completely free of any caring responsibilities. This has never been the case – or at least, it has only ever been the case for a small number of families where the (usually) male partner earned enough for his wife to remain at home, doing, well, wife-work. Working-class women, for example, have always worked – were, in fact, the original bearers of the curse of so-called having it all, having to work back-breaking shifts and then come home and care for a husband who somehow missed the fact that she had been working all day too. So too those who live in non-'traditional' households, lesbian and gay couples, single parents, the list goes on. The model of work that relies on a heterosexual couple where only one person has to work simply does not reflect the vast majority of the population.

Alongside this shift in working practices, we must challenge the expectation that giving birth somehow predisposes women to care work. There is no connection between possessing a womb and possessing finesse in nappy-changing. If the basic logic of that statement doesn't convince you, this was demonstrated in a recent study reported on BBC Radio 4's *Today* programme, which revealed that men and women were equally competent at looking after their baby immediately after its birth. Women only became more competent if, as time went on, they shouldered more of the care burden; conversely, where men shouldered an equal share of the care burden, they remained just as competent. The idea that women are predisposed to wiping bottoms is nothing more than practice being interpreted as innate function. The simple truth is that when you wipe many bottoms, you come to be something of an expert in it. And it's a vicious circle, because the more you wipe, the better you get, and the more you are considered to be an innately expert wiper, so the more you, and all the women who come after you, are expected to wipe.

And it's not just women. There are also many men who don't fit into the straight white male default human around which the world has been designed – so this is an issue for the majority of the world. 'There are so many people who can't do this type of stuff because of who they are,' Victoria says, 'and I think [the] activist community in general – I'm not talking about Greenpeace here, I'm talking about everything from Occupy to Uncut – hasn't left enough room for people of colour, say, for example, or trans people who can't really be safely taken to a male prison or a female prison, you know that's been a big concern of many trans people and I've known people who are poor, people who are illegal immigrants, people who can't afford to go to prison, there are so many people who just can't get involved in this kind of thing, it's certainly not just limited to women with children.' Victoria was, she tells me, 'really active with trans rights back when I worked in Vancouver and loads of the people I knew *would* come to protest, but had an agreement with everyone that we would do everything we could to protect them and get them out of there if anything started to go down because they were just not able to go to a gender-segregated prison.' Victoria's example shows how so much change can be down to small, practical solutions that address a precise problem. As for the other women on Victoria's climb team, 'we ranged in age from twenty-five to thirty-four. None of us have kids.' She laughs ruefully.

But although the political implications of the childlessness of her team matter, at a certain point in the life of an action, these considerations fade into the background, as the activists focus on the often dangerous task ahead. Greenpeace released a video of the women in the run-up to the climb. One of them spoke about the moment she realised what they had let themselves in for: 'I think when we first saw the building yesterday, and saw what we'd got to climb, like the landings were so tiny, and it was so high, we were all just a bit like, pfff – wow.' Another team-member was even more dubious: 'When I first came here and we were looking at the structure, and really *understood* what we were going to do, I wasn't really sure that I wanted to do it.' Victoria mused, 'It's a weird thing knowing that you're going to be scared and doing something anyway. You have to be very young or very foolhardy to feel no fear when you do something like this. I have a very average fear of heights, but it's very much what you do with that fear,' she concludes.

What she did with it was to embark on a gruelling fifteen-hour climb up 306 metres of sheer glass building. Arriving in a van while the city was still dark, the team quickly got out the ladder that was going to get them onto the roof of London Bridge station, from where they would begin their ascent. 'When they put the drawbridge down to get from one building to the other,' Victoria says, 'it was really far down, but suddenly it was just: *Run!* Go!'

They were noticed almost straight away by police – but not quickly enough to put a stop to the climb. 'As soon as you're attached to the building, no one would normally try and mess around with you, but of course the police had asked some emergency rescue climbers to come. And they just went…' (she mimes looking up, before adopting a deeply unconcerned voice), '"Nah, they're fine."' She laughs with pride. The climb had begun.

'There were six of us, three on each side of the building, and each person had a role,' Victoria tells me. The two women who led on each side were free climbing (Victoria was one of these), and the two women who brought up the rear did rope-access climbing. The rope-access climbers were needed, Victoria tells me, because 'we had a huge banner that we were hoping to be able to put up, and it was too heavy and too big for any one person to carry on their back. But because you're just hauling your own weight on a rope they were able to suspend these bags from themselves, and come up like that.'

Victoria is a distance athlete by training, so she coped well with the physical challenge of the climb. 'It was more mentally exhausting than physically exhausting,' she says. She felt the weight of the time and money that had been spent preparing the action – and the weight of her gender, worrying that, if they failed to complete the climb, it would be put down to their being women. 'I felt this huge pressure about us being all women: that was weighing *really* heavily on my heart and mind beforehand.' This had been felt by the other women on the climb, too, and the team developed 'summit madness' as a result.

'Summit madness is how they describe the mentality of

people when they go up Everest and one of their team members dies and they just leave them there and keep going.' She adopts a robotic tone: '*We've got to reach the top.*' She tells me that the team on the ground would periodically ask them if they were OK: '"It's taking a long time, are you sure?" And we were like, there's absolutely no way we're gonna come down!' At one point the police came out with megaphones, shouting '"*You are breaking the law by continuing to climb; come down*"' – again the robotic tone that I realise is her 'humanity lacking' voice – 'And we're like: no, shut up!' She laughs.

Another thing they hadn't expected was the presence of the many male builders inside what was still, at the time, something of a construction site. 'I was really nervous about that factor at first,' she tells me. 'That was definitely a gender thing: they were all men, we were all women. And of course at points we wanted to go to the bathroom and we had to tell them,' she starts to speak shiftily out of the corner of her mouth, 'Turn around!' She mimes hand gestures. 'Because it's all glass, of course, and everyone's standing there, right there, you're as close to them as we are now. So, at first, I studiously avoided eye contact or anything. But actually, they were really, really supportive, that was one of the biggest surprises of the day. Giving us the thumbs up, and showing pictures of us on their phones. One of them did try to give their phone number to one of us,' Victoria laughs. 'She was like, "I don't have a pen, sorry!"'

The police presence was also very heavy, and not just on the ground. 'There were helicopters as well,' Victoria tells me. 'So many of them, and being at that height, where a helicopter is nose to nose with you, is pretty weird. I'm sure they were actually quite far away, but in my memory, they were really loud and really close and it was terrifying. It made it hard to communicate with each other because we had to shout so loudly. It was very windy and really cold.'

In spite of the helicopters and the builders, the women made it to the tip of the shard to hang their banner. When they climbed back down to the observation platform on the seventy-second floor, the whole team was arrested for aggravated trespass. 'Obviously, we were wearing all this heavy gear, and they looked at us and said' – she breaks into a parody of a manly mumble – '"Yeah, you can take that all off."' Victoria says, 'We were wearing probably thirty pounds' worth of stuff which I had to put into two garbage bags: the harness plus the bag with all the banners and all the other stuff we'd taken up with us. And the policeman went to pick this up so he could take us somewhere and he went, "Ooph," as he picked it up.' Victoria then play-acts the exchange of gestures that followed this: her looking at the policeman with a wryly raised eyebrow and cocked head, and his acknowledging he had underestimated her strength with a respectful 'fair dos' nod of the head. It was a moment of victory I suspect Felicity Aston would have relished witnessing.

On the whole, Victoria says, the public were on their side. She was in charge of live-tweeting the climb as they ascended the Shard, and at first she hadn't been checking her Twitter mentions. 'But eventually I did, and they were so supportive, it blew me away. There were the inevitable one or two people who said things like' – Victoria breaks into robot – '"*I hope you fall and die.*"' Another joker came out with the outstandingly original quip, 'If these ladies are climbing the shard, who's making their boyfriends' breakfast?'

The media coverage was also mainly positive, but Victoria admits, 'There was one headline that really annoyed me: "Angry Women Get to the Point". I just thought, there's nothing about this that was angry, *nothing*.' She tells me about the video they put together, singing the music for me, 'It was really nice and happy and none of our tweets were saying, like, "F★★★ Shell", and you know, f★★★ everyone, they were just saying "Yay we're going to make it, we're sending this important message."' She draws in her breath. 'I don't know where they got that from. Why can't it be Women of Conviction? Instead, it has to be *Angry* Women, as though a woman gets really *angry* and then she does something crazy.' She laughs in exasperation. I reflect on how this would have been reported if it had been an all-male, or even mixed, group. I also reflect on how assigning emotion to women is so often used to undermine and trivialise our actions of, as Victoria puts it, conviction.

Not long after I interviewed Victoria, hostilities between Gaza and Israel erupted again. There was, as ever, much hand-wringing from the UK government over what, if any, action to take. Unhappy with the lack of a strong line, one government minister, Baroness Warsi, resigned. Cue the following headline from the *Daily Mail*: 'Warsi flounces out in a fit of righteous fury over Gaza', accompanied by the subtitle, 'But was her bitter attack on Cameron fuelled by her rage at reshuffle snub?' The language choice makes the intention to trivialise Warsi unashamedly evident. Flouncing, the idea that your sense of having been personally wronged is so great that it carries over into theatrical bodily motions, is a term that is for the most part applied to women (apart from when we want to demean a man by suggesting that he is effeminate). It carries clear connotations of childish, over-dramatic pique (this sense of flounce entered the English language at around the same time as the sense 'an ornamental appendage to the skirt of a lady's dress' – both in the early eighteenth century). The rest of the headline continues in the same vein by assigning irrationally overblown emotion to Warsi's actions. Warsi is not resigning, she is having a 'fit': her actions, this word tells us, are not rational. She is fuelled by 'fury' and 'rage', not conscience. She is 'bitter', not reasoned. Even 'righteous' implies a sense of her being puffed up on a cloud of her own self-importance. Nearly every word in this headline undermines Warsi in gendered terms.

Of course, this is just one headline – and who is to say it doesn't happen to men too? The respective reporting of Clare Short and Robin Cook's resignations is instructive in this regard. Both government ministers resigned within months of each other over the Iraq War in 2003. Both released letters explaining their reasons. But they were read very differently. The *Daily Mail* issued a very sober rendering of Cook's resignation. 'Robin Cook resigns from Cabinet', ran the headline of an article that began, 'Commons Leader Robin Cook has become the first Cabinet casualty of the planned war on Iraq'. The passive tone here is interesting. Robin Cook is not presented as the aggressor: he is simply a 'casualty' of the 'planned war'. The piece goes on to quote from his resignation letter, using neutral words like 'Mr Cook said', and 'He added', before quoting a fellow Cabinet minister's designation of his action as 'honourable'. Compare this with how the same paper reported Clare Short's resignation less than two months later. 'Clare Short quits Cabinet' – not for this angry lady the honour of a dignified 'resign'. 'Clare Short savaged Prime Minister Tony Blair and Foreign Secretary Jack Straw': unlike 'Commons Leader Robin Cook' – indeed, unlike 'Prime Minister Tony Blair' and 'Foreign Secretary Jack Straw' – Short was shorn of her role as International Development Secretary in her opening appearance. And again, not to labour the point, she antagonistically, viciously, unreasonably 'savaged' rather than resigned. While Robin Cook 'said', Short 'accused'. Cook's letter was quoted from at length and in full sentences, whereas the actual words of Short's letter were barely cited. The treatment of Short is more subtle than that of Warsi, but it is no less loaded.

When it comes to emotion – as with so many things – women are damned if they do and damned if they don't. When I was on the receiving end of a relentless stream of vicious rape and death threats in the summer of 2013 for having campaigned for female historical figures on banknotes, I was criticised for not displaying enough emotion – she isn't breaking down on TV, ergo this isn't upsetting her much, ergo she's making a fuss over nothing. The way I held it together in public was even mentioned by the Crown Prosecution Service as a reason for not prosecuting one of the more disturbing men who had fixated on me. But when, after a few months of non-stop threats, I did start to lose my composure, the line became: *Whoa, this woman is unhinged. Better disregard everything she has ever said*. It was disconcerting to see how easily I was branded 'mad'.

Women have for centuries been aligned with irrationality – it's part of the Men are from Mars, Women are from Venus thing. They are rational day; we are mysterious, scary, irrational night. So when we do not behave irrationally, we are breaking the boundaries of appropriate 'womanly' behaviour. This is unacceptable, even frightening, because if women can be 'rational', where does that leave the hierarchised binary of man/woman? Whence male superiority? So this behaviour must be punished by shaming the woman. She is cold, lifeless, untrustworthy, *unwomanly*. When, by contrast, we do display appropriately feminine 'irrational emotion', all is right with the world and we can be mocked, safely dismissed and looked down upon as the silly women we are.

It is always a source of wonder to me how male anger, which so routinely explodes on our newspapers in the form of rape, beatings and murders, hasn't earned men the label of 'irrational' – this is not a slur on men, merely an observation that as a species, none of us can lay claim to being fully rational beings. This is simply a feature of our humanity, as the field of behavioural science increasingly reveals. And yet women alone are considered irrational. Some of this can be put down, as ever, to 'that's just as it is'. Sometimes, however, this form of sexism almost by default becomes something we do consciously, as a way of delegitimising and subjugating women. Sometimes it is a form of sexism that is knowingly entrenching the 'difference' between men and women's access to 'rationality' with the deliberate aim of upholding a form of male supremacy that some of us old-fashioned feminists like to call patriarchy. You might, in fact, call such sexism 'misogyny'. It can be found in abundance within the world of professional sport.

If I had read, just a few months earlier, that the English Premier League boss Richard Scudamore had been exchanging emails from his work account with someone who referred to women as 'gash', in which he dismissed the 'big-titted broads' as 'irrational' 'double deckers', I might have been surprised. Similarly, when I read in 2014 that former Australian rules football player and now football pundit Sam Newman remarked of women in football, 'They serve very little purpose at board level. What do they do?' shortly before flashing his penis live on air in front of a scantily dressed nurse (and a 1,000-strong audience), I might have been shocked. Not because of the misogyny itself, but because of the context. I had naively assumed that the public expression of such antiquated and demeaning attitudes to women would have something of a career-dampening effect.

But when it comes to sport – and in particular football – nothing much surprises me any more. Not since I spoke to Anna Kessel, veteran sports journalist. The world she described for me was one that left me slack-jawed. It wasn't just the openly sexist 'banter' that permeates the world of sport, it was the unashamed nature of the discrimination and the way it seemed to be entirely condoned, even encouraged, by the sports establishment. I didn't expect sport to no longer be sexist, but I *did* expect those who are part of that establishment to feel the need to hide it, even if only a little bit.

Anna tells me that when she decided to be a sports journalist, she had no idea that she was stepping into a 'huge political quagmire'. She just liked sport and thought that reporting on it would be interesting and fun. She was prepared for it to be a challenge, she tells me, 'in the sense that being a tomboy at school could be a bit of a challenge, but there's a difference between having to be a bit of a plucky woman, and encountering actual physical barriers and outright hostility. I didn't expect it to be that serious.'

But it was. 'There are areas in sport that women are not allowed to access, because they are male-only.' The most famous of these are the last few golf clubs holding out against the invasion of the *ladies*, a word that in this context is simply dripping with tender derision. Anna tells me about Rachel Anderson, a top football agent, who was denied entry to the Professional Footballers' Association Awards in 1997; she had to fight the PFA all the way to the High Court and had the UK Sex Discrimination Act changed in the process. Strangely enough, waitresses didn't have to lay out £210,000 in legal costs to be allowed entry to the black-tie event.

Women are not just prevented from participating or socialising; they are prevented from doing their jobs. 'The dressing room tends to be one of those no-go areas for women,' says Anna, and that presents something of a problem for female press officers, club photographers and medical staff, whose job it is to access the players. The rules don't seem to apply when it comes to female cleaners, however: like the waitresses at the PFA dinner, they can come and go as they please. There are, Anna explains, 'awful double standards about what roles women can perform in what areas'. It seems that it's fine if women are carrying out one of the many invisible caring roles that enable the whole machine to run smoothly, but not if they're doing a professional role that involves engaging directly with the players and managers.

Less well known outside the inner circle are the football clubs that don't allow the fairer sex into the 'tunnel'. The tunnel is where the post-match press interviews take place – so not being allowed into this area is something of a problem if you happen to be a female press officer or a female journalist. You have to ask a kindly man to get your quotes for you. Or, if you happen to be Vicky Kloss, Head of Communications at Manchester City, you loudly announce you will not be barred from the Notts County tunnel, and force a change. It is striking that, having had the issue flagged up so publicly, the Football Association did not then force all remaining clubs that ban women from the tunnel to follow suit: that they didn't merely serves to highlight how unique a position Kloss occupies as a woman in football able to wield even such limited influence. It's an issue across the Atlantic too – one female football journalist working in North America told Women in Football, 'Security has barred me many times [from the press area] so then I have to go to the club to get them to talk to security so I can get my interviews done after the match. It's a huge hassle that's not needed.'

As with the issues over inclusivity in direct-action environmentalism, there may be an explanation beyond direct sexism that causes this particular problem, at least when it comes to changing rooms. In the case of Greenpeace it is that of wider society and the unequal sharing of care work; in this case, there may be legitimate reasons for not allowing women into an area where men may be naked. Nevertheless, if we take this at face value and accept that there is no deliberate sexism behind such a policy, there is a simple solution that does not require us to accept another 'that's just how it is' reason that discriminates against women: wherever female journalists are barred access, male journalists should also not be allowed. Otherwise, football will remain a boys' club where ladies get to serve and men get the scoop, simply because they are allowed to be in the right place at the right time.

Direct discrimination of the kind that prevents a whole class of people from being able to competently carry out their job is no trifling concern, but sexism within football can be even more serious. In Anna's position as co-founder of Women in Football, she has received reports of people being verbally, even sometimes physically, abused at work. 'It is shocking that anybody would be slapped round the face by a colleague during work hours,' she says, shaking her head at the absurdity of the idea, 'in daylight, in their workplace. I find that amazing.' But, perhaps it's not so amazing when you consider that this is an industry that welcomes a convicted rapist back into the fold with open arms.

And it's a pattern that is replicated more or less worldwide.

A US-based respondent to Women in Football's March 2014 survey reported that in the course of her work as a referee, '[I was] yelled at by a player I had sent off for violent conduct on an opponent. He continued to yell abusive things to me from the side-line, calling me a "fucking dyke", [and shouting that] "she likes to lick pussy".' In 2009 in Australia, a female referee was threatened with rape and warned she would not leave the ground alive during a rugby match – her brother, a former player, informed the press that 'there was not even one security guard to be seen', while in May 2014, a director of Football Federation Victoria (again, in Australia) was summoned before a disciplinary tribunal for abusing a female referee during and after a junior boys' soccer match. In New Zealand, Tina Karreman, a female referee tipped to represent New Zealand internationally, stepped down as a result of continual abuse: 'You get abused by players, parents, everyone. They think females have no idea about sport, especially a male-dominated sport,' she said, going on to describe 'the look of disgust' on a new player's face when told she would be his coach.

Perhaps it is inevitable that the misogyny in which sport currently festers seeps into sports journalism. The sexism ranges from the institutional and male-normative (as in the assumption that the male experience is representative of all humanity) to the flagrant. A good example of this spectrum is illustrated by the press box, which is, like other sports spaces, and like the Greenpeace wetsuits and the Afghan fighter pilot uniforms, designed around being male. Anna tells me, 'When you go into it, there are really narrow seats and you have to squeeze your body between a desk and a row of men. And so nearly every time you cover live sport, there are smirks and sexualised comments. I remember one time I had to crouch down on the floor to plug my laptop in, and a guy who was old enough to be my dad joked, "Oh well while you're down there, love, hahaha." And everyone else laughed, hahaha, isn't that funny.' From the normative to the actionable in one ill-thought-out space. And never mind women when they are pregnant – their bodies simply don't fit, and their increased need to urinate is hampered by a fifteen-minute half-time and the fact that the women's loos are often located a ten-minute walk away.

It's not just the sports clubs that are causing problems for female professionals; women don't get an all-access pass within sports journalism itself, either. 'Every sport has a journalist organisation,' Anna tells me. 'It's a kind of union in a way,' that organises professional networking events and high-profile annual awards dinners. Athletics writers have one, cricket writers have one – and boxing writers have one. Anna tells me that it's an all-male one. When I contacted the Boxing Writers' Club to check whether this was still the case (their website proudly proclaims that in 2012 they 'broke with tradition and allowed women to attend the Annual Dinner for the first time') they failed to respond. Women boxers have been officially recognised in the UK since 2001, and in 2012, Great Britain's Nicola Adams won Gold at the first Olympics in which women were allowed to compete. Yet women have to be 'allowed' to attend a journalists' party as if it's a special favour.

And then, of course, there's the expectation that you have to be a bit of eye candy. 'It's a massive problem for female TV journalists,' Anna tells me. She particularly singles out Sky Sports as the worst offender, with their stale dynamic of 'a male newsreader who's often quite old, with white hair, alongside a female newsreader who's in her twenties and often got her cleavage out'. The message, Anna points out, is that 'you can be any male body type, but you can only be one female body type'. She tells me that Women in Football is aware of pressure still being put on women to be sexy in their job. Many of the women who speak to her in private tell her how frustrated they feel that 'they're not able to do anything beyond reading autocue. That they're not able to get a senior role as reporters.' Still, maybe they should be grateful to have a position at all – when *Match of the Day* boldly flirted with having a female match commentator in 2007, the media and football world erupted with outrage. It hasn't repeated the experiment. Far better to leave commentating to serious journalists who complain about female lineswomen, sniggering that they won't understand the offside rule, or joke that a striker who missed a shot at goal should have put a skirt on.

A recent episode in North America highlighted how sexism in sports and sports journalism is mutually reinforcing. Karen Thomson, a female sports reporter, was interviewing one of the players after an ice hockey match, when he insinuated that she didn't know what she was talking about, based on the fact that she was 'female'. The exchange was later picked up on *The McNeil and Spiegel Show*, a US sports radio programme. Although the presenters initially condemned the comments, McNeil went on to say that he 'doubted a woman's ability to speak authoritatively about sports, and later in the broadcast commented that they should call Karen Thomson, hoping she would be available to talk about sports after getting the kids off to school, cleaning the kitchen, and making breakfast'. *SB Nation*, a sports news website, reported that they also read the following email from a listener: '"Here are [*sic*] a list of my favorite women in sports media." The list was blank.'

But Anna keeps going. Partly because, in an echo of the other women I spoke to who have trespassed into the male inner sanctum, being told she can't do something, she tells me, is 'a bit like a red rag to a bull'. And, like Felicity and Candie, she also feels a sense of responsibility to the younger generation. 'There is no way am I quitting now, if this kind of stuff is still going on.' Anna is contacted regularly by young women curious about getting into the profession: 'They ask about doing our jobs and you feel like you owe something to them to make a difference. I want it so that in fifty years' time it's just not an unusual thing to be a female sports journalist.' She pauses. 'Or twenty years' time, please. Ten years' time? Come on! Where *are* the female commentators on *Match of the Day*? *Why* was it even acceptable to have a national debate across national media outlets about whether a woman could commentate on football? Even in the supposedly liberal *Guardian*, a columnist wrote that it was tokenistic to have a woman.' Her tone is one of despairing disbelief.

Anna wasn't encouraged to play any kind of sport at school – or not what she at the time considered to be 'proper sports'. While boys played football, the girls played netball and hockey – 'but those sports were never on TV and I didn't know anyone that played those sports, so I didn't feel like it was anything that I needed to respect'. It's a particularly interesting example of the myriad ways in which we deliver the message that anything marked with the taint 'female' is lesser. Without anyone having to tell her, Anna understood the clear implication of being made to play sports that were not the ones we revere enough to watch as mass entertainment. It is the same dynamic as when we qualify any activity with the word 'female' and thereby disqualify it from being the 'real thing'. Men play football; women play women's football. Men are novelists, women are women novelists – at least on Wikipedia they are. I am reminded of Candie and Dana's resistance to being classed – and, implicitly, dismissed – as a 'female graffiti artist' or a 'female beatboxer'. It's all part of a sexist value system that establishes the male experience as default, capable of encompassing all humanity, and the female experience as deviant, even niche – despite the fact that we make up over half of the global population.

And it's everywhere. Gwen Sharp, Associate Professor of Sociology at Nevada State College, began a blog page in 2010 listing examples of products that betrayed this underlying cultural assumption. It contains such highlights as a 'LEGO Time-Teacher Minifigure Watch & Clock' and a 'LEGO Time-Teacher Girl Kids' Minifigure Watch & Clock'. No prizes for guessing which is blue and which is pink. She also includes a Walmart sign which reads WOMEN'S DEODORANT and, below, DEODORANT. A user submitted a screenshot from the US Post Office's website that lists magazines such as *Cosmopolitan* under 'Women', while the equivalent publications aimed at men, such as *GQ*, appear under 'Lifestyle'. In 2012, having for so long had genderless pens, Bic developed 'Bic for Her', rendering the unmarked version the de facto 'For Him'.

Indeed, this trope that men are human and women are deviant men is so entrenched that it even crops up when we are actively trying *not* to be sexist. A Berlin-based blogger called Sophia Gubb wrote a post called 'Sexism in Our Culture: Male as Default'. In it she provided a number of examples of how when males and females are pictured, it is almost invariably the female who has something added to mark her out as female, leaving the unmarked version as the male – the standard from which the female deviates. Examples included a picture of Moomins in which the genders were differentiated by the female Moomin having hair and sniffing a flower; and the traditional public convenience sign, where the distinction between the genders is indicated by one figure wearing a dress. (To hammer home her point about the arbitrariness of this choice, Gubb doctors the images to have the male Moomin sporting a moustache, and the male lavatory sign wearing a tie, so that the females are now the default.)

The cultural conception of women as anomalous can have even more obviously damaging results. Up until April 2014, the vast majority of animals used by medical researchers to develop new drugs and treatments were male. Only in a society that considers the female body to be an anomaly could this rationale, reported by the *New York Times*, have been acceptable: 'Researchers avoided using female animals for fear that their reproductive cycles and hormone fluctuations would confound the results of delicately calibrated experiments.' It seems rather odd that a researcher would conclude that the fault rests with the female body rather than with the experiment – and that perhaps the experiment should be changed to suit a body possessed by over 51% of the population. But it took an intervention by the US National Institutes of Health to force researchers to start using female animals – and if the time it took to reach gender parity in clinical drug trials is anything to go by, this process could take years. The upshot of all of this is that researchers tend to know far more about the effects of any given drug on men than on women, resulting overall in women experiencing more severe side effects and less effective treatment.

For example, the *New York Times* reports that in 2013, the US Food and Drug Administration had to tell women to cut their doses of the sleeping pill Ambien in half 'because new studies showed they metabolize the active ingredient more slowly than men do'. That seems like a pretty drastic difference to have missed. Statins, those supposed wonder drugs which so many people of a certain age are prescribed as a matter of course in order to lower cholesterol, were tested mostly in men:'evidence of their benefit to women is limited'. Even when researchers study diseases 'that are more prevalent in women – anxiety, depression, thyroid disease and multiple sclerosis among them – they often rely on male animals'. But research by Dr Irving Zucker, a professor of psychology and integrative biology at the University of California, Berkeley, shows that rather than women having particularly irrational, unpredictable bodies, it is in fact male bodies that are more variable.

This male bias, which is not just limited to drugs, can sometimes have fatal consequences. Writing on the topic, journalist Joy Goh-Mah pointed to research revealing that 'the largest body of knowledge on health and illness is about men and their health'. The male body, she writes, 'is assumed to be universally applicable, with women having "extra, womanly issues" like childbirth, period pains and breast cancer, neatly cordoned off into an exclusive section called "women's health"'. This is a mistake, as Goh-Mah illustrates with the example of heart attacks. 'Now almost everyone can tell you the symptoms of a heart attack', she writes, detailing the traditional symptoms of a squeezing, painful feeling in the chest, and pain in the left arm. 'Well, as it turns out, that pain in the chest is a classic male heart attack sign, and female heart attacks often have very different symptoms, more comparable to indigestion than chest pain. According to Katherine Kam on health information website *WebMD*, "many doctors still don't recognize that women's symptoms differ, [and] they may mistake them for arthritis, pulled muscles, indigestion, gastrointestinal problems, or even anxiety and hypochondria… many emergency room doctors still look mainly for chest pain".' Clearly, mistaking a life-threatening condition for something as minor as pulled muscles or indigestion is less than ideal. Similarly, a revolutionary new artificial heart designed for transplant fits 86% of men – but only 20% of women, even though heart disease is the leading cause of death for women in the United States.

But, as Anna reminds me, women have a role to play in this too. Many female journalists don't want to write about women's sport, in part because of this illogical framing of half of the global population's experience as statistically insignificant. Women's sport is much less high profile (because it's not the 'real thing'), and female journalists don't want to be pigeon-holed. Anna has sympathy with this point of view but, partly because of her own experience at school, she feels strongly that women's sport has to be represented in order to stop perpetuating the idea that it's irrelevant. 'I felt an obligation and a duty to make sure I was doing women's sport as well as male sport.'

Watching her daughter's enthusiastic reaction to sport has strengthened her resolve. Anna's husband is also a football journalist, so they often have men's football on in the house. 'My daughter's never been that interested and has talked about how Daddy likes football.' Last summer, however, the women's European Championships were shown, and her reaction was very different: 'It's the first time I've ever seen her *sit* and *stare* at the TV at these women playing football. And I thought, if you're two years old and that makes a difference… I found that incredible.'

This anecdote is striking for what it reveals about how early in life and how acutely we can be socialised into an awareness of what is important and what is niche, what is and isn't 'for us'.

Anna's story reflects the prevalence and power of the millions of unsaid messages beamed out into children's minds from toy aisles, from clothes, from television shows, from adverts, from children's books, from children's songs – even from schools and parents. But Anna's story is also hopeful. It shows, as all the women in this chapter show, that we don't have to accept that the world is 'just as it is'. We can change it. We can break out of these limiting stereotypes that tell us who we are and what we can do. We can imagine a world where a future generation of women will be able to take for granted, as men do now, that a society constructed with their full humanity in mind is 'just as it is'. And we can start to bring that world into being by making changes as small and as simple as calling men's football 'men's football'.

2

Speaking Like a Woman

'I am shouting but you don't answer / One day you'll look for me and I'll be gone from this world.' Not long after writing these words, Rahila Moska was indeed gone from this world. She was dead. She was sixteen years old.

Rahila was a member of the Mirman Baheer poetry society, a Kabul-based group where women come together every week and share their poems – and with them, the thoughts and feelings that they are forbidden to express in wider society. Rahila lived 700 kilometres away in Helmand, so she used to phone in to the meetings and read her poems down a crackling line to the assembled women. On days when the group did not meet, she would still try to call Ogai Amail, the coordinator, and read out her poems. It was a compulsion for Rahila; she had to speak. She had to be heard. 'Why am I not in a world where people can feel what I'm feeling and hear my voice?' she wrote. Unfortunately for Rahila, her family were listening.

When she was caught for the second time reading her two-line poems, her traditional *landai*, down the phone to Ogai, her family thought she had taken a lover – and beat her severely, locking her away. Shortly afterwards, Rahila phoned Ogai and recited, 'On Doomsday, I will say aloud, / I came from the world with my heart full of hope.' She never told anyone, not even Ogai, what she was planning. It seems her hope ran out, and less than two weeks later, on 8 April 2010, Rahila set herself alight.

Like Rahila, many of the other members of Mirman Baheer also write *landai*, a traditional form of Pashtun poetry. The word literally means 'short, poisonous snake' in Pashto, and this seems appropriate for a brief, often biting oral form that could prove as poisonous to its author as it was to its subject. It is for this reason that *landai*, historically seen as a female form, have always been anonymous and oral, passed down from mother to daughter, whispered in rooms where men can't enter. The subversive voice of the underground.

'*Landai* belong to women,' says Safia Siddiqi, a poet and former parliamentarian. Her proprietorial tone strikes a poignant note in a country where so often women are themselves property. 'In Afghanistan, poetry is the women's movement from the inside,' she continues. Sahira Sharif, founder of Mirman Baheer, echoes Safia's positioning of poetry as resistance. 'A poem is a sword,' she says. 'It's our form of resistance.'

In her formative text *Intercourse*, Andrea Dworkin wrote, 'Men often react to women's words – speaking and writing – as if they were acts of violence; sometimes men react to women's words with violence. So we lower our voices. Women whisper, Women apologize. Women shut up. Women trivialize what we know. Women shrink. Women pull back. Most women have experienced enough dominance from men – control, violence, insult, contempt – that no threat seems empty.' The women of Mirman Baheer are doing the opposite of withdrawing into silence in the face of a masculinity that suffers an existential crisis every time a woman opens her mouth.

The historical anonymity of the *landai* complements this particular form of resistance: although a lone woman raising her voice is an act of dangerous rebellion, there is safety in numbers. Studies over the years have repeatedly demonstrated that in mixed groups women speak much less than the men in the group, but in Mirman Baheer, not only do women outnumber men, the usual gender roles are reversed; while the women declaim, discuss, recite, the men are relegated to the act of silent support, seated in chairs edging the room.

In a country whose received narrative has for so long been dominated by images of active men fighting other men, while women perform the passive roles of weeping, rending their hair and beating their breasts, this role reversal is in itself a radical act. The words of their poems belie the idea that Afghan women have nothing to say about the state of their country. 'May God destroy the Taliban and end their wars. / They've made Afghan women widows and whores,' reads one *landai*, offering a little-heard female perspective on the outcome of conflict, one that has nothing to do with land and property lost and gained. 'Hamid Karzai came to Kabul / to teach our girls to dress in dollars,' reads another, its metaphorical punch at odds with the traditional image of a subservient Afghan woman hidden behind her veil.

For all the stereotype-smashing of the Afghan women poets, the hope they represent almost feels lost in a country where many women lack even the most basic tools of literacy. Indeed, access to learning is a theme that repeatedly emerges as the women talk about their poetry. 'Most women here are not educated. That's why we started a poetry club: to encourage women to grow,' says Gulalai, another member of the Kabul poetry society, in an interview with Al Jazeera. Although *landai* are traditionally oral poems, the women of Mirman Baheer do not restrict themselves to just one form – and those women among them who have been denied the right to read and write will recite their poems, while other members of the group transcribe for them. It's another way in which female solidarity can prove a powerful impediment to subjugation. But again, this hope comes with a major caveat. In Kabul, the meetings can take place in relative openness and security, but for female poets who, as three-quarters of the Afghan population do, live in rural areas, expressing themselves is more fraught with danger. Even for women with a high public profile, the private repercussions can be fatal – as they were for Nadia Anjuman, a well-known poet and journalist who was murdered by her husband in 2005, reportedly for writing poetry. She was twenty-five years old.

Karima Shabrang nearly became another of these permanently silenced women. Karima studied Farsi and Dari literature at university in Kabul before moving back to her native village in Baharak, in the Badakhshan province in north-eastern Afghanistan, where she became a popular and successful teacher. And then, in 2012, she published a book of her poetry, *Beyond Infamy*.

> Leave the buttons of your shirt open.
> Allow me to look at your eyes.
> And a little lower let me feel the heat
> and understand the warmth of the sun in your chest.

Such a potent expression of desire was too much for the local mullahs. When the news of Karima's scandalous writing reached them, '[t]hey said I should be got rid of. They meant I should be killed.' This was no idle threat. Karima's life was in serious danger. She fled to Kabul – and although she has been forced to live in exile, she is one of the comparatively lucky ones. She has not been killed. She still has her poetry. She still has her voice.

'Most Pashtun women are not allowed to express their emotions in society, not even in poems,' Sahira Sharif explains. 'But the spirit to raise their voice is always alive in them.' The resilience of these women is awe-inspiring. Despite the dangers, despite the framing of their voices as both irrelevant and dangerous, they insist that their voices must, *will*, be heard.

'I miss you… my hands are stretching from the ruins of Kabul,' reads one of Karima's latest poems. The unashamed expression of her sexual desire, alongside the evocation of an exile that resulted from that exact expression, is striking in its refusal to comply. 'I want to invite you to my room for a delicious smoke… and you will give me refuge in your shivering red body,' she continues, relentlessly. 'Even if it costs me my life, I will continue,' she says. 'To a life lived as a hostage, in silence, I prefer a dignified death.' Defiance, boldly evoked, shimmers under the surface of shivering red bodies and stretching hands in her poem; it spills out in plain language. She has made her choice. She has chosen her voice. She is prepared to die for that right.

Eliza Griswold, an American journalist and poet, encountered the same irrepressible desire for expression when she travelled to Helmand in search of Rahila Moska's family. Finding herself in a room where women were being instructed about the exaggerated health benefits of tomatoes and okra (an initiative dreamed up by the Afghan government to curb poppy cultivation), she asked if any of the women liked poetry. In response, Gulmakai, who 'was twenty-two but looked forty-five', stood up and started 'what looked like freestyle rapping in Pashto'. She brought her performance to a close with a final grotesque *landai*: 'Making love to an old man / is like fucking a shrivelled cornstalk blackened by mould.' The room burst into raucous laughter. It somehow seems less funny when Gulmakai delivers her punchline, 'I know this is true. My father married me to an old man when I was fifteen.' She tries to go on, but is silenced by the workshop leader – a man.

Gulmakai's delivery is contemporary and her scornful laughter is overt, but her experience and her rage are all too familiar, and echo the traditional *landai*:

> You sold me to an old man, father.
> May God destroy your home, I was your daughter.

'When we recite our poems, we remove our pain,' says Seeta Habibi, a journalist who shares the fate of so many other women writers, having been forced out of her home province by threats.

> When sisters sit together, they always praise their brothers.
> When brothers sit together, they sell their sisters to others.

Seeta is listed as Country Director for the Afghan Women's Writing Project – an organisation that supports women who want to tell their stories. 'To tell one's story is a human right,' runs their strapline – and there are shifts towards the acceptance of this claim: in 2012, a literary prize open only to women was established in Afghanistan. One of the winners, eighteen-year-old Shkola Zadran, said that she hoped to be an example for other women and girls who may be struggling with a voice inside them that won't be repressed.

The anonymous silhouette that is used instead of a photograph to illustrate Seeta's brief listing on the Afghan Women's

Writing Project website is a brutal reminder of how contentious that right is for women. Seeta's biography on the website is short and free of details, saying only that, along with her family, she was forced to 'relocate' – that ominously neutral-sounding word – and give up her position as the only female journalist in Farah province. It is hard not to look at the weight of the forces set against these brave women who refuse to be quiet, and wonder how they can ever prevail. 'I dream I am the president. / When I awake, I am the beggar of the world,' reads the *landai* that inspired the title *I am the Beggar of the World*, a collection of Afghan women's poems edited by Eliza Griswold. And yet these women who dream of presidency but awake to the penury of womanhood keep going – which in itself is cause for hope. 'We talk to the paper with our pen and we fight for our rights on paper,' Seeta says. 'Someday, we hope we will win.'

Another woman who puts her faith in her pen is Mae Azango, a journalist from Liberia, whose unflinching reporting forced her government into outlawing female genital mutilation in 2012. It is in her pen, she tells me, that she learned her power lay. She discovered this power, it seems, by sheer chance, while on a journalism course she took just for something to do. 'To pass the time,' she says.

She had recently returned from years in exile in the Ivory Coast, at the end of the second Liberian Civil War. 'It was awful,' she says of her time as a refugee. 'You have no rights. You are expected to know your place, and it is the place of a second-class citizen.' She corrects herself, 'Less than a second-class citizen.' She found herself pushed in the street, called a dog, subject to the cruel whims of rapacious private landlords. 'That's how life was in Côte d'Ivoire. You are a refugee, you are being trampled upon, you are desperate, *nobody* to speak on your behalf, so.'

Eventually in 2002, after almost six years in exile, Mae was able to return to Liberia permanently, but her joy at coming home was tempered by what she saw when she got there. 'I met people in my country living in utter poverty,' she says. Utter poverty combined with endemic violence, carried out with impunity. 'I saw domestic violence, sexual violence, gender violence, I saw all this violence.' But she saw no punishment. 'When these people go to court it's the same thing. The perpetrators have money and they bribe the police, but the poor have no money, and without money, *nobody* speaks on your behalf.' It was a state Mae knew well from her time in the Ivory Coast. But she wasn't a refugee any more, so she set about putting the skills she'd learned on her journalism course into practice.

Mae started off working as a police reporter for the Liberian *Telegraph*, before moving on in 2005 to write for the *Daily Observer*. She was fired from the latter position after she spoke up in 2007 about the widespread sexual harassment of female journalists in Liberia, but was soon picked up by the more liberal-minded *FrontPage Africa*, where she still works today. And, as was to become a pattern for Mae, she chose not to accept any kind of moral from this lesson that would have led to her being cowed into silence in the face of injustice. 'I decided to use my pen to shock the destiny of my country,' Mae says. 'And in using my pen I decided to talk to the poor people, because they are the ones whose rights are being violated, and they have a story, but they don't have a voice.' Mae felt that if she didn't tell that story of the people she saw every day, 'the government wouldn't know'. Or, perhaps it's more accurate to say, the government wouldn't be forced to care and forced to act. Forcing action is something Mae prides herself on. Her motto, she tells me, is P-U-S-H.

'I write for results. I don't just write. I write for something to *happen*. It is PUSH! P is for push! U is for until, S is for something, H is for happens! Push until something happens! That is what I pushed for, something to happen that stopped it.'

The 'it' she's talking about is female genital mutilation, or FGM. Because so few people speak about it, it is hard to gather exact numbers of women who have undergone the procedure. Globally, it is estimated that more than 125 million women have been mutilated, often by a practitioner with no medical implements or training, without anaesthetic or even antiseptic. In Somalia, Guinea and Egypt, among other countries, over 90% of girls will have experienced this trauma. In Mae's home country of Liberia, it is a practice that is carried out by ten out of Liberia's sixteen tribes. A 2007 Department of Health Services study showed that 72% of Liberian women had been cut. All these women were being 'violated', Mae told me, and yet 'they don't *talk* about it'. I had only been chatting to Mae for about ten minutes, but I already knew that this combination of violence and silence would have been enough to trigger her fierce sense of justice. She decided to address her pen to this most unspoken of taboos.

Her first piece, published by *FrontPage Africa*, reported on the long-term effects of the procedure on women's lives – specifically, on their relationships with men. Many women who had undergone FGM couldn't find husbands, Mae discovered. Others who found sex painful as a result were left by their husbands. The piece passed more or less without comment.

In her next piece Mae turned her attention to the procedure itself. One of the cases she focused on was that of Ma Sabah (not her real name), who had been cut as a teenager and whose husband had later left her ('And why do you think he left her?' Mae asked me, rhetorically). Ma Sabah told Mae what had been done to her out in the bush by the secretive Sande society. 'There were four women who knocked her to the ground, and the fifth woman sat on her, used the knife, and cut her brutally, without even sterilising. Without even anaesthesia… This woman still recalls that incident. She is now in her fifties, but she still recalls that incident. They did it to her when she was thirteen.'

The piece was published by *FrontPage Africa* on International Women's Day 2012, and it spread across the international print media, the airwaves and the Internet like bushfire. A group of angry but ominously silent women went to find Mae at her office; another troop of women turned up at her house, looking for Mae's nine-year-old daughter. 'They told me that the penalty for what I did was death.'

That the enforcers of this shadowy, threatening group are women may seem shocking. When people find out that women traditionally carry out FGM, when people hear about women hurting other women, as they themselves have been hurt in their turn, they are confused. Sometimes they use it to defend the practice – if women are doing it to themselves, it can't be that bad, so the refrain goes. This same attitude was expressed in a baffled response by the UK media to 2014 research by the think tank Demos which found that women were using misogynistic language towards each other on Twitter. But to be shocked at this, to think that women behaving badly towards other women disproves the existence of misogyny, is to misunderstand how society works.

Women are brought up in the same women-hating society as men – there is no logical reason why they should be free of misogynistic thinking. Self-preservation would, you might think, kick in, and cause women to stop the cycle. But there is safety in joining in and attacking other women, far more so than standing up against it, where you become a focus for attack. Better to deflect it onto others, in the hope that the executioner will spare you. Of course, the dynamic is different when it comes to FGM, since the motive of deflection is missing, but the fear of what is portrayed as monstrous womanhood, the belief in the horror and shame of femaleness – and particularly of female sexuality – is the same. It is noteworthy that the words women were using on Twitter, as highlighted by Demos, were 'whore' and 'slut'.

Mae was threatened not only with death, but also with being cut herself. 'They threatened to drag me to the Sande bush and have me circumcised, so that when I leave from there I won't tell. They said I would have to swear an oath not to tell, and if I tell, then my family will find me dead one day, one way or another. They said the penalty for what I did was death. But first they wanted to catch me and initiate me. That was my punishment.' The act that is promoted by its defenders as a joyous initiation into womanhood can also be unblinkingly wielded as a threat, a means by which wayward women can be corrected. Ma Sabah, the woman whose testimony Mae had given voice to in her article, had also been cut as a punishment: 'she had been forced into the Sande bush for a crime her mother committed in her village in 1976'.

As a result of the threats, Mae was forced into hiding, as the police and government refused to protect her. Mae was not surprised the police wouldn't help, as she had previously reported on the rape of a thirteen-year-old girl by a police officer. 'That guy was walking around for *three months*,' Mae says. He was arrested two days after her article – but that made her no friends in high places. She made enemies within the government too, when one of her pieces on police brutality was published on Liberia's Independence Day. Foreign dignitaries arrived on what was meant to be a day of celebration to see embarrassing headlines about corruption and violence. But eventually, the international row sparked by Mae's article forced the government to publicly announce that the Sande society's practice of FGM was to be suspended indefinitely. Once again, Mae had got something to happen.

The 'something' that Mae brought about in a country where the majority of women have been subjected to legally sanctioned FGM is remarkable. The extent of Mae's achievement is borne out by the struggle Nimco Ali has faced in her battle to get the issue of FGM acknowledged and taken seriously in the UK, a country where the practice is against British law. Here too very few women affected by FGM dare to speak out about it. Not only this, but the conspiracy of silence is enabled, Nimco tells me, by well-meaning statutory agencies that, in a bid to respect cultural norms, frequently only engage with often self-appointed male leaders – leading to farcical situations described by Nimco as 'people talking about me to the people who were talking at me'. And no one was talking to her. Nimco sees the silence of women as a mark of their subordination and oppression. And for her, the oppression of women begins in childhood: it all starts with female genital mutilation.

'You're violated in order to be accepted into society, for these men to own you,' she says. 'That's why they think they can do all these things, because ultimately, they claim ownership over your body as soon as you're born, because you're initiated [through FGM]. They're scared that if it doesn't happen, you might actually grow up to be a woman who stands up for herself.'

She tells me how a 'so-called cousin' of hers emailed her to tell her she was wasting her time campaigning against FGM. 'FGM is always going to go on,' he told her. He ended his email by saying, 'if you could drop the name Ali from your surname, you would do us a great favour'. Nimco looks deeply unimpressed as she relates this story; she rejects the idea of being disowned, 'as though you own me in the first place', and ends with what I discover is a typical dismissal: 'you'd better just shut yourself and pfff be quiet'.

Nimco has never suffered fools gladly. Her description of her first reaction to hearing as a child about the practice of FGM and the idea that it would make her into a woman is typically forthright: 'I just thought it was really stupid. It just didn't make any sense. You know, [cutting me is] not actually going to turn me into an adult overnight, so... why would you do that?' When she puts it like that, it seems so simple. She shrugs. 'Sometimes you can make the simplest things really complicated.'

This propensity to follow her own, rather than received, wisdom has sometimes made her path a lonely one. 'It was literally Planet Nimco, population one,' she says of a childhood littered with unanswered, maybe unanswerable, 'Why?'s. She struggled to find people who shared her concerns about FGM. 'I was like, seriously, what is wrong, why are you guys not reacting to this? But they just thought, why is this even an issue?' In the end, she gave up. 'They didn't want to talk about it, and I didn't want to be isolated again, being the only person considering this thing to be wrong, and being seen as crazy.' So she stopped talking about it, went off to university and got a job in public health.

But it all changed when she was twenty-five and gave a talk to a group of schoolgirls. When the teacher left the room, the talk quickly turned to taboo subjects. They asked her about boys, STIs, pregnancy, anal sex, all the things that Nimco knew no one else was educating them about – so she did. And then one girl stuck up her hand and asked the question that was to alter the course of Nimco's life. 'Miss,' she asked, 'is FGM halal?'

'What would you guys know about FGM?' Nimco quipped back. It was a moment of defensive flippancy that Nimco has since deeply regretted, but at the time she couldn't actually believe any of these girls had undergone the procedure. She hadn't spoken about FGM herself for years, hadn't heard anyone else talking about it; surely it wasn't still happening? 'How many of you have had FGM?' she asked, thinking, 'I know every single one of you is born in nineteen-ninety-something, so, maybe you're going to say your grandmother had it, but you wouldn't even think someone my age had had it.' Out of the thirteen girls in the room, twelve raised their hands.

'They went from being really… you know, kids who live in urban cities, all in their tracksuit bottoms, acting really loud, to the point where I was feeling kind of intimidated by them, to… actually regressing back to children.' They all went quiet, she says. They had never spoken about it, even to each other, so deep ran the conspiracy of silence. 'Then one of the really angry ones just snapped out, snapped out like a child, and said to the other one [the lone girl who hadn't had the procedure], "Listen, don't think you're special. I know your Mum's gonna take you to Somaliland this year and they're gonna…", and she graphically described what probably must have happened to her. I went back to my office and just burst into tears. And then I started to work.'

Nimco started speaking again about FGM. About what it

meant, why it happened. About how to stop it. Together with Leyla Hussein, she founded the campaigning charity Daughters of Eve, whose members go out into FGM-practising areas and, unlike traditional agencies, engage directly with young girls who are at risk of being cut. As the group grew in influence and notoriety, as it started to prove its worth and effectiveness, government ministers began to invite it to advise on policy. The voices of women were being silenced no longer, with Daughters of Eve acting as their 'unedited voice'.

But it still took Nimco years to admit she herself had undergone FGM Type III, the most extreme form of the practice, where a woman's entire genitalia, her clitoris, her inner and outer labia, are cut away. The flesh is then sewn up, leaving only a small hole open from which to urinate and menstruate. Or at least theoretically to urinate and menstruate – the reality is the hole is often too small, and many women suffer serious medical problems, with backed-up menstrual blood collecting within their body.

As in other countries, the silence surrounding the practice means that there are no exact figures for FGM in the UK, but the most often quoted numbers are 66,000 and 23,000. The former is the number of women living with FGM in the UK today; the latter is the number of girls, like the one in Nimco's class, at risk of experiencing this trauma.

Trauma is one word for it. Nimco describes it as 'a war on our genitalia', and it's not hard to see why. Beyond the universal pain, shock and bleeding, the immediate effects of FGM include tetanus, HIV, hepatitis B & C, inability to urinate and damage to nearby organs. Over the longer term, women can face chronic vaginal and pelvic infections, kidney damage (Nimco was rushed to hospital when she was eleven with kidney failure), pain during sex, infertility and complications in childbirth. And that's before we address the chronic levels of post-traumatic stress, depression and anxiety. It's before we address the number of girls who die.

It was seeing another woman's psychological trauma that finally convinced Nimco to speak up about her own. 'She'd had FGM Type III when she was about five and she [later] legit-imised it by saying, this is going to get me the guy that I love and he's going to be with me for the rest of my life.' Grace (not her real name) got engaged at nineteen to a man who broke up with her when he discovered she'd had FGM. She had a nervous breakdown and was sectioned – and when Nimco met Grace upon her release, she realised she herself had to speak up. 'I saw my silence as complicit,' Nimco says.

After telling Grace that she too had suffered FGM, she went back and told her fellow campaigners that the woman she'd previously spoken about in the third person, the angry young girl with the trust and mother issues, 'that's me'.

'Before meeting Grace I just wasn't ready for a fight,' Nimco tells me. But now, the counter-offensive started in earnest, and Nimco began campaigning in the first person. When she deliv-ered workshops, gave talks, spoke to ministers, spoke to the media, she said 'I' – although she started spelling her name Nimko, in the hope it would offer her some protection. It didn't work. Nimco was bombarded with threats. Rape threats, death threats – someone offered to kill her for £500. A woman's worth. Many other family members besides the 'so-called cousin' are no longer speaking to her. It's gone on for years now – and in fact has started to get worse. Not long before we spoke, as she was walking down the street, a man threw liquid in her face as he screamed that she was a slag and needed to learn some shame.

Nimco thought it was acid – maybe next time it will be. And now they've started on her grandmother in Somalia. 'Psychologically, they know exactly what they're doing… it's a form of torture.'

Nimco puts the deepened aggression down to the inroads she and her fellow campaigners are starting to make. In February 2014, seventeen-year-old Fahma Mohamed fronted a petition on change.org that attracted 230,000 signatures, and which forced the government into writing to every school in the country ahead of the main FGM 'season', warning teachers to be alert to the dangers. In March of the same year, the first prosecution of FGM began in the UK, with two suspects being formally charged and entering pleas in court. A few months later, David Cameron, Britain's Prime Minister, announced that parents who fail to prevent their daughter from being cut will be prosecuted. Nimco's voice has forced the perpetrators onto the offensive. 'They've seen that there is more traction, that it's not just one lone voice. They see that it's getting to the point where young people are starting to question FGM.' She describes their attempts to shut her up as an attempt to 'cut off the snake's head', and so quieten the increasingly restive body. It's an effective strategy, Nimco acknowledges. 'If women see something horrible happening to me then they'll get scared and think, well obviously I'm not going to risk speaking out because it's dangerous and crazy.'

And so Nimco feels it's her duty to carry on speaking up, to not give in to the fear that could envelop her if she let it. 'I'm one of the lucky ones,' she says. 'The fact that I *can* talk about it.'

And talk she does. Her words come tumbling out, sentences abandoned halfway through as her mind races ahead to the next connection, the next story, half-spoken words left inchoate in the air. The only time she slows down is when the phone rings towards the end of our interview. Nimco is telling me about how inspiring she finds her three-year-old niece ('she wants to be a tree, and if she wants to be a tree, she can be a tree'), and she stops short. It's her grandmother. Afterwards she tells me, 'When I get phone calls like that, my heart just… I don't know what she's going to say…' Her grandmother is sixty, and the terrified calls relaying the threats she's heard directed towards Nimco ('they're really going to burn you alive, walking the street, I don't think you'll be able to walk the streets') have increased recently. But, Nimco says, 'I can put the phone down and I can go to my friends' house and have a glass of wine and be really angry about it and really scared. But at the same time, I know I'm also safe. And so many other girls are not.' So she keeps going despite it all. She has started calling herself Nimco again. She keeps fighting, she keeps speaking up. And increasingly, it seems like she might be winning.

Mona Eltahawy shares Nimco's sense of duty. Mona is a journalist who was born in Egypt but spent some of her childhood in the UK before moving with her family to Saudi Arabia when she was fifteen. 'To move to Saudi as a teenage girl was like the lights being turned off. And I understood that as a woman I had two options: to lose my mind, or to become a feminist. And at first I began to lose my mind – and then I became a feminist,' she told Mehdi Hasan in an interview for Al Jazeera, the Qatar-based broadcasting network. The privilege of education, of work, of being able to travel freely 'obliges me to fight ten times as hard as women who don't have that privilege,' she says. When she was attacked in Egypt during the 2011 anti-Mubarak protests, 'twelve other women were assaulted in the same street where I was assaulted. None of them had been able to speak.' Some had been silenced by their families, some by shame. 'As a society,' Mona continues, 'we do not encourage women to speak out about violence or sexual assault especially. [So] when those twelve other women cannot speak for whatever reason and I can… I'm obliged to speak very, very loud.'

And so she has. Having spent three months with her arms in casts following the assault, when she was finally able to write again, Mona was angry. Out of that anger came a clarion call of an article for *Foreign Policy* titled simply 'Why Do They Hate Us?' The 'they' was Arab men, and the article questioned the use of revolutions where nothing changed for women. 'Until the rage shifts from the oppressors in our presidential palaces to the oppressors on our streets and in our homes, our revolution has not even begun,' she wrote.

The Internet exploded. A debate was ignited – but Mona was also faced with renewed attacks, abuse, accusations that she was actually the one who was doing the hating, only it was men she hated. They said she was racist; they said she was mad. 'I think it's really interesting that women are always accused of personalising everything, that you know when a woman is angry it's because "Oh my god you've had such a terrible life". Well, first of all what happened to me was horrific and it made me angry, of course it's made me angry, who wouldn't be angry?' But, she says, it was also a political position – as well as a political decision to speak out.

'Women understand what they need to say in order to be accepted,' Mona says. She made a deliberate choice to say what she knew would render her unacceptable. In response to a young woman who accused her of being 'too extreme', Mona explained that this was a calculated decision. 'It's up to you to decide where upon a spectrum of activism you stand,' she said.

But for as long as 'there are extreme elements in my society and in my culture and in my religion, who are willing to basically strip women of as many rights as possible, I will be on that extreme end'. In this way, she hopes that 'because I'm pulling on this end, it opens up a bigger space for you. You don't have to have the exact same views as I have. You can say Mona's crazy, she's way out there…' Mona is essentially choosing to be the archetypal madwoman, to take one for the team. 'I'm proud of that,' she says. She sees her role as being 'a provocateur. Someone out there who will say things that few people want to say. Who will be controversial, because I believe that it is the role of a writer and somebody who considers the words that she uses as part of her activism. To disturb people. To find the place where it hurts and to push. That's what I believe my role is.' And so we are back to Mae, and her allegiance to P-U-S-H.

'Women and girls are the vulnerable group in society,' Mae says. 'And if we women don't talk about what affects women most, men journalists won't. If female journalists keep quiet, those things will keep happening to us.' She's stopped writing about FGM for the time being, out of concern for her daughter's safety. 'I went quiet on it for a while, but I have collected enough information that once I get my daughter into safety I will open. Oh I will open up! Mmm!' She laughs. 'Once a journalist, always a journalist. As long as I see ill in the society and I can talk about it, I will continue to write.'

If we women don't talk, male journalists won't. The statistics bear Mae out: the 2010 report by the Global Media Monitoring Project (GMMP) found that 'stories by female reporters contain more female subjects than stories by male reporters'. For both male and female reporters, however, men are still the focus in the majority of stories. Only 24% of the people we hear or read about across the news media are female, and only 13% of stories focus specifically on women.

Ah, say the overwhelmingly male newspaper editors, but we are simply 'representing the world as it is'. Don't blame us: blame a world where power is concentrated in the hands of a select bunch of men. When the worlds of politics, culture and sport are not so saturated with male faces, neither will our pages be. The thing is, though, the media paints the world as more male-dominated than it actually is.

For example, in research recently carried out on the UK media by Lis Howell of City University London, in political news stories, men outnumbered women by ten to one. The UK Parliament, with just under five men for every female MP, is bad, but it's not that bad. On global news stories that affect women disproportionately more than men – for example, those on HIV and AIDS – women made up only 42% of news subjects. When the story is about gender-based violence, that figure goes down to 40%. During the 2012 presidential elections, only 12% of those who spoke in the US media on abortion were female, according to research by 4th Estate, an organisation that conducts statistical analysis of the US media. Even when we look at news stories that are expressly about women, men dominate as the subjects: the GMMP found that only 37% of global news stories about the women's movement featured women as the main subject. Perhaps even more bizarrely, this figure goes down to 30% when the story is about female electoral candidates. This final statistic is particularly baffling – it is hard to even begin to imagine how it was achieved.

To be fair on the global media, it is improving – albeit at a glacial rate. The GMMP's figure of 24% for news stories that feature female subjects represents an increase of 3% over five years. This figure, however, is largely down to an increased female presence in health stories, a topic that 'occupies the least space on the news agenda when compared to the other major topics', such as the economy or the government. During the same five-year period, women's presence in stories on politics increased from 14% to 19%; in stories on the economy, it remained at 20%. The GMMP report concludes that 'the percentage increase in female news subjects is less pronounced in topics of high priority on the news agenda'. Which means that the stories featuring female subjects are being shunted off the front pages and squeezed in somewhere before the sports section, from which, at 11% globally, they are almost entirely absent.

So, the media aren't just representing the world 'as it is'. But even if they were, even if only 30% of female electoral candidates were actually female, we would still need to question what the media have decided are the most 'important' stories, and why. We need to question whether it's just coincidence that the stories the male-dominated news media think most important happen to be stories dominated by men. The choices editors make over what stories to cover are just that: choices. They are not fixed. They are subjective, and therefore, they are value-laden. There is no 'objective' reason why a story like the National Security Agency (NSA) surveillance scandal (based on security analyst Edward Snowden's leaked files) that dominated front pages for weeks on end is of more inherent interest than, say, the ongoing global epidemic of men killing women ('epidemic' is the World Health Organization's word, not mine). And yet the two women who are killed every week in the UK alone barely get a mention in the national press, let alone make the front page. Or, to compare one epidemic with another, the flu epidemic of 2009 dominated UK news headlines for weeks on end – and yet for only 0.5% of those whose case was bad enough to seek medical help was the flu fatal. Any death is, of course, tragic. But, for the media it seems that some deaths are more tragic, more terrifying, more pertinent, more *newsworthy*, than others.

But why does all this matter anyway? Well, if you need an answer beyond the simple discrepancy of 51% of the population getting 24% of the news space, there's always the business case: if 51% of the population is female, so must 51% of the potential media audience be. And don't try to placate us with mentions of a few puny and patronising 'women's sections', which only serve to entrench the view that the 'unmarked' news that makes up the rest of the paper is, like 'football' rather than 'women's football', for men.

As well as giving a disproportionate amount of space and airtime to stories featuring men, the media also gives a disproportionate amount of space and airtime to stories *written by* men – and this inevitably offers a narrower and less diverse set of perspectives on the world. 'There's this whole swathe of human experience that we just assume is not interesting,' Helen Lewis, Deputy Editor of the *New Statesman* in the UK, tells me. The first time she became aware of the unique angle a woman writer could bring was when she was at university and chose to rebel against the male-centric literature canon by reading the letters of the eighteenth-century aristocrat Lady Mary Wortley Montagu. 'She went to Turkey with her husband, who was the ambassador, and wrote beautiful letters back home, describing her experiences. Because she was a woman, she got to visit the Turkish baths, and she saw inside a hareem.' Helen found the insight Lady Mary's letters offered fascinating and felt that their exclusion from the canon was simply because 'people haven't gone to find out and make the case for why it's interesting'. If a male writer as talented as Montagu had letters surviving, the case would not need to be made. We're still in the realm of the female perspective being niche, and the male perspective universal.

Eleanor Mills, Editorial Director of the *Sunday Times*, agrees that a female perspective can be a valuable asset. 'If you look at somebody like Ann Treneman, the political sketch writer of *The Times*, the kind of things that she picks up on, even when she's writing about male politicians, are different from what male writers do. I just think if you have a woman's perspective on things, they see things differently, or they pick up on things that men don't think are important. So it's just a question of having a kind of balanced view of the news, not seeing it always through a masculine prism.' Because as much as a female prism may only reflect the eyes of half the population, so does a male one. The idea that a male perspective is automatically universal and unmarked needs to be challenged in every sphere.

To challenge such entrenched thinking is not easy in any field, but it is more than usually difficult in the context of the media because of the deeply intertwined and reciprocal nature of the relationship between the media and politics. 'The thing that it's always really hard to explain, and that no one fully appreciates, is that the media is to a huge extent a feedback loop,' says Helen. 'The media is interested in what other bits of the media are interested in. So, what's on the front page of the *Telegraph* or the *Daily Mail* will lead Radio 4's *Today* programme the next morning. The *Today* programme's coverage then means that all the people who work in politics feel compelled to tweet about that item. That means that people then commission the follow-up story. That then makes the front page of the *Daily Mail*. And so it goes on.' When this is extrapolated out to a global media market, particularly given the dominance of a few particularly powerful multinationals, the navel-gazing becomes ever more far-reaching.

On a local level in the UK, we find ourselves in a situation where there has been limited coverage of the way in which the government has focused its budget cuts disproportionately on women's services, precisely at a time when women are more likely to need them, as domestic abuse always rises in a time of austerity. Result? On a single day in 2012, 180 women were turned away from refuges, because there was no space. These women then faced the choice of returning to abusive partners, or living on the street. And then, when the media notice at all, they blame the women for staying with those abusive partners.

There's also the issue of what the media say about gender roles. A 1999 study found that 80% of pictures that were considered irrelevant to the story they accompanied – that were there purely to provide some visual stimulation (what the industry calls a 'lift') – were of young women. In the UK, a young woman standing and gazing alluringly into the camera in nothing but her knickers is pretty much guaranteed to appear on the third page of the *Sun* newspaper from Monday to Saturday. The GMMP found that the gender breakdown of those who appear in the global media as experts on an issue in the news was 80% men and 20% women; a UK study by Women in Journalism found that the figure was almost exactly inverted when you exchange experts for victims or case studies, where women make up 79%, and men 21%. The overall message is that men do (important) things and women have (not very important) things done to them.

This discrepancy bothers Eleanor. 'Women make up 50% of the population,' she points out. 'So yes, I think it matters that in a world that has a 50:50 population, the news that's seen as the most important and on the front page is written by and for men. It's a wonderfully reinforcing loop and things won't change if we allow that to go on unchallenged.'

For this reason, she is opposed to the tabloid tradition of putting pictures of topless women on page 3. 'If we're trying to say to our girl children, women are equal to men, we have a role to play in society, we can run things, we can be leaders, then for the biggest picture in a newspaper to be of a woman with her breasts out, sends completely the wrong signals about what we think women are for and what we think their role is.' Although the topless photos on page 3 are at one extreme, this is a trend across the global media. The reality is that while men are more likely to feature in the words of a newspaper, women are far more likely to feature in the pictures (we have to be allowed supremacy somewhere). The GMMP found that female subjects of news stories were more likely to appear in photographs accompanying the article than male subjects (the figures were 26% and 17% respectively), and that where men, when pictured, tended to be shown from the head up, women tended to be pictured in full-body shots and 'in various states of undress' at a rate 'much higher' than that for men.

Eleanor continues: 'It's easy to say, oh well, page 3 doesn't matter, it's just one small thing, but it sets the whole tone. You don't see men in those roles, portrayed in that way every day. I don't think we're going to get anything like equality until it's not acceptable to do that.' A US study by Name It. Change It. reinforces her point. It found that whenever a news report mentions the appearance of a female politician – it doesn't matter whether it's negative, positive, or even neutral – the poll ratings for that politician were negatively affected. Voters are less likely to think she is 'experienced, strong, effective, qualified and confident'. When the *Daily Mail* runs a double-page spread of the 'Downing Street catwalk' in which all the female cabinet members have their appearance raked over as they walk to work; when newspapers run features on Hillary Clinton's decision to wear glasses and hair bobbles; when the female MPs serving in Tony Blair's government get dubbed 'Blair's Babes' – career prospects are materially damaged. And then there's the detrimental effect on women as a whole, not only on their confidence, but on how they manage their time. Eleanor clarifies the issue by offering me one of her own favourite statistics: 'The average woman could learn a language or climb a mountain or get another degree with the time that she's spending worrying about how she looks.'

The way in which women are so often reduced to a decorative role in the media alongside news stories in which men are seen doing and saying things bothers Helen Lewis too. 'In every way that the media is unrepresentative, it is a bad thing,' she says. 'I think it's very easy for people who are in the majority not to be able to see that.' She tells me about a piece one of the *New Statesman* columnists, Mehdi Hasan, wrote about race in the media, in which he talked about looking at columnists and people that make opinions, and not seeing any faces that look like his looking back at him. 'And I think a similar thing happens for women,' says Helen. 'When you look at the subjects women are encouraged to write about, you look at the kind of positions they're encouraged to hold, it does shrink down your options.' She acknowledges that 'it's become quite trendy now to dismiss representation, as not being a 'proper' feminist issue, not like low pay, or more concrete things, but I think that the signals the world sends back to you, about what you can be and what you're allowed to do, are really important.'

Both Helen and Eleanor are trying to change this. Eleanor tells me, 'one of my constant internal monologues when I look at a news list is to ensure that there are stories about women with agency in the newspaper. Women who are not in the newspaper a) because of what they look like, b) because of who they're married to, or c) because they're a rape or murder victim. I want to make sure there are always enough stories about women doing things, in their own right.' So does Helen and, increasingly, so do others. In the past, Helen has felt that she's had to be the one who always has to point it out, but things do now seem to be changing. She tells me about a recent meeting where one of her male contributors asked if they had a woman to talk about a particular issue. 'I thought, yes! That's it! I've now bored everyone sufficiently about it that they've internalised it!'

It's not easy to be the person always speaking up. It's not easy to keep pushing. Sometimes, Sara Khan wonders why she goes on. In 2009, sick of a stagnation of women's rights within Muslim communities in the UK, she co-founded Inspire, a counter-extremism organisation that attempts to be a conduit for the voices of British Muslim women. It provides leadership training for Muslim women and fosters local women's networks, as well as providing training for statutory agencies and acting as a conduit between them and the communities they are trying to reach. This is an improvement on the traditional model of speaking to male 'community leaders': 'often some of those community leaders are the very offenders,' Sara says. 'They are the ones who have been making their daughters have forced marriages. They are the ones that are beating up their wives at home and not allowing women to have a voice in the mosque committee.'

Speaking out on such sensitive subjects, Sara had been braced for abuse from both Muslim and far-right misogynistic extremists – and it came. She's been spat at and shoved. She is regularly called *kafir*, *munafiq*, a dirty disbeliever, a hypocrite, an apostate. These may not sound particularly threatening to an outsider, but, Sara tells me, they position her 'outside the folds of Islam', which means, in her own chillingly clinical words, that she can be 'legitimately killed'. And all for daring to challenge misogynistic extremism within Islam while not wearing a headscarf.

While abuse might have been expected from those for whom a woman's voice is a threat, what Sara hadn't been prepared for was the lack of support from white feminists – some of whom, in a striking example of cognitive dissonance, have called her racist. Despite her successes with Inspire, she has still found herself ignored and spoken over by statutory agencies, many of whom still automatically reach for self-appointed men 'in charge'. Men talk to men about women, and then tell women how it's going to be. When Sara tells me about her battles to be heard by the people whom one might imagine to be her allies in the fight against misogyny and extremism, she laughs – and it is the laugh of someone who is choosing to laugh rather than cry.

In the face of such hostility, there are days when Sara questions her decision to take a stand. 'I wonder, why am I doing this? I've got two lovely kids. I could just be hanging out with them and doing fun stuff.' But she keeps going because she must. And there are signs that things are shifting. Despite continual attempts to silence it from every side, her voice is still confident and what she is saying has resonated. Sara has been asked to provide advice to government panels; she has appeared across the print and broadcast media. People are slowly learning to accept that British Muslim women can speak for themselves. That they don't need men talking to men to speak for them, or about them.

When things seem too difficult, Sara has two trump cards that she holds close to her for inspiration. The first is Aisha, wife of the Prophet Muhammad. A seventh-century scholar of law, Aisha narrated 2210 Hadiths (sayings from the Prophet Muhammad, which alongside the Qur'an, provide Muslims with guidance on various matters, particularly relating to jurisprudence), which Sara says can account for a quarter of Islamic Law. 'She was a great orator, very eloquent,' Sara tells me, and she wasn't afraid to challenge misogynistic statements made by the Prophet's companions. 'She reminds me that knowledge is indeed power and in the battle against patriarchy today, it is imperative that we continue to speak up and speak out.'

Sara's second source of inspiration is derived from all the women she's engaged with over the last twenty years. 'The women whose stories will remain untold, whose voices will be unheard, whose names no one will recognise, and whose tears will be ignored. The countless marginalised Muslim women whose very dignity and worth is trampled on a daily basis, who are denied the most basic of freedoms and human rights. Whose freedom of movement is curtailed, whose dreams and aspirations are crushed. They are told put up and shut up, and few speak up for them and their rights, either in Muslim communities or more widely in British society. When, at times, I've wanted to pack it in, it is these women who inspire me to fight for them. It is their unacceptable experiences of injustice which make me continue to do what I do.'

★

The importance of continuing to doggedly speak up and fight back even in the face of life-threatening hostility is a sentiment that Nadya Tolokonnikova, Yekaterina Samutsevich and Maria Alyokhina would recognise, particularly after their experience with the Russian justice system. These three women are members of the female punk protest group Pussy Riot, who hit headlines around the world in 2012 when they were arrested, prosecuted and sentenced to two years in a penal colony for the crime of hooliganism.

One of the rare times Pyotr Verzilov had been allowed to visit his wife, Nadya Tolokonnikova, a founding member of Pussy Riot, in the penal colony, the conversation turned towards Nadya's closing statement in court. Pyotr was surprised at what Nadya described as her 'fit of absolutism'. In the face of a court with a slippery approach to facts, Nadya had been loquacious in her closing statement on the fundamental and inalienable importance of Truth with a capital T. 'The truth is not a political concept at all,' Pyotr now informed her.

It may have been a reaction to his patronising implication that she didn't know about the questionable standing of truth in fashionable postmodern theory. It may have been the jarring clash between his abstractions and the all-too-concrete reality of Nadya's incarceration in a labour camp where inmates were sustained on the delusional and paranoid edge of exhaustion and hunger. Either way, she flashed back, 'So what that it's not a political concept? I just wanted to be understood. I could have used constructions from contemporary philosophy that are better suited to describing this precisely, but I wanted to be understood.'

There is something poignant about her repetition: I wanted

to be understood. It had been a long time since she could have felt that basic human affirmation. Not perhaps since Pussy Riot's performance at the Christ the Saviour Cathedral in Moscow, more than two years previously. Pussy Riot had worked up to their pièce de résistance by ticking off a series of stunts, including an illegal performance in Red Square – a basic requirement for any self-respecting activist group. But now they were graduating to what they saw as the real thing: a strike at the heart of Putin's empire of propaganda. On the morning of 21 February 2012, five members of the group made their way to the imposing cathedral at the heart of Moscow. Once inside, they removed their coats to reveal brightly coloured mismatching tights and dresses, donned neon balaclavas and walked up the steps to the altar. Once there, they erupted in a mess of bounces, screams and high kicks as they exhorted 'Virgin Mary, Mother of God' to 'become a feminist' and 'banish Putin'. They were escorted outside by security in less than a minute, but short as the performance was, it instantly made the group famous around the world – and infamous within Russia. And it delivered Putin the scapegoat he had been waiting for, enabling him to clamp down on the biggest demonstration of popular dissent in Russia's recent history: the burgeoning mass protest movement against his unprecedented third term in office.

With the performance in the cathedral, Pussy Riot had pushed themselves to the centre of that movement. And while their stunt has been dismissed by some as foolish, naïve, and damaging to the cause, the absurdly draconian reaction by the authorities suggests that, at the very least, Pussy Riot's analysis of the Church's role in Putin's corrupt edifice was spot on.

Yekaterina Samutsevich used her closing statement in court to make this point. Having described how Putin's government appropriated the Russian Orthodox Church's 'historical sense of loss' in order to 'present their new political project of restoring the lost spiritual values of Russia', she went on to explain the level of media manipulation it took to maintain this facade. It required, she said, 'a large amount of multi-ton professional lighting and video equipment, airtime on the central television channel for live broadcasts lasting many hours and, subsequently, many more hours of filming for news stories aimed at reinforcing the moral fabric by means of transmitting the patriarch's seamless speeches, meant to help believers make the right choice at this difficult time in Putin's life, before the election. The filming had to be ongoing, the necessary images had to be burned into memory and continuously renewed, creating the impression of something that is natural, permanent and non-negotiable.'

Pussy Riot's appearance at the Cathedral of Christ the Saviour, Yekaterina said, 'disturbed the integrity of this media image, created by the authorities over time, and exposed its falsehood'.

The authorities did not take this exposure lightly. Three members of Pussy Riot were arrested – the two others who had performed at the cathedral fled the country. These three women, Nadya Tolokonnikova, Yekaterina Samutsevich and Maria Alyokhina, deemed a violent danger to the fabric of society, were held in prison for four months while they awaited their trial.

Reading the trial transcript is an exercise in the experience of disbelief. In its farcical dependence on equivocation and doublespeak, it could not have been bettered had it been written by Kafka. The three defendants were repeatedly denied their right to a meaningful defence; nearly all their witnesses were disallowed on specious grounds; they were denied chances to speak; their words were twisted beyond recognition. Meanwhile, the prosecution called witness after witness, all of them pronouncing themselves victims of the abomination that had been Pussy Riot's performance in Putin's holiest of holies. One poor woman was traumatised by their high kicks and their dresses, some of which were (the horror!) sleeveless; another described how she pleaded with them not to climb up onto the stage, as only men could step onto such sanctified ground without soiling it irrevocably.

One scene relayed by Masha Gessen in her account of the Pussy Riot protest is particularly instructive, seeming to capture in a single exchange the trial in its entirety. It begins with Maria's condemnation of the prosecutor:

> 'I also want to say that the things the prosecutor says make me suspect he's a provocateur. And I can't even respond to him because I don't have that right.'
>
> 'You want to talk about it?' asked the judge.
>
> 'Yes!' said Maria. 'It hurts being unable to say anything!'
>
> The judge said it was now [Yekaterina's] turn to speak.

No surprise, then, that when the three defendants did finally get their chances to speak uninterrupted, they clung to 'truth', to freedom, to precious words that had universally understood meanings.

'It's not the three Pussy Riot singers who are on trial here,' Nadya declared. Instead, she said, the trial had exposed the Russian state for the puppet theatre it was. 'We have more freedom than the people who are sitting opposite us, on the side of the accusers, because we can say what we want and we do say what we want.' The prosecution, she continued, 'say only that which political censorship allows them to say. They cannot say the words "Mother of God, chase Putin out", a punk prayer. They cannot utter those lines in the punk prayer that have to do with the political system. Maybe they think it would be good to send us to jail because we have spoken out against Putin and his system. But they cannot say that because they are forbidden. Their mouths are sewn shut.'

But they had sewn her mouth shut too, and in her brief moment on the witness stand, she drew attention to the way the trial itself had attempted to silence them. 'Back when we could stage our punk performances we screamed as loud as we could and knew how to, about the lawlessness of the regime. But they have stolen our voices.' The court, Nadya said, 'refused to hear us'. Still, though, she maintained her faith: 'Words,' she said, paraphrasing Aleksandr Solzhenitsyn, the Russian novelist exiled for his critique of Soviet totalitarianism, 'will break cement.'

Like Nadya, Maria clung to a faith in truth and freedom, the final freeing of her tongue inspiring her to soaring rhetoric, as she honed in on the prosecutors' fondness for debasing the women and their actions as 'so-called'. The same phrase, she said, was 'used in the trial of the poet Joseph Brodsky. His poetry was referred to as "so-called poetry" and the witnesses who testified against him had not read it. Just as some of those who testified against us did not witness what happened but only saw the video on the Internet.'

The prosecutors might denounce Pussy Riot's statements apologising for having offended Russians by referring to them as 'so-called'; they might denounce all contemporary art as 'so-called', but, 'For me,' Maria burst out, 'only this trial can rightly be referred to as "so-called". And I am not afraid of you. I am not afraid of lies and fictions and of poorly coded deception in the verdict of this so-called court, because all you can do is take away my so-called freedom, the only sort that exists in the Russian Federation. But no one can take away my inner freedom. It lives in my words and it will survive thanks to the public nature of my statements, which will be heard and read by thousands. This freedom is already multiplying thanks to every caring person who hears us in this country… I believe that openness and public speech and a hunger for the truth make us all a little bit freer. We will see this yet.'

The notes of hope on which all three members of Pussy Riot end their closing statements are inspiring, but their faith in the power of words is up against another faith. Its adherents also believe in the power of words, but it is a faith that places them in violent opposition to everything Pussy Riot stand for – not only as dissident activists, but as women who demand a voice. In the context of Russia and Pussy Riot, perhaps the distilled essence of this faith can be found in the Carriers of the Cross, a shadowy and seemingly self-styled gang of bearded protectors (or, more accurately, enforcers) of the Orthodox faith, who appeared in the documentary film *Pussy Riot: A Punk Prayer* wearing 'Orthodoxy or Death' T-shirts. Frankly, for all their posturing and self-importance, they seem more reminiscent of a Hell's Angels troop than an influential religious congregation.

'Pussy is a devious word,' they say suspiciously. 'It means kitten but also the uterus… the best translation [of the group's name] is "deranged vaginas".' They must fight against these deranged vaginas, they say, noting that 'in the sixteenth century, they would have burned her, hanged her'. The 'her' they refer to is Nadya, of whom they say, 'That main one, she's a demon with a brain… you can tell from her lips, her eyes… there have always been witches who don't repent.' A clue as to how Pussy Riot might like to repent can be found in the chants of Carriers of the Cross as they march through the streets of Moscow: 'You are a blessed wife... blessed is your womb.' Childbearing organs do tend to be less mouthy than women in their entirety.

The style of their delivery may be idiosyncratic, but the misogynistic message of the Carriers of the Cross is age-old. Unlike the 'blessed womb' of the Virgin Mary, physicians from the ancient Greeks through to the sixteenth century held that mortal wombs had a dangerous propensity to wander – trailing psychosis for women in their wake, and even, occasionally, threatening to swallow hapless men. The Bible tells us that only the grave, fire, and 'the barren womb' are never satisfied. Meanwhile, Milton freestyles on the dangers of the 'wide womb of uncreated night', where one might 'perish rather, swallow'd up and lost', and Shakespeare's Lear warns that 'Down from the waist they are centaurs, though women all above. But to the girdle do the gods inherit, beneath is all the fiend's: there's hell, there's darkness, there's the sulphurous pit, burning, scalding, stench'. In more recent history, W.H. Auden reiterates one of the central rhyme pairings in English poetry when he writes 'womb /... is rhyme to tomb', and Ted Hughes conjures up the 'splitting-grin' of 'infernal' 'cunt-flesh' – a not exactly subtle reference to the myth of the *vagina dentata*, or toothed vagina. And an Idaho preacher from the 1920s began a sermon with a request to his female congregants to cross their legs. This being done, he said, 'All right folks, now that the gates of hell are closed, I can begin my sermon.' Yes, the Carriers of the Cross are inheritors of a grand tradition of misogyny informed by fear.

In 1792, Mary Wollstonecraft devoted much of the fifth chapter of *A Vindication of the Rights of Woman* to critiquing 'woman' as defined by eminent male writers of her generation.

This 'woman' is 'formed to please and be subject to [men]'; 'it is her duty to render herself agreeable to her master – this being the grand end of her existence', Wollstonecraft wrote. The Carriers of the Cross are merely one group in a long line of disappointed, self-appointed 'masters'. Although they dress their condemnation up in the language of religious morality, the sheer intemperance of their reactions suggests a level of sexual frustration too, a sense of horror at the inkling that what these women are doing is not wholly engineered for their benefit. The Carriers of the Cross do not appreciate vaginas with uncontrollable mouths of their own: they would prefer wombs that have been 'blessed', or impregnated, by men.

Sadly for the Carriers of the Cross, the outrage they feel at the discovery of women with mouths and minds of their own has had no effect on Pussy Riot. Released from their respective penal colonies in December 2013, Nadya and Maria have gone on to set up Zona Prava, a non-governmental organisation (NGO) that agitates for prisoners' rights – and they have not ceased to speak out about Putin's regime. The only difference now is that their every word is reported by the world's media. They have written articles for international publications; they speak regularly to audiences in packed international venues. Far from being burned as witches, these women now have a platform the Carriers of the Cross could only dream of. I can't help allowing myself a smirk at just how cross the zealots must be at how this has all turned out for those mouthy, deranged vaginas.

Although some members of Pussy Riot have now been outed and are famous under their own names, the original concept of the group was one of anonymous collectivity – and it is striking how often this dynamic crops up. A woman speaking alone is vulnerable – to disbelief, to dismissal, to attack. In a brilliant essay printed in the *London Review of Books*, Mary Beard, a professor of classics at the University of Cambridge, explores how the de-authorising and silencing of women's voices is embedded in our culture and history. She starts off with Greek culture, highlighting a passage in Homer's *Odyssey* where Telemachus, whom Beard describes as a 'wet-behind-the-ears lad', officiously sends his mother to her room, informing her that 'speech will be the business of men, all men, and of me most of all; for mine is the power in this household'. The passage illustrates a repeated theme in Greco-Roman literature, Beard tells us, whereby 'an integral part of growing up, as a man, is learning to take control of public utterance and to silence the female of the species'. Public speaking and oratory 'were not merely things that ancient women didn't do: they were exclusive practices and skills that defined masculinity as a gender'. Public speech 'was a – if not the – defining attribute of maleness'.

Beard draws attention to the specific word Telemachus uses for 'speech': *muthos*, the term which in Homeric Greek 'signals authoritative public speech (not the kind of chatting, prattling or gossip that anyone – women included, or especially women – could do)'. Beard goes on to present other examples of this distinction between male and female speech: an ancient scientific treatise pontificating on the way a 'deep' voice indicates manly courage, while a high voice alerts us to the presence of female cowardice; a Roman anthologist from the first century AD describing the 'impudent' 'barking' and 'yapping' of a woman in court. In the nineteenth century, Henry James is even more explicit on this point, in one of his essays comparing women's voices to the 'moo of the cow, the bray of the ass and the bark of the dog'.

Like the undermining of women's voices as shrill, nagging, whining, this reduction of female speech to animalistic, unintelligible noises serves a purpose beyond denying women access to human speech. It highlights the more fundamental denial of access to rationality and knowledge. It suggests that women don't have legitimate political opinions and analyses and their voices have no place in the cultural arena. Mary Beard picks out an old *Punch* cartoon that neatly parodies this framing of women's voices as unintelligible. A group of five men and one woman are sitting at a table, wearing business clothes. 'That's an excellent suggestion, Miss Triggs. Perhaps one of the men here would like to make it,' runs the caption. The cartoon wouldn't work if it were five women and one man, because at that point, the women's voices achieve strength in numbers.

It may be easy to intimidate a lone woman into silence, but it's harder to dismiss a whole group of them speaking together, saying the same thing. It is harder to say they are unintelligible when they all understand each other. The power of the anonymous collective is what protects the Afghan women scribbling their two-line venomous snakes; it's what gave Pussy Riot the strength to defy Putin.

The strength that comes from numbers is something Laura Bates discovered when she set up the Everyday Sexism Project. Throughout our interview she always says 'we', not 'I' – when I ask her why, she tells me, 'When I talk about the Everyday Sexism Project I really feel incredibly strongly that the reason it's so powerful and has this strength is because of the voices of the 50,000 people who've shared their stories. So when something happens, when we achieve something, it's not anything to do with me alone.'

She tells me about the #FBrape campaign that, by targeting

its advertisers, forced Facebook to deal with the many pages dedicated to glorifying rape and domestic violence. 'I would never describe that as something I did,' Laura says, 'because 60,000 people tweeted and sent messages to advertisers and that's absolutely why it's succeeded. But also the project is run by volunteers, so we're a very grassroots organisation. We don't have any kind of funding really, apart from a very small amount that we were able to crowd source. But we have about 30–40 volunteers all over the world who run the individual country websites and also run the day-to-day admin side of moderating the website and copying entries across from Twitter. So that's what I mean when I say "we".'

Still, though, there wouldn't have been a 'we' if one day Laura Bates hadn't decided to set up a project that has taken the world by storm and been covered by pretty much every global media outlet. The Everyday Sexism Project has changed the terms on which feminism operates in the modern world. And all this from a woman who, a few years ago, wouldn't have even called herself a feminist.

'It wasn't that I was anti-feminist, or that if someone had talked to me about it and explained it to me, I wouldn't have called myself a feminist, I think I would,' she tells me. 'But it was just that I hadn't been exposed to the idea of feminism or what it meant at all really.' That changed in early 2012, when a series of 'experiences of varying degrees of severity' made Laura angry.

'By coincidence, they all just happened within the space of a week or so,' she says. 'There was a guy who followed me off the bus and was making comments about my looks really insistently even though I made it clear I didn't want to talk to him. He followed me all the way home and I had to walk past my house and call a friend. Then there was a guy who approached me when I was sitting outside a cafe one evening, grabbed my hand and wouldn't let go and was talking about how beautiful I was and wouldn't take no for an answer. There was general street harassment which was quite severe, guys shouting out of their car windows about my legs, about things that they wanted to do to me. There was a night when I was on the way home on the bus quite late and speaking on the phone to my mum, and a guy next to me started groping my legs and, when I said what was happening, everybody on the bus looked away, no one stepped in to help. And then there was another time where I was walking past a lorry that was unloading some scaffolding and one guy on the back of the lorry turned to the other and said, "Look at the tits on *that*," as I walked past.'

As Laura tells me about these experiences, she doesn't make eye contact with me, but looks off into the distance, as if she is disconnecting herself from her memory of what happened. Her voice – level, calm and measured – jars with the sordid behaviour she describes. 'The thing that really shocked me,' she says, 'was recognising that had these things not all happened within such a short space of time, I really never would have thought twice about any one of them individually. And it made me start thinking about how many other things like that had happened over the months and years that I hadn't mentioned to anyone or really stopped to think about myself, because it was so much a part of my daily experience.'

When she says this I am reminded of one of the first times her project really resonated with me personally. She had started a discussion about the harassment women face in clubs, and as I watched the stories come in – as woman after woman talked about how men would grind up behind them as they danced, invading their space, and often their body – I was suddenly flashed back to my clubbing days. I remembered how that woman – girl really – had been me, how I'd developed coping strategies, how I'd weaved my way around the dance floor, never confronting these men head-on, how I'd always dithered about going to Fabric on a Friday night – even though I preferred the music there and my favourite DJ would invariably be on – because the men were always worse on a Friday. I now felt such a sadness for that girl, for all of us, who just wanted to go out and dance for hours, and had never even considered that it didn't have to be this way.

I'm intrigued, though, to know how it came to Laura – who was by her own admission someone unschooled in feminist theory – that what she had experienced was 'sexism', a structural phenomenon, rather than a series of unpleasant incidents. 'I think it started that week, with my strong sense of indignation when I recognised that this was so normal to me that I'd never stopped to think about it,' she says. 'I felt really angry. I felt I shouldn't have to live this way. Every one of those instances that I've told you about happened within half a mile of my house and most of them happened on the same street that I live on. It had made me scared and it made it difficult to go out of the house. So it started affecting how I walked down the street, how I crossed the road to avoid the particular fishmonger where the guys would always mutter under their breath and look me up and down. Or I wouldn't go to the coffee place that was nearest to my house and had convenient Wi-Fi because that was where I was sitting outside when the guy came up and grabbed my hand and started going on at me, and it was my local bus stop I was getting off at when the guy followed me. It was having a real impact on my day-to-day life, and that made me really angry. And I think that was when I first really recognised that this was something that was unequivocally happening to me that didn't, for example, affect my boyfriend who lived with me, and walked that street without ever thinking twice.'

Laura decided to see if other women were living this way too. 'I started asking other women, older women, younger women, friends, women I didn't know, if they'd ever experienced anything similar and I was blown away by their responses. I really thought that maybe one or two people would have one or two instances to share. And instead, every woman I spoke to had so many things, you know, on my way to meet you this happened, not just in the street, but in the workplace, in the home, in education. And I just could not believe that the problem was so huge. But just like me, they hadn't mentioned it to anyone until I'd asked them, because it was so normal.'

So she set up a website where women could submit stories of the harassment they experienced, and women who had for so long been told, 'No, sexism doesn't exist any more, women are equal now, you must be making a fuss about nothing, you've got the wrong end of the stick, you're overreacting, it was meant as a joke, you need to get a sense of humour' suddenly erupted with stories – 50,000 within the first year. I ask Laura why she thinks it took off so quickly. 'It was genuinely total word of mouth,' she says. 'When it started, I had my own private Facebook account with maybe four hundred friends and I put it on my own wall there, and I started the Twitter account from scratch with zero followers.' Which suggests that women have felt that they weren't allowed to speak about these things – and that once someone, in the shape of Laura via her website, gave them permission, no one was going to shut them up.

Laura agrees. 'I think that there's a real sense of relief in something finally being talked about when it's been denied or brushed aside or belittled for so long.' In contrast to the early days when she was first asking other women if they'd ever experienced sexism, now she doesn't even have to bring the subject up. 'If I go out to dinner, everyone I meet tells me their Everyday Sexism story. Everyone.'

From the beginning of the project, women and girls started to write to Laura to tell her that Everyday Sexism had given them the courage to speak to their families for the first time about their experiences; that the existence of the website, full of so many stories from other women, had helped them to explain these experiences. 'I heard from older women who said that they'd carried the burden of their rapes with them for their whole lives, and that reading these other women's stories was this cathartic moment for them and the first time they started to realise that maybe it wasn't their own fault.' She regularly receives emails from women all around the world thanking her for her work. Women who have not told anyone about their abuse have suddenly found their voice. They've lost their shame. Some have gone on to report assaults they hadn't realised they had a right to report. And they've been inspired to start up their own anti-sexism projects. She's also had countless emails from men thanking her for opening their eyes to a problem that had previously been invisible to them – telling her they have changed their behaviour as a direct result.

Still, not everyone's a fan. A few women – and Laura stresses that it's a very few – 'have suggested that Everyday Sexism is a bad thing because it makes all women into victims and that what we're doing weakens women'. She understands their reaction, she says. 'But for me, what's weak is to be in a situation where you don't speak out and where it's just normal and you have to put up with it, and that's where I think we were before. So while

I understand that it's hard to speak out about these things, and that it does feel like you're making yourself vulnerable by admitting them, for me it's a strong thing to do, to speak out and to refuse to be silenced any more.'

Others have asked why feminists are wasting their time on things like 'harmless flirtation' when we should be focusing on rape and FGM. Laura has little time for such arguments. For a start, she points out, Everyday Sexism is not a space only for the arguably more minor end of the sexism scale: entries range from experiences of wolf-whistling to stories of rape and domestic violence. But she doesn't think that we shouldn't sweat the small stuff either. 'There's no other field in which they say don't bother with these things, only focus on the more important ones,' she says. 'Feminism is tackling the big issues, and rightly so: there are charities doing brilliant and important work on domestic violence and on FGM. But I don't see why that means that we shouldn't also tackle the kind of lower end of the scale. Nobody would say, let's abandon all fraud investigations because we should be focusing on murder.'

But it's not just a matter of fairness. It's a matter of looking at the bigger picture – the spectrum of sexism. 'If the project has shown anything,' Laura says, 'it's the connections between these different forms of gender inequality, how the ideas and attitudes towards women that underlie these more minor things that we're told to brush off, that are often seen as insignificant, are the same ideas and attitudes at the root of the more severe cases like sexual assault and domestic violence.' She talks about how we're told just to not buy the *Sun* newspaper if we don't like the daily topless woman on page 3, that we should be focusing on more important things than a titillating picture in a daily newspaper, and yet women have written in to the project about men who whispered to them about page 3 as they raped them. 'Women are told that they shouldn't make a fuss about street harassment, that they should just ignore it,' she says, 'but we hear from women who've tried to ignore it and found that it escalates into serious verbal violence and aggression, into being followed and pursued and in several cases into serious physical assault as a result.' Any woman who has experienced how an ignored 'harmless' cat-call or a 'come on, love, give us a smile' quickly shifts to 'frigid bitch' will recognise this dynamic.

'I don't think it would work to tackle the issue of the lack of representation of women in business if we ignore the fact that the media is still presenting women as dehumanised sex objects,' Laura says. 'I don't think it would work to tackle, let's say, workplace discrimination if, as soon as a man from within that workplace walks out into the street, he's in an environment in which he sees that it's perfectly acceptable for men to objectify women, and demean them, and rate them sexually, and shout out what they think about them. I don't think it's possible to compartmentalise something which is essentially attitudinal at its root.'

What we need, Laura says, is 'a cultural shift in our ideas and attitudes and we can only achieve that through a broadly focused approach'.

And there's no denying that she's having a serious impact. The success of the #FBrape campaign that forced the mighty and seemingly untouchable Facebook to change its policies is just one example of the power of the project. A clutch of companies have been forced to reconsider and often withdraw sexist products and marketing campaigns: Apple was forced to remove a plastic surgery Barbie game aimed at nine-year-old girls from its App Store; the supermarket chain ASDA, which used to file publications like the *New Scientist* and the *Economist* under 'Men's Interest', was forced to reorganise its magazine sections in all stores; Bike Treks Ltd, a cycle store, was forced to withdraw an ad for a bike that read, 'Like a good woman; light, supple and ready to ride when you are.' Everyday Sexism has forced apologies from *FHM* men's magazine (for joking that '[n]o matter how cold it is it's never acceptable to wear your girlfriend/mother/victim's socks'); from @Footy_Jokes, a Twitter account with nearly 500,000 followers, for tweeting a domestic violence cartoon; and from BBC Radio Cumbria for running a segment entitled 'If you could have a Filipino woman, why would you want a Cumbrian one?' Everyday Sexism has even had a direct impact on crime: within the first few weeks of its campaign with the British Transport Police, reports of sexual offences on public transport were up by 20% and detection of offenders by 32%. And the project has now gone worldwide, by September 2014 boasting offshoots in nineteen countries.

But it's not just companies that are running scared of Laura and her newfound influence. There's another group that is seriously disturbed by the change Laura is effecting in the world – and it is fighting back with a relentless and vicious campaign of rape and death threats. It started almost immediately, Laura tells me. 'Before there was any kind of wider support network or awareness about Everyday Sexism at all, I was suddenly getting two hundred of those messages a day and my phone would just be buzzing and buzzing and buzzing.' She was completely unprepared for it. And she was scared.

Some of the abuse came in the form of explicit sex and rape fantasies submitted as project entries under her name, 'making it look like I was contributing stories about myself and describing the things that would happen to me'. Some of it was in the form of 'horribly violent descriptions of rape and domestic violence. Men were boasting about stuff they claimed to have done, in a "And what are you gonna do about it?" way.' The third category 'was just outright threats that they would kill me or rape me, often with very long, specific descriptions of which weapons would be used, what order it would happen in and different ways that they were able to track me down'. She found this particularly scary, she says, 'because they would describe how they could use the IP address that I'd registered the website with to find where I lived'.

Like Nimco Ali, Laura has found that her abusers know how to maximise the psychological impact of their attacks. 'Hundreds of them would all send me abuse for a couple of days and then they'd all stop, as though they had called it off. And for a few hours, I would think that it was over. And then they would all start trickling back in and with messages like, "Oh hi again Laura, did you think we'd forgotten you?"' She tells me how they followed her around online, finding her private social media accounts, and 'they would quote back to me things that I had said elsewhere to show that they had access'.

'I found it difficult to sleep,' she says. 'I was worrying all the time about very odd irrational things. The main one was that these people who said they were going to come and do things to me would turn up at the house when I wasn't there and do things to my fiancé instead. Eventually, when they kept saying they knew where to find us, we actually moved out for just a short period of time from our flat because I was unable to concentrate when we were there.'

Despite the persistence of her abusers, Laura has been told, like women who protest against street harassment, to just ignore it. 'People say, oh just turn it off, or oh you know it's just some-one in their mum's basement right? And the fact is that, yes, in the cold light of day, I do know that, but we're not all logical all the time and actually, when you're lying in bed at night, and those things are going through your head, it doesn't matter what someone's said in the daytime about how it's probably fine. You hear a noise outside and you can't help your emotive reaction to that, and you can't help the way that it makes you feel. And there's also part of you that just thinks about the 0.001%. I think about Jill Dando all the time and I get scared when the door goes. I don't know why, but that case just comes back to me and I just kept thinking probably someone will have said to her, you know, it's just someone trying to scare you. But every now and then, someone does get obsessed with someone in the public eye and these things do happen. So you can't help thinking: what if?'

When Laura mentions Jill Dando, I get a shock. It reminds me of something I had completely forgotten until that moment. When I had been trying to keep my sanity under a similar wave of extreme and explicit rape and death threats, I too had thought of Jill Dando, shot dead on her own doorstep in 1999. It was her murder that made me scared every time the doorbell went; every time I stepped outside. And I felt stupid about it, so embarrassed about this overblown fear that I hadn't even told my boyfriend. But the fear lingered. I also couldn't help thinking: what if?

For me, it also started with a campaign. In April 2013, the Bank of England announced that Winston Churchill would be the new face of the £5 note, replacing social reformer Elizabeth Fry. This meant that every note issued by them would have the face of a man on the reverse. The only woman on the notes was the Queen – and she didn't form one of the gilded group chosen for their historical achievements. She was there simply for the achievement of being born without any brothers. The message of an all-male line-up was clear and damning: no woman had ever done anything worthy of being celebrated. What the Bank itself called 'a unique and rare opportunity to promote awareness of our nation's history and acknowledge the life and work of great Britons' was being squandered.

When I started the campaign, I blithely assumed the Bank would cave in immediately – it was so clearly an unnecessary and damaging decision. Those in charge there just needed it explained to them. They needed to be told about the studies that show how important role models are to growing girls and grown women. How role models have been shown to affect women's involvement in politics, their academic course decisions, their ability in maths tests, even their ability to give good speeches. They needed to be told about the young girl who wrote on the Everyday Sexism website that she wanted to be a boy so she could be an astronaut; about the boy who in answer to his mother telling him about his great-great-aunt being a spy in World War II incredulously exclaimed, 'But, Mummy, spies are men!''; about the children who asked, 'Mummy, can a woman be Prime Minister?' They needed to understand the impact that these silent, seemingly unobtrusive daily messages that this world is a man's world have on us. So what if many people would struggle to name who was on our banknotes? An entire multi-billion-dollar advertising and marketing industry has been built up around the power of our subconscious to store up messages and alter our behaviour (indeed, as Cordelia Fine reports in *Delusions of Gender*, studies prove the sponge-like – and therefore often politically incorrect – quality of our associative memories)

– so why did people think they were any less suggestible when the message wasn't explicit or consciously deliberate?

But they did seem to think that. The campaign ran for three months, with a combination of online petition, offline protesting, legal challenge and fundraising – and almost until the final moment, the Bank stonewalled, telling us the Queen was on the banknotes and refusing to respond to a freedom of information request about its decision-making process. Its lawyers repeatedly mischaracterised our complaint, ignored direct questions, and patronised and dismissed us. They told us the Bank had considered women for the slot, as if that fulfilled its obligations under the public sector equality duty, which stipulates that all decisions by bodies acting in a public capacity have to pay due regard to promoting equality of opportunity. What this meant for the Bank is that that it didn't matter who it had considered: what mattered was whether its decision helped to level the playing field for women. It clearly didn't.

But eventually sense prevailed. I was invited to a press conference at which the Bank announced that not only was it bringing forward the introduction of the new ten-pound note and putting a woman (Jane Austen) on it, it was also going to hold a review of its selection process and criteria for selecting banknote characters, with the aim of ensuring that 'the full diversity of British people' was represented. Having repeatedly denied the relevance of the public sector equality duty to its decision (although it hedged its bets by claiming that, if the PSED were engaged, it had been complied with anyway, via the aforementioned consideration of women for the slot), it was particularly gratifying that now it specifically intended to ensure that future decisions would 'operate within the spirit of the Public Sector Equality Duty'.

The choice of Austen herself was serendipitous, and not just because of how Churchill had implied her work was trivial because her novels explored women's lives rather than the Napoleonic Wars or the French Revolution. At the time there was some mumbling across the media about why we couldn't have a scientist or someone else who had actually made a substantial achievement as the female representative – but if this chapter has shown anything, it is that for a woman to use her voice is no small thing. 'Men have had every advantage of us in telling their own story. Education has been theirs in so much higher a degree; the pen has been in their hands,' Austen wrote in *Persuasion* in an exchange concerning the misrepresentation of women. It was fitting that a woman whose work was so intensely engaged with the various ways in which women are misrepresented or not represented at all should be the woman chosen as the antidote to an all-male line-up on banknotes. 'The quarrels of popes and kings, with wars or pestilences, in every page; the men all so good for nothing, and hardly any women at all — it is very tiresome,' says Catherine Morland of history books in *Northanger Abbey*. We had won. It was an amazing feeling – not least because I had a master's dissertation to write, which I could now finally get on with.

But just as they had for Laura, the men of Twitter had other plans for me. The day after the decision was announced, I received my first rape threat. And then another. And another. They streamed in second after second, minute after minute. More people joined in; the same dynamic that had enabled a group of people without access to traditional forms of power to take on a huge institution like the Bank of England and win was now turned against me at terrifying speed. Except I wasn't a big institution. I was just a woman alone in her flat, watching these threats roll in. And I was terrified.

'You never know what it's like, because no mainstream paper will print it, nobody on the radio will let you say it, and so it came to look as if I was worried that they said I hadn't done my hair.' Until it had happened to me, I had no idea how true these words were. They were spoken by Mary Beard in an interview with the *New York Times*, after she had been a victim of online abuse in early 2013. Less than six months later, the same thing happened to me. I read newspaper reports that spoke vaguely of 'online abuse'; I turned up at radio studios to be told I could only describe in polite terms what was still coming in every minute. I was forced to shield members of the public from something from which no one had been able to shield me. And I have been labelled a 'delicate flower' by certain commentators as a result. They thought I was just complaining that someone had sworn at me.

PUT BOTH YOUR HANDS ON MY COCK AND STROKE IT TILL I CUM ON YOUR EYEBALLS. DO AS I FUCKING SAY OR I'LL SLIT YA THROAT

Go on your knees and suck my dick. I will teach you to learn your place as a woman in this world. Then you will eat my cum.

i will find you :)

I will rape you. Fucking pathetic slut.

a car bomb will go off outside your house at 11:04 pm. I will be watching to make sure it does. Do not call the police.

FIRST WE WILL MUTILATE YOUR GENITALS WITH SCISSORS, THEN SET YOUR HOUSE ON FIRE WHILE YOU BEG TO DIE TONIGHT. 23.00

I will shove a three foot pole in your vagina. You deserve nothing but pain

I will find you – just think, it could be someone who knows you personally

WOMEN THAT TALK TOO MUCH NEED TO GET RAPED

enjoying having the media at your doorstep? Better hope there isn't a rapist disguised as a reporter

I'm going to pistol whip you over and over until you lose consciousness while your children (?) watch and then burn your flesh

You'll never get me… you'll only feel my cock when it's raping you slut

Im gonna rape you, be very afraid

I have a sniper rifle aimed directly at your head currently. Any last words you fugly piece of shit? Watch out bitch.

UR DEAD AND GONE TONIGHT CUNT. KISS YOUR PUSSY GOODBYE AS WE BREAK IT IRREPARABLY

SHUT YOUR WHORE MOUTH… OR ILL SHUT IT FOR YOU AND CHOKE IT WITH MY DICK

It went on like that for weeks. Months. By the end of the first weekend, the police had 300 A4 pages of threats against me. Those making the threats went by names like CarolineIsDead, YoureDead, RapeHerNOW, Rapey1. They got hold of an (incorrect, thankfully) address and telephone number and started posting it all over the Internet. I had a panic alarm installed in my home.

There is no doubt that women disproportionately suffer from the bile that for some reason we seem to think is just part and parcel of online life. In 2006, the University of Maryland conducted a study in which fake accounts were set up and sent into chatrooms. Those with female names received an average of 100 messages every day that included 'sexually explicit or threatening language'. Those with male names received an average of 3.7. This finding is backed up by numerous anecdotal accounts from men who have posed as women online and from male journalists who watched their female colleagues' inboxes for them when they were away. Some of these men started off thinking, 'Come on, how bad could it possibly be?' Without exception, they were all shocked and even traumatised by their experiences.

There's also little doubt of the results: women shut up, back off, power down. Kathy Sierra's popular blog on software development was rated number twenty-three in the Technorati Top 100 technology blogs in 2007, when she started receiving messages like: 'i hope someone slits your throat and cums down your gob'. It is striking how often the threats women receive focus around the speech area: the threats I received also centred on my mouth and throat, and in 2014, Michael Fabricant, a British MP, tweeted that he would end up 'punching Yasmin Alibhai-Brown [a British journalist] in the throat' if he had to debate her. The message could not be clearer: shut up, or we will commit acts of violence that will force you to be quiet. And it often works – in no small part because, as Andrea Dworkin said, '[m]ost women have experienced enough dominance from men... that no threat seems empty'. For Sierra, eventually, the attacks became too much and she stopped writing. She's far from alone: a Pew study found that from 2000 to 2005, the percentage of Internet users who participate in online chats and discussion groups dropped from 28% to 17%, 'entirely because of women's fall off in participation'.

For a while, I was one of those silenced women. For weeks I had maintained, or tried to maintain, a defiant front. Most of all, I knew my abusers wanted me to 'shut [my] whore mouth', and I wasn't going to give them the satisfaction. But, I found, there are limits to what a human being can cope with, and one day in early September 2013, after two months of constant abuse, I had reached mine. I remember I could hear screaming in my head, non-stop screaming that I had no power to shut up. But somehow, through the brain-fog, I knew one thing that would shut it up, and that was to close down my Twitter account. At that moment, I was no longer a defiant feminist campaigner, I was just a woman on the edge of a nervous breakdown – and my survival instinct kicked in. I clicked 'suspend'. The screaming stopped.

For me, it wasn't just the threats. They were undoubtedly what drove me to the edge of my sanity; but they were also given a helping shove by the incompetence of the police and the officiousness of the thousands of people who felt it was their duty to inform me that I was an unsatisfactory victim. I was too loud, too gobby, too sweary. I didn't do my hair nicely before being interviewed on TV. I hadn't followed the conventional Internet wisdom that 'trolls' should be ignored, that they are looking to be fed and I was feeding them great dollops of their favourite sustenance. I have no doubt that some of the thousands of people who took it upon themselves to provide me with a minute-by-minute analysis of how I was coping genuinely thought they were being helpful; but then again, I'm sure the police think they're being helpful when they tell women not to dress like 'sluts', rather than telling men not to rape. It all comes down to the same thing: blaming the victim, rather than the abuser. And so, after about a month of 'helpful' advice, I started responding less politely to it. That made me even less of a satisfactory victim.

From an outsider's perspective, it might be hard to understand why having thousands of strangers advising you on how to cope with your abuse should be particularly traumatic. At the very least, it shouldn't be anything close to the trauma inflicted by the abuse itself. But that would be to miss the central message of the advice – and its significance. Because, like the man who told me that if I didn't shut my whore mouth he would shut it for me, like the man who told me that women who talk too much need to get raped, the central message of all these communications was, 'Shut up'. The only thing that marked the 'advice' out from the abuse was that I was to be patronised, rather than threatened, into silence. When you look at it that way, this 'advice' amounted to more people telling me that women who talk too much deserve to get rape threats.

When Professor Lorna Martin of Cape Town University conducted research into the injuries suffered by victims of femicide in South Africa, she found that a large proportion of the injuries were in the face and neck area: as with the threats suffered by women online, the focus of this violence has a clear message. It is about shutting women up by any means necessary. And it starts so early: a recent study into patterns of interruption among young children showed that boys interrupt at almost three times the rate of girls – and that those girls who interrupt do so more than twice as frequently when they are in a group with only girls than when they are in a mixed group. Of course, this isn't violent silencing, but it shows how early the dynamic that males speak and females listen begins. From interruptions of girls at play, to stopping women talking about their abuse, to stopping women talking *through the use of abuse* – both verbal and physical – in a way, it's a wonder women talk at all when everywhere they turn people are telling them, trying to force them, to shut up.

And yet they do. Not all of us and not all the time. But enough. And increasing numbers of us. And at any one time when one woman is being silenced, maybe permanently, another woman is inspiring still another to find her voice by showing her that she doesn't have to shut up. By showing her how to fight back, and urging her not to give in. By speaking, together, like women.

3

Leading Like a Woman

From December 2010, squares across the Middle East began to fill with people. Hundreds, then thousands, turned up day after day. The dictators and despots who ruled these people turned up too, in the shape of police and army forces that tried to quell by violent compulsion the growing show of mutiny. But something had snapped in the long-subjugated people, and they refused to be cowed. They continued to show up. One by one, decade-long dictatorships were toppled. First went Ben Ali of Tunisia; next was Mubarak of Egypt; in Libya, what had originally been peaceful protest erupted into civil war, culminating in the killing of Gaddafi, who had ruled Libya by dictatorship for forty-two years.

In the West, we were used to looking patronisingly at women in Arab countries as subjugated, silenced victims who lack a voice, a political will, a public presence. Yet images from what was dubbed 'the Arab Spring' confounded this view. These squares were full of *all* people: young and old, middle- and working-class. Men and women. They stood shoulder to shoulder in demanding their freedoms. More than this, women were often instrumental in the protest movements' ascendancy. In Egypt, Asmaa Mahfouz's video calling on Egyptians to join her in Tahrir Square to publicly protest against the regime of Hosni Mubarak sparked off Egypt's revolution; in Tunisia, Lina Ben

Mhenni, one of the few bloggers to write under her real name, was also one of the only people documenting the atrocities committed by the state against its people and keeping up international pressure on the Tunisian government; and in Libya, according to an interview in Mona Eltahawy's documentary *The Women of the Arab Spring*, it was women who began the Libyan revolution by gathering together outside a police station in Benghazi on 15 February 2011.

Gradually, however, something changed. The optimism that these revolutions might mean more than a 'change of management' for women (to borrow the words of US progressive blogger Melissa McEwan) started to fade. The sexual assault of women became a discordant accompaniment to the beat of revolution. By early 2014, over six thousand women had been raped in Syria, while one study in Egypt has revealed that up to 86% of Egyptian women had been sexually harassed. In the words of Mona Hussein Wasef, after standing side by side with men in Tahrir Square for so long, 'now we are fighting just for the right to walk down the street without being assaulted. It is so hard, so shocking. To see the rights we had being ripped away and lost in the power struggle. To see us go backwards.'

In Tunisia, reports emerged of women being forced to wear the hijab, and being attacked at universities and schools. Mariz Tadros reported for *openDemocracy* that 'ultra-radical Islamist Salafis emerged in public since 2012 and have claimed the authority to verbally (and sometimes physically) "chastise" unveiled women for their attire, with the police doing nothing to refrain or hold them in check'. One woman who filed a complaint against two police officers for rape was charged with public indecency. In Egypt, the now-deposed Muslim Brotherhood government removed parliamentary quotas for women and left the door open for the legalisation of FGM and child marriage – otherwise known as child abuse.

In Syria, women were at the heart of the revolution in its 2011 beginnings in Daraa. They organised the 'declaration of milk', a demand for the government to provide milk for the children of the besieged city. By the time I speak to Mouna Ghanem, a Syrian activist, in February 2014, she tells me that Islamists are enforcing the hijab and segregated protests for men and women; in the last ten days, she tells me, a woman was stoned to death in Raqqa for having a Facebook account.

Mouna has already aroused the ire of her fellow opposition activists for alerting the world to the existence of Jihad Al-Nikah, or sexual jihad, 'where they bring women to satisfy the sexual desires of the fighters'. When she informed the audience at a Women in the World event in New York that the practice was on the rise in Syria, she was swiftly censured. 'They don't want to address the sexual violation which is committed by the opposition or by the jihadists, because they think this might destroy the image of the revolution.' Mona Eltahawy noted the same dynamic in her article 'Why Do They Hate Us?' in which she wrote, 'while we are eager to expose assaults by the regime, when we're violated by our fellow civilians we immediately assume they're agents of the regime or thugs because we don't want to taint the revolution'. But Mouna is unrepentant. 'I would never accept any revolution or any regime which would come to power on the money of women's bodies or sexual health or sexual life. And for me women, human rights, is more than any revolution. We wanted to change the regime for a better life for women and children. And we could not—' she corrects herself, 'we would not accept less than that.'

Since I spoke to Mouna, things have worsened for women in

the region with the ascendancy of the terrorist group that calls itself (at the time of writing) Islamic State (IS). Another woman has been stoned to death in Raqqa, this time for adultery, under a sentence handed down by new courts which boast of not meeting international standards of justice. This boast is voiced by a judge interviewed for a *Vice Magazine* documentary called *The Islamic State*, in which women are notable for their absence. The only time a woman features significantly in the entire forty minutes of the documentary is when a man walking down the street is summoned over by a patrol leader of the newly set up *Hisbah*, or religious police. 'Is she your wife?' he asks the man, indicating a veiled woman with whom the man was walking. Upon confirmation that she is his wife, the religious enforcer says, 'First of all tell her to change the fabric of her veil. And second, tell her not to hold her gown up, because we can see what she is wearing underneath. She is your wife, my brother, preserve her.' The patrol leader explains to the journalist sitting in the car with him, 'We told him, "This is your wife. She shouldn't be on display. Is she a product? Is she your wife or are you sharing her with people?"' It is now seen as a come-on for a woman to hold her skirt in such a way as to facilitate walking.

Across the now-bulldozed border between Syria and Iraq, women of the Yazidi faith have been captured and are being 'coaxed' by IS into converting to Islam, at which point they will be married off to jihadist husbands. The *Independent* article in which this is reported claims that the 'more lurid rumours of mass rapes and sexual enslavement of the women who were caught appear to be exaggerated'. But if these women are married to their captors, then mass rape and sexual enslavement is exactly what will have happened. And a later report from the BBC confirms that this is still happening. Young girls and women are 'being treated as spoils of war'; Adla, one of the few women who managed to escape, told reporters how every day 'men would come and make us take off our headscarves so they could choose which of us they wanted. Women were dragged out of the house by their hair.' Adla was moved from place to place and saw her friends being violently beaten and raped; she was left alone as she was pregnant. She eventually decided to attempt to escape because 'even if they captured and killed us, we'd prefer to be dead than to stay'.

Other women are fighting IS in their own way. In the UK, Kurdish women chained themselves to the railings outside Parliament to protest. In Syria, Kurdish women fighters boast of being 'the bravest fighters'. Diren, 19, says, 'We're not scared of anything… We'll fight to the last. We'd rather blow ourselves up than be captured by IS.' She claims that when IS fighters 'see a woman with a gun, they're so afraid they begin to shake. They portray themselves as tough guys to the world. But when they see us with our guns they run away. They see a woman as just a small thing. But one of our women is worth a hundred of their men.' Another brave woman living in Syria recently managed to get a film of life in IS out to the French media, risking her life in the process. The film shows people wandering the streets with Kalashnikovs slung over their shoulders, and women telling distraught families back home that they do not intend to return. The woman herself is forcefully chastised by a man in a car (we can see the tip of his gun poking out): 'Come over here! You have to behave better in public.' When the woman asks why, he informs her that he can see her face. 'I am truly sorry,' she replies. 'My niqab might be a bit transparent. I'm sorry.' The man tells her, 'You have to pay attention by covering up. God loves women who are covered,' before driving off.

Mouna is clear that female leaders are crucial if peace is ever to come to Syria. 'Women see war from a different perspective,' she tells me. 'They don't see it only from the perspective of power or influence, but from the perspective of the family.' She points to World Food Programme guidelines for humanitarian assistance that stipulate rations should be given to women rather than men, 'because research has shown that if you give it to a woman, all the family will eat, but if you give it to a man, only the man will eat'. This is only one example, but Mouna sees it as symbolic of the difference in perspective female leadership can bring: because women are brought up to be more invested in community and family, this is how they see the world. And when it comes to peace rather than war, a community approach, or what Mouna calls 'a wider influence', is essential.

But women are being shut out from negotiations. 'Men are telling women, "Go back home, it's not your time now, we want to build democracy, you should be home,"' Dalia Ziada told the *Christian Science Monitor* in October 2012. 'It's not proper that the people who led the revolution are now completely out of the scene,' she said. In a similar vein, in January 2014, Pakistan announced talks with the Taliban. At these talks, no women would be present – and yet on the table for discussion was the plan to ban women from appearing in public in jeans or without a headscarf. The day after the talks were announced, I spoke to Hibaaq Osman, founder of Karama, an organisation that lobbies for the UN's own stipulations that women must be included in peace talks.

'I mean, what are we talking about?' she said. 'Instead of talking about the security and the economy and the political...' She paused. 'They will spend so much time talking about whether a woman's going to wear jeans, I mean it just shows you what's wrong with this world! How can you take people who make this part of their negotiations seriously? Honestly. I think that's an indication that this is a joke.' Her frustration was spilling over as she asked me, 'Don't you think so?'

Women need to take care of themselves, Hibaaq insisted, because no one else is going to. 'The only way women can sustain the rights that they have gained is to make sure that there are people in parliament and policy makers that are supporting them. This is just what it's going to take. People who are going to negotiate on jeans, what are they going to do tomorrow? Today it's the jeans, tomorrow of course it's going to be your face, and then it's going to be you can't go to school, you can't work, don't go out of your house and stay there…' She trails off slightly disconsolately.

In her paper 'Rape, Genocide and Human Rights', Catharine MacKinnon wrote about how violations against women are not seen as human rights' violations – only as women's rights violations. When we are, like men, beaten and disappeared by the state, our human rights have been violated. But when, as more often happens to women, we are captured, beaten, raped, held prisoner, tortured and disappeared by men we know, we simply become 'the *desaparecidos* [forcibly disappeared] of everyday life', not awarded the dignity of being victims of human rights violations, because 'what was done to [us] smells of sex'. Even when the state is the actor, unless it is a violation that also happens to men (so, for example, being forced to cover your face would not qualify), these violations of basic freedoms are seen as, at most, a violation of women's rights, an implicitly less serious category than the grander *human* rights. 'Atrocities committed against women are either too human to fit the notion of female or too female to fit the notion of human.'

MacKinnon's argument may feel alienating at first reading. Obviously we know women are human beings. But culturally speaking, women's footing in humanity is less secure. The way women are always told to wait until after the revolution is secure before agitating for their rights adds heft to this analysis. Why are women to ignore rapes and beatings meted out from their own side, while men fight against beatings meted out by the state? Why does one sex being beaten matter less than another? Why are women told that they are splitting the movement when they highlight the injustices within it? The way the Arab Spring seems to be failing women has been most often compared to the Algerian and Iranian revolutions back in the 1950s, '60s and '70s. In both cases, women fought and resisted alongside men; in both cases, women were sent back to the kitchen (and in Iran, back behind a veil) and not included in post-revolution state-building. But there are other examples too.

Back in the 1970s, when 'the only position for women' in the Student Nonviolent Coordinating Committee was, in the words of Stokely Carmichael, a prominent civil rights activist, 'prone', Shulamith Firestone complained about the failure of the New Left to address women's concerns, to discuss the need for women to have 'control over their bodies'. The men in charge dismissed Firestone as a 'little girl' (one of them literally patted her on the head) and told her they had 'more important issues to talk about'. Later, at the New Left's counter-inaugural to Richard Nixon's first inauguration, Marilyn Webb and Firestone's speeches were both drowned out by rape threats from the crowd. Firestone's ultimate response? 'Fuck off, left. You can examine your navel by yourself from now on. We're starting our own movement.'

And it goes on today too. In 2012, feminist journalist Laurie

Penny attended a panel on 'The Future of Occupy Wall Street in New York'. She put up her hand at the end, asking about the make-up of the panel. Surely, she reasoned, 'if the crisis here is a lack of political imagination', to have a panel talking about 'the future of what is the largest honest-to-god countercultural movement we've seen for generations' made up of 'four middle-aged [white] guys' was, to put it mildly, jarring. Deeply affronted by the temerity of this young female upstart, Mark Crispin Miller, the panel organiser, began by patronising and mocking her, while David Graeber, on the panel to Miller's left, giggled inanely. Miller reminded Penny of the 'more important issues', before launching into a bizarre conspiracy theory about feminism being a plot concocted by the CIA in the 1970s to split the Left. He would later refer Penny to a bizarre rant from Daniel Brandt, something of a self-appointed CIA watchdog, about how '[o]ne yearns for the good old days, when issues were big, [and] women didn't want to be imperial spies'.

The thing is, though, that the 'good old days' when men were accepted without question as leaders are still with us. Over the past thirty years, only one in every forty signatories on global peace agreements has been a woman. Even in 2014, the UK sent an all-male delegation to a NATO summit. And it's no surprise to find that Anonymous, the biggest countercultural movement for change in a generation, has a white male face: the bearded, vacantly smiling Guy Fawkes mask of comic book series *V for Vendetta* fame. Anonymous occasionally edges into white knight territory. In 2013 it forced the Steubenville police force into action over one of the most notorious US rape cases of the year (members of the high school football team filmed their rape of a young woman and the media wrung their hands over the boys' ruined lives). But Anonymous stemmed from the infamously anarchic 4chan online forum, famed for its casual misogyny dressed up as lulz (their word for 'laughs'). Offline, the Occupy movement proved utterly incapable of dealing with the string of sexual assaults against women that took place in its camps. As in Egypt and Syria, sexual attacks by the authorities, 'the pigs', were swiftly and roundly condemned; when they came from within the movement itself, however, victims were on their own, asked to keep it as a private matter, so as not to 'taint' the movement.

While it is easy to feel disheartened by revolutions and movements failing women and sometimes actively oppressing them, there is, as ever, hope. And it is found in the women who are not waiting for an invitation from men to become leaders, but who are just going ahead and doing it anyway. In February 2014, Cynthia Cockburn reported for *openDemocracy* from Sarajevo, where a conference between Syrian and Bosnian women was being held. Like Bosnian women, Syrian women live in 'hyper-masculinized societies featuring the sexual abuse of women as men's weapon of choice for humiliating enemy males', she wrote. Like Bosnian women, Syrian women deal with 'misogynistic religious conservatism encroaching on their secular and civil space'. And like Bosnian women, Syrian women had been left out of the UN-mediated peace talks that were to decide their, and their country's, future.

This time, lessons really would be learnt. 'Bosnian women recalled how the war had galvanized them in projects of self-help and mutual help. Memories of unity in Yugoslav days had enabled some of them to reach out across ethnic conflict lines and support each other in work for women refugees and survivors of war rape. But the negotiation of a peace agreement, when the moment came, had taken place five thousand miles away at an airbase in Dayton, Ohio. The negotiators, dragged to the table by international actors, were the male war leaders, their sole motivation to retain territory and maximize power. Women and civil society had no presence and no voice in that process.' Don't let this happen to you, the Bosnian women told their Syrian sisters. And although there are obstacles to unity within the Syrian sisterhood, there are visions of hope, too, not least from the Syrian Women's Forum For Peace, a coalition of forty women from across the political landscape, set up by Mouna Ghanem. They hold meetings, workshops and training sessions. Mouna has hope that Assad's government will listen to them – if only because they want to show the world that it is only terrorists they oppose.

So too in Tunisia, where despite the reports of increased social conservatism, women are playing a crucial role in leading the country out of revolution. In her BBC documentary *Women of the Arab Spring*, Mona Eltahawy speaks to Amira Yahyaoui, a Tunisian human rights activist and founder of Al Bawsala, an NGO she set up to oversee the new Tunisian government and advocate for transparency. In January 2014, Tunisia passed its post-revolution constitution – which included an article specifically guaranteeing gender equality. Amira explains that Al Bawsala informed all parliamentarians that anyone who voted against the article would have their picture prominently displayed along a busy avenue in Tunis. 'Everyone will see you,' she warned. The constitution passed – even the most hard-line fundamentalist member of the government eventually voted for it, despite having delivered a speech the day before the vote in which he railed against the constitution. 'I took him and I hugged him,' Amira says. 'I think it was the first time he hugged someone who wasn't his wife.'

In Jordan, protests which originally began about the

economy quickly expanded, under the influence of women's groups, to include a focus on 'child marriage laws, so-called honour killings and domestic abuse'. The political reform that followed included a 12% quota for women in parliament – which now has 18 female MPs, one of whom, Wafa'a Bani Moustafa, is working to abolish article 308, under which a rapist can escape punishment if he marries his victim. She tells Mona Eltahawy that every female MP attended the session to sign the petition, and not one opposed it. 'This indicates that more women in parliament will naturally lead to there being better laws for women outside of parliament,' she says.

And there are women like Hibaaq Osman, who tells me, 'I think I'm just one of those people who never has the sense of fear. I don't have that.' She corrects herself: 'I just *cannot* have that, you know?' When it comes to women's rights, the difference between a leader and someone who just follows the crowd, Hibaaq argues, is that a leader is prepared to pay the inevitable price that comes with advocating for women. 'As a woman, for every accomplishment in life, you *have to* pay a price.' Women grow up facing red lights at every turn, she says. 'You always feel this red light, you know, don't go to that street because it's dark – something might happen to you. Don't talk like that because people will misunderstand you. Don't dress like this. But I haven't met any red light that I was not willing to cross and then take the consequences.'

Hibaaq echoes Mouna's point about women being particularly invested in their communities as she emphasises the strength women can bring as leaders. 'You can't change the community if they can't relate to who you are. Or what you are. You have to look like them and be like them and think like them in order for them to trust you and to *change* their lives.' We look for leaders and leadership in the wrong places, Hibaaq says, 'when it's right there in front of us. Like every time I go to these communities where I grew up, I learn so much. I have learnt so much in a few days from Eritrean fighters, women fighters, just by the way they stood! The way they put their hands in their pockets. The way they carried themselves. These women were breastfeeding in one hand and carrying a Kalashnikov in the other.' What did the way they stood teach her, I wondered. 'Fearlessness,' she says. 'They had no fear.'

When Hibaaq tells me that we look for leaders and leadership in the wrong places, that local people are needed to address local needs, I think of Camila Vallejo. In 2011, she emerged as the leader of a student movement that has revolutionised Chilean politics and, in the process, thrown a global question mark over the inevitability of neo-liberal economies. Her success certainly took her own government by surprise.

In September 2013, Paula Escobar Chavarría wrote that Chile was '*un país engaño*', a deceptive country, when it came to matters of gender. It has had (and now has again) a female president. But only 3% of boards are female; some large companies don't have a single female manager; the gender wage gap stands at around 30%; and female participation in parliament is a lowly 13%. Or at least it was.

Back in 2011, Chile's president was Sebastián Piñera, a billionaire businessman who headed up a centre-right Alianza Por Chile coalition. By the usual economic markers, Chile was doing well. In 2010, its economy was strong enough for it to be granted entry to the Organisation for Economic Co-operation and Development (OECD), a group of (currently) 34 countries committed to democracy and a market economy. By 2012, the

Economist reported that Chile's economy was growing by 6% a year, wages were rising, and unemployment was virtually nil. Inflation was low, gross domestic product (GDP, related to the size of the economy) was high.

But in terms of its score for equality and social mobility, Chile wasn't doing well at all. Although the number of Chileans living below the poverty line had fallen dramatically since the mid-1980s, Chile's income distribution was still the most unequal in the OECD, with the wealthiest 5% earning 257 times more than the poorest 5%. Discontent amongst Chileans that there was no 'trickle-down' of the country's growing wealth meant that when students took to the streets in May 2011, their complaints about a system that benefited the few while leaving the many floundering and saddled with debt resonated with a wide sector of society.

As well as having the questionable distinction of boasting the highest income inequality in the OECD, 40% of the amount spent on education in Chile comes from households rather than the state, and this is also the highest percentage in the OECD. In the OECD, the average amount of spending on higher education from public funds is 70%; in Chile it is only 16%. In 2009, Chile outscored all other Latin American states in the OECD's Programme for International Student Assessment (PISA) rankings – but out of 65 countries, it ranked 64th when it came to social segregation. Only in Peru were school students more divided by socio-economic background.

University tuition fees in Chile cost $3,400 a year, which, in a country where the average wage is $8,500, means Chile has the highest education costs in the world. And while theoretically Chile's universities, which are 75% privately owned, are legally barred from making profits, they routinely exploit loopholes that enable them to sell services such as housing to students at inflated prices. In 2012, a report revealed that eight universities had sidestepped the laws that prevent them from turning a profit by outsourcing services to companies under the same private ownership. These profit-making entities enjoyed non-profit tax status.

Enter stage right 'Comandante Camila', as she was crowned by some of her hundreds of thousands of supporters, railing against a system that one student banner summed up as '*5 años estudiando; 15 pagando*' (five years studying; fifteen paying). Education, she said, should be a public good. All students should have access to quality, state-funded primary and secondary education so that entry to higher education would no longer be dictated by socio-economic background. She denounced and rejected Piñera's solution of legalising the illegal profit-turning of Chile's universities.

Students turned out en masse on the streets again and again. Hundreds of schools and universities across the country were occupied, and thousands were arrested in heavily policed protests where gas canisters and water cannon were used, and that turned into violent clashes. Workers joined the protests, and by August 2011, after just over three months, Piñera's approval ratings slumped from the 63% high he'd held since the successful rescue of thirty-three trapped miners in October 2010 to 26%. According to a BBC report from the time, this is the lowest rating for any Chilean president since the return to democracy in 1990.

Panicked, Piñera tried a range of approaches to handle the growing discontent. He forcefully repressed the protests; he reshuffled his government; he presented the protesters with various concessions. The students, led most visibly by Camila

Vallejo, were unimpressed and continued to reject the government's proposals. Camila knew that she had the country behind her, and that the government was running scared. It simply didn't have a clue how to handle this popular movement that, with its propensity for flash mobs and kiss-ins, alongside more traditional marches and powerful speech-making, knew how to exploit social and traditional media.

Camila was the second-ever female leader of the Federación de Estudiantes de la Universidad de Chile (FECH), the University of Chile's 150-year-old student union. She had become president of the union in November 2010, six months before Chile's students took to the streets. As president she oversaw forty-two protests between June and November 2011 – and although she lost her re-election bid in December 2011 to Gabriel Boric, her talent for rousing speeches and canny media sound bites ensured that she remained the face of the student movement, leaving its actual president to play second fiddle to her charismatic de facto leadership.

By November 2012, Camila was nominated by the Communist Party as its candidate for the La Florida district in the upcoming elections for Chile's House of Deputies. In 2013 Camila won her seat with one of the largest majorities of the whole election. By this point, she was still only twenty-five years old.

As is the case for most female politicians, Camila's rise to prominence was quickly followed by a backlash. Camila was demeaned and belittled, her leadership reduced to 'attention-seeking', her solidarity with other social justice groups interpreted as an opportunity to parade her latest fashion and make-up choices in the media. Even those on her side seemed to focus more on her beauty than on her prowess: the *New*

York Times called Camila 'the World's Most Glamorous Revolutionary' in an article stuffed with references to the student leader's looks. The first two paragraphs informed readers that Camila is a 'Botticelli beauty who wears a silver nose ring' and related how a local bartender pronounced her '*bien buena la mina*', or 'hot'.

It got worse. A right-wing politician took to Twitter to call her 'una putita' (a little whore – an attempt at both belittlement and sexual shaming); another advocated that 'the bitch' should be killed in order to end the unrest. Violent threats started amassing and Camila was placed under police protection; her address was published online, forcing her to move out of her home. 'As a woman, I can see and relive in my own skin the current forms of oppression of which we are victims in the current misogynistic configuration of society. In Chile… there is a history of oppression and sexism that lasts to this day. Us women still suffer all kinds of discrimination, when we look for work, in healthcare plans, in wages, even when we participate in politics,' Camila says.

But she keeps going – and keeps delivering results. By August 2014, less than a year after she had been voted into office, she had witnessed the approval of a bill on education that contained new regulations on profit-making and student selection, as well as tackling the loopholes educational establishments were exploiting to get round the law on profiteering. It was a clear result for Camila, addressing the demands she had been championing ever since her emergence in 2011. As she sat in the House watching the votes come in, she began to cry. 'I don't know how others might have responded, watching the session live,' she told Francisca Miranda for the daily newspaper *La Tercera* a week later, 'but for me, it was hugely emotional, to be there in the commission, defining something that for me, and for the people I represent, is so very important.' She was perhaps too politic to mention it, but given the doubts voiced about her ability to carry these changes forward, her achievement must have been even more satisfying. 'Many sectors say we won't be able to make these changes because we don't have the votes in Congress,' she had said back in November, but, she insisted, 'we've learned that there's no limit to what the social movement can achieve.' And now she has been vindicated again: Camila makes things happen.

Of course, not everyone likes what she is making happen, and Camila has seen her approval ratings plummet since she took office: a survey released only days before the approval of her education bill placed her at the bottom of all the politicians who were assessed. Camila is sanguine about the poll, putting it down to inevitable fear of the kind of fundamental change she is pushing. But I can't help wondering if there's something else going on here too. Talking to Camila, I remember the findings of the Name It. Change It. study, showing how any mention of a female politician's appearance in the media has a negative impact on her poll ratings. And Camila's beauty has had more than its fair share of media attention.

Camila remains determined to see her radical project through. 'I'm convinced that it is necessary to advance, despite all the difficulties that you have to face along the way. And it is because of that that I have been prepared to put up with all the criticism and all the bad times that I've had to go through, because I believe in the project.' And then there's her daughter Adela. 'You think about those who are to come,' Camila says. 'I don't want Adela to be in a classroom with just Adelitas... I want her to know the diversity of our country.' Thanks to Adela's mother's efforts, that is now increasingly likely, where only a year before it was an increasingly remote possibility.

Something else Adela will have in her favour is Camila herself, as a role model to look up to, an example from which she can learn. As a campaigner on education, Camila will know about the dramatic difference education makes to a child even before the age of five. In 2011, a US paper based on the findings from numerous studies found that education provided for children under five was 'crucial in the fulfilment of an individual's future potential'. Children who participated in early childhood education did better at school – and by the age of 40 they were more likely to be employed, own their own home and car, and have higher median earnings that the control group. They also developed what the study called 'non-cognitive' abilities, such as higher self-esteem and social skills. Perhaps most impressively, the study found that early childhood education could 'mediate and even prevent the skill gaps for children from disadvantaged families'.

When we say education, we tend to mean the type of learning that we associate with school. Learning to speak, to count, learning the names of objects, the names of colours, the alphabet. But there is another set of skills we are taught from the day we are born that is related to the non-cognitive abilities mentioned in the US study. Research findings on this particular branch of early childhood education are not accepted as readily. Rather, there seems to be a keenness to attribute this set of learned skills to biology. I am talking, of course, about skills related to gender.

Cordelia Fine is a cognitive neuroscientist who wrote a brilliant book called *Delusions of Gender*. With precise and voluminous research, she shattered the various claims of what she dubbed 'neurosexism' – the field of supposedly scientific research that claims men and women simply have different brains, which explains why women do laundry and men do maths. And yet, she writes, when she told parents what she was working on, the number one response was 'an anecdote about how they tried gender-neutral parenting, and it simply didn't work'. It doesn't matter what the research says: I personally tried to give my girl a truck and she ended up putting it to bed like a dolly. Therefore, gender is innate. The thing is, by the time you've given your three-year-old daughter a truck, she's already extremely well-trained in feminine behaviour. And, as Fine's book shows, you're probably not parenting in quite as gender-neutral a way as you may think.

Even before your baby is born, you are likely to be treating it according to its gender. Fine shares the finding of a study by sociologist Barbara Katz Rothman that when mothers didn't know the sex of their babies there was no distinction, in terms of the baby's eventual sex, in the way the movements of the foetuses were described, but when mothers *did* know the sex of their baby, the differences were striking. Male activity was 'more likely to be described as "vigorous" and "strong"'; female activity was gentler: '*not* violent, *not* excessively energetic, *not* terribly active'. Once the baby is born, parents are more likely to place a birth announcement if the baby is a boy; and they are more likely to express pride if the baby is a boy, and happiness if she is a girl.

The difference in how children are treated continues as the baby grows up. Mothers are 'more sensitive to facial expressions of happiness when an unfamiliar six-month-old baby is labelled as a girl rather than a boy', and although boys are no less responsive to mothers' speech and no more likely to leave a mother's side, mothers talk and interact more with girl babies. This continues as infants reach toddler and pre-school years, a finding that Fine points out is consistent with the stereotyped belief that females are the emotion experts (a supposed expertise that tends to bite us on the bum as girls grow up into supposedly over-emotional, irrational women).

This research chimes with a very telling study quoted by Kat Banyard in her book *The Equality Illusion*. Beverly I. Fagot from the University of Oregon monitored the behaviour of infants between twelve and fourteen months old and 'found no differ-ence in the frequency with which males and females displayed "assertive behaviours" (such as shoving, hitting, and grabbing) and "communicative behaviours" (such as talking, gesturing, and babbling)'. They did, however, find a difference in the way adults responded to this behaviour. When the babies displayed assertive behaviour, males got a response from the carer 41% of the time – females got it 10%. When they displayed communicative behaviour, girls came out on top, with a response rate of 65%, leaving boys trailing at 48%. And when the behaviour was aggressively attention-seeking (screaming, crying, pulling at the caregiver), male babies got a response 55% of the time and females 18% of the time. When the babies were revisited a year later, the girls were more interactive with their carers, while the boys were more assertive and aggressive.

Let's pretend for a moment that parents really are parenting in as gender-neutral a way as they think. Even if they are, there's only so much parents can do. Fine mentions the experience of one couple who tried very hard to parent their children neutrally. They shared care responsibilities equally; they edited books so that there were equal numbers of male and female characters in both key and background roles; all toys were devoid of gender markings and offered with equal enthusiasm. And then their children went to school. '[O]ur son Jeremy, then age four… decided to wear barettes [hair slides] to nursery school. Several times that day, another little boy told Jeremy that he, Jeremy, must be a girl because "only girls wear barettes". After trying to explain to this child that "wearing barrettes doesn't matter" and that "being a boy means having a penis and testicles", Jeremy finally pulled down his pants as a way of making his point more convincingly. The other child was not impressed. He simply said, "Everybody has a penis; only girls wear barrettes."'

Fine doesn't tell us if Jeremy persisted in his gender-deviant habit of wearing barrettes after this experience, but she does mention the experience of another child, a girl this time, who turned up to school on fancy dress day as a cat. Every other girl was wearing a princess or fairy outfit. The girl burst into tears, wailing that she should have worn *her* princess outfit. And next fancy dress day, she did. This ties in with the way that pre-school children spend more time playing with gender-appropriate toys when among their peers than when they are on their own. There is a rather terrifying study mentioned by Fine that shows how little time it takes for children to learn to 'choose' what they are expected to like. A classroom of children between the ages of three and five were classified as either blue or red, it only took three weeks of being classified in this way to bias children's view. They 'preferred' toys they were told were liked by children of their colour, and they wanted to play with children of their colour. Fine also mentions another study where children were shown a video of a man and woman playing a game where the man performed one type of ritual and the woman another. The girls did copy the woman and the boys the man – but only after having confirmed that these rituals were what men and women did *in general*, rather than just in this particular instance. The lesson: parents can only have so much influence in a society where every TV channel, book, magazine, advert and friend says the opposite.

And they do. Studies of gender representation in children's books, TV shows and films all show that male characters are dramatically over-represented. A study looking at children's books found that males were almost twice as likely as females to appear in title roles, and that they appeared about 50% more in pictures, while an international study of children's TV programmes found that only 32% of characters are female – and this goes down to 13% if the figure isn't human – for example, where it is a robot or an animal. A US study from 2011 by the Geena Davis Institute found that 'a large percentage of stories [in children's TV programmes]' were 'extremely' male centric, casting boys or men in 75% or more of the speaking roles, with female characters only representing 28% of speaking roles. Another Geena Davis Institute study found that female speaking roles in G-rated (for general audiences) Hollywood films also sat at 28%, while women only represented one in five (17%) of the characters in crowd scenes. (Incidentally, 17% is also the proportion of women in a mixed-sex group that it takes for men to think both sexes are equally represented; when women hit 33%, men think women are in the majority.)

Men and women are also represented differently. A study into children's books found that one sex was most commonly described as 'beautiful, frightened, worthy, sweet, weak and scared', and the other was 'big, horrible, fierce, great, terrible, furious, brave and proud'. A study into films found that over half of female characters in children's films were depicted as 'nurturing', and females were over five times as likely as males to be shown in sexually revealing clothes. '[A]lmost all of the females in the sample were praised for their appearance or physical beauty.' In the context of research showing that learning tends to happen when *positive* rather than negative reinforcement is delivered to media characters, the report concludes that 'a child viewer watching these films may vicariously learn that beauty is an essential part of being female'.

What children are unlikely to learn, however, is that an essential part of being female is having a career. A study of every first-run G-rated film theatrically released in the United States between 5 September 2006 and 7 September 2009 found a 'pronounced gender gap' in the employment of the over 800 speaking characters analysed. Across the sample, a total of 333 speaking characters were shown in a job-related light; 268 of those characters were male. In contrast to the men in the films sampled, not one female was depicted in medical science, executive business, law or politics. Almost all business owners and military/law enforcers were male. A later study taking in children's films and television between September 2006 and September 2007 found that women comprised 25.3% of employed characters in children's TV shows, and only 20.3% in family films. As the study points out, women comprised 47% of the US labour force in 2011.

As in the earlier study, women did not tend to be depicted at the top of their field. Across the entire sample there was not one woman to be found at the top in the financial sector, the legal arena or journalism – this in comparison to the reality, which is a paltry, but still better than zero, 25.5% of chief executives being female in the United States in 2010. There were only three female characters presented as being at the top of the political sphere, two of whom did not speak and are only referred to by name, and all three of whom were 'inconsequential to the stories they populate'. This was in contrast to men, who held over forty-five different prestigious political positions. When it came to science, technology, engineering and mathematics (STEM), there was not a single female protagonist or co-lead who worked in the field, compared with 14 men.

Does any of this matter? Well, it matters if we care about level playing fields and free choices. One Canadian study demonstrated the impact of sexist adverts on female students who were 'invested in doing well in maths'. The study showed one mixed-gender group a selection of 'gender-stereotypic' adverts (a woman so excited about a new skin treatment that she bounces on her bed for joy; another where a female student dreams of being homecoming queen), and the other group – also mixed gender – a selection of 'neutral' adverts. Then both groups were given the same test, which included both maths and verbal problems. Both men and women in the neutral condition, and men in the gender-stereotype condition, attempted more maths than verbal problems (remember that these students are invested in doing well at maths). By contrast, women in the gender-stereotype condition displayed the exact inverse propensity, being more likely to attempt verbal problems. They also became more likely to express a preference for careers that rely on linguistic rather than mathematical abilities (in contrast to the three other groups, who chose mathematical careers), and became less interested in taking on leadership roles.

The phenomenon that is being highlighted in this study is called 'stereotype threat' – and it is worryingly easy to trigger. Something as simple as asking women to record their sex at the beginning of a quantitative test has been shown to negatively affect their performance; and women being in the minority when they take a test has also been shown to trigger the stereo-type-threat effect. And the impact is not minor. In one study from Italy, women who were told that a gender difference has been observed in 'logical-mathematical tasks' ended up per-forming more than 20% worse in a test held immediately afterwards. In an American study, more than 100 students (both male and female) who were enrolled in 'a fast and difficult calculus class that was a pipeline to the hard sciences', and who had, on average, received more or less the same course grades, were given a particularly tough calculus test. One group was told that the test was designed to try to understand what makes some people better at maths than others; the other group was told this as well as that, despite thousands of students having been tested, no gender difference had ever been found. Both men and women in the first group, and men in the second group, scored on average 19%; but women in the second group scored on average 30%.

As I've hinted earlier, there is a solution to this problem – namely, using female role models, which have been shown to dramatically alleviate the various effects of stereotype threat. A Harvard study gave two groups a maths test. One group was given the test by a woman presented as incompetent at maths, while the other group was given the test by a woman presented as competent at maths. By now it shouldn't be a surprise to learn that the women who were given the test by a positive female role model did better than those who were given the test by a negative female role model; the same researchers also found that women did better when they were given the test by a woman rather than a man.

★

So, role models matter. Unfortunately however, they are in short supply, particularly in STEM subjects. In a self-perpetuating cycle, women don't choose to study STEM because they don't perceive these subjects as being for women. A University of Michigan study cited by Cordelia Fine showed women were quicker to pair words like calculate, compute and maths with words like he, him and male, than with female words. And the higher up you go in maths, the fewer women there are: in the United States in 2013, women earned 43.1% of undergraduate degrees in maths – but only made up 25% of the workforce. (In 1986 the percentage of maths degrees earned by women was 46.5%, so it's not simply a case of waiting for the numbers to trickle through.)

But all hope is not lost, because some women do make it through – and some of them are using their success to make it easier for their female colleagues to follow them up to the top. One of those women is Sara Seager, an astrophysicist at the Massachusetts Institute of Technology (MIT). Sara was awarded tenure at MIT when she was 35, but she is still a rarity as a woman in her field. 'It's still male-dominated,' she tells me, 'I'm still unusual.' Her reputation tends to rule out outright sexism: 'Because I'm so senior now and I'm an MIT professor, I have all these awards, people won't mess with me, I won't get treated badly.' She is still, however, regularly met with puzzlement: 'people expect an older male professor'. Sometimes, as when she first met the man to whom she is now engaged, Sara tells me, laughing, she is mistaken for someone's wife: she was actually the keynote speaker.

Sara's experience chimes with the findings of a 2008 report from the Center for Work-Life Policy, which commented on the tendency for men to assume their female colleagues work in admin, or that the woman is the most junior person in a meeting when she is the most senior. This is more than merely irritating: the research shows that each time a female engineer is mistaken for a junior worker or admin assistant, she is being reminded of the stereotype that she does not belong in her job, making it harder for her to do her job effectively.

Sara's gender has been salient throughout her academic career. It was obvious right from when she was an undergraduate that her field was male-dominated, she says. 'In my programme in physics there were hardly any women. In the first year there were a fair number, but basically they all dropped out.' And the women who were there were often assumed to be less capable. When she and two other women received astronomy summer internships about a year into the course, a guy on their course informed them that 'the reason you got your jobs is because you're female'. Their grades were around 80 and 90 out of 100, and his were around 60. 'We just looked at him like he was an idiot, because everyone knows each other's grades.' And yet, he was still convinced that he belonged more than they did.

But it wasn't just the students. Sara tells me about the professors who, instead of answering the question she asked, would repeatedly answer an easier one. 'Like three times in a row. But a guy asks a question and it's answered.' A pivotal moment for Sara was when her traditionally nerdy-looking male lab partner in her physics lab got a letter grade above hers: 'I was smarter. I did a better job… I knew I knew more.' But he was 'perceived as just being smarter and I knew that wasn't true'. She understood then how 'subjective' it all was, that how she presented herself was as important as the work that she produced, and that she could 'lose out'. Things like this were 'always happening, always', she tells me.

MIT was making an effort to address these issues even when Sara was an undergrad, and she tells me about supportive professors who encouraged her, noting that it tended to be those who had daughters of their own. But given the gender-biased environment, it is hardly surprising that so many of Sara's female peers dropped out. Even now, women have to be 'so many light years ahead of their peers to succeed', Sara says. One of her current students 'is such a brilliant physicist, unbelievable. If she was lesser, she never would have made it through all the struggles. I think, if you're so talented, people will let you pass no matter what… I feel like that's what happened with me and other women.' I am reminded of the aphorism that we will have achieved gender equality when there are as many mediocre women at the top as there are mediocre men.

But in the end, does it really matter that STEM is still so male-dominated? 'You know, I've thought about that for a long time,' Sara tells me. 'And people throw various rules around, like some people say, well our talent pool is cut in half if we don't have women. But you know, the only reason that I could actually like… was that it's a measure of equality.' Until we live in a world where women can 'do whatever they want, and be treated well, and get to do what they've set out to do', Sara says, 'I think we lack equality. So for me, that's the main reason.'

But how are we going to get to that point, Sara wonders, when women themselves feel so inadequate? 'That's the reason these women are dropping out, that they're not asking questions, that they're not pursuing what they really want to do. It's a lack of confidence in themselves.'

As we have seen, the building blocks for this lack of confidence are set in motion from before a baby is even born. But when does it come to fruition? Since having children, Sara has become interested in this question. Girls her sons' age – that is, up to the age of eight – are 'the most confident people alive. These little girls, they're like they own the world.' But by the time Sara sees them in college, their self-confidence is notable by its absence. Sara is missing a chunk of data ('I don't see them in between, because I don't know high school students, not yet anyway'), so she asked one of her students what happens. 'High school happens,' she was told.

'High school happens' reminds me of a memory of my own that has always stuck with me. I was sitting at the lunch table at school. I was about eleven. And suddenly, it occurred to me that I was talking and the boys were talking – but the other girls were more or less silent. More than this, it came to me in a flash that the boys didn't *like* that I was as loud as they were. Somehow, even at the age of eleven, I knew that it mattered what boys thought of me. I knew they had social power that I didn't. So for the next seven years or so, I tried to tone it down a bit (without much success). I chastised myself on the rare occasions I was self-aware enough to catch my loud mouth taking over. Just as I never thought to question the fact that I would be harassed if I went out clubbing, so it never occurred to me to question why I had any less right to talk than the boys.

Fast forward nearly twenty years (to the day before I interviewed Sara, in fact), and I'm at a seminar on poetry publishing being given by a male friend of mine. After his talk, my friend took questions from the audience – and the session developed into a general discussion among the men in the room. I tried to think of something to say, just to even out the balance, but sadly my lack of expertise, or even passing acquaintance with poetry publishing, proved to be a hindrance. After the talk, the women all immediately melted away, and the men stayed to continue the debate. I particularly noticed one young man who had just finished his PhD and was engaging in lively conversation with a much older professor – the head of department, in fact. As I saw these vital homosocial career connections being made, I found myself thinking, 'This is how it happens.' Afterwards, as I walked to the station with my friend, I asked him what he'd thought of the gender dynamic. He hadn't even noticed it. We are just so used to men doing the talking, that women's silence doesn't strike us as noteworthy – perhaps explaining why men think women are in the majority when they represent 33% of a group. Perhaps that is the figure it takes for most women to feel comfortable talking in mixed groups.

Sara tells me that she'd been in a similar position on the very day I spoke to her, when she'd attended a talk on astronomy. 'There were maybe fifty to seventy-five people in the audience, maybe only one woman for every fifteen men. And I was the only woman who asked a question. I always try to, you know, to sort of make it OK for the other women to.' It didn't work in this case – but I know anecdotally from friends who teach that if a female member of the audience is called upon first, other women are far more likely to ask questions too.

Sara has also implemented more systematic, practical solutions. She 'started a programme to mentor younger women who had huge potential, but were limited' because they didn't believe in that potential. A scientist to the core, Sara carried out experiments with these women to find out what was at the root of their particular strain of impostor syndrome (a phenomenon whereby high-achieving women do not believe in their own competence). Once the root was identified, she would set tasks for each woman to get them over whatever their particular fear was. Some women were forced to ask questions after lectures;

some had to go up to unknown senior scientists at events and start chatting to them. 'The exercise would make them get way outside their comfort zone until that became the norm, and then they would go a step even further outside their comfort zone until *that* became the norm.'

When I ask Sara why she herself doesn't seem to have needed a similar programme to overcome feminised confidence issues, she tells me, 'I was born with a risk-taking gene.' This gene, she says, was developed by two key figures in her life. One was her stepfather, who, from Sara's description, might most flatteringly be described as an authoritarian. Sara's childhood under the control of this man can hardly be recommended as an ideal incubator for confident women, but she does credit him for what she considers a crucial factor in her success: 'I wasn't afraid of authority, and I had disrespect for people that I didn't like. So I think in retrospect, do I thank him for this?' She laughs. 'You know, I don't think I can *thank* him.' As a child, there was nothing she could do about the situation, but later it would prove to have been her making. When older professors tore apart her lectures, her work, her ideas, she says, 'I just didn't really care that much, because I was torn apart many times by my stepfather and I could just categorise them as a jerk. I didn't take it personally. I couldn't. I had to learn how to not take stuff personally.'

This ability makes Sara something of an outlier: stereotype threat and impostor syndrome affect most women and mean that the majority would not be able to rise above such criticism, because to them it simply confirms the suspicions they themselves already hold: that they don't belong, that they are indeed inadequate and incompetent. Because the derision fits with what they have been told over and over again in magazines, newspapers, adverts, films and books, by teachers, by friends, by their parents, it rings true, and this makes it that much harder to shake off. If girls are brought up to hold a belief in their innate access to objectivity and rational, hard-headed, emotionless 'facts', their ability to overcome prejudice will be more developed.

The second figure to shape Sara was her father. He actively encouraged his daughter, Sara says, and 'told me I'm *allowed* to take risks'. He told her she must never be dependent on any man, and he taught her to 'think big', even at the risk of seeming pushy. (An analysis of the 450-million-word Corpus of Contemporary American English found that women in leadership roles were labelled 'pushy' twice as often as men.) It was on a car journey with her father that, as a child, she discovered a wonder for the universe that she has never lost: 'my early memories are associated with my dad and the stars'. 'The moon was following me in the car,' she tells me. 'I just couldn't understand why, no matter which way the car turned, or how far we went, the moon was always right there. And I just couldn't figure this out. I was just so stuck on it. And I asked my dad and he didn't have an answer.' Not long after, Sara saw the moon through a telescope for the first time – 'and it just took my breath away'. On her first camping trip, she saw the stars in a dark sky. 'I *really* had no idea that existed. I saw so many stars, I just couldn't believe it. It was just so phenomenal. I just was shocked, I had no idea it was *there*.' The next shock was discovering at a university open day that she could look at the stars as a career. The day she made this discovery was 'probably one of the best days of my life. I was just thrilled. I was like *wow*: I just can't believe you can do this for a job.'

But this is exactly what she does do for a job. Sara is a planet hunter. She is one of the leading scientists investigating the atmospheric composition and interior structure of exoplanets (planets that orbit a star other than our sun). It's not easy to find exoplanets. Sara and her team are looking in what's called the 'habitable zone', not too far from or too close to their star. But in this zone, the planets are still pretty close to a very bright star. Just as 'our sun is ten billion times brighter than the earth at visible wavelengths', as Sara says, so hunting these planets is like 'looking for a firefly next to a searchlight, when the firefly and searchlight are thousands of miles away'. Nevertheless, over the past twenty years or so, thousands of exoplanets have been found, with about two dozen residing in the habitable zone. It is Sara's job to detect life on these planets by searching for gases that might be produced by life – again, no easy task. It involves using a hugely powerful telescope and a specially shaped screen, positioned between the telescope and the star to block out enough of the starlight that the planet can be seen by the telescope – but it's a very delicate business. This star shade and the telescope have to be aligned despite being tens of thousands of kilometres apart (in terms of space distance, this is tiny); and the shade has to be manufactured to be precise to a micron. Sara believes that within her lifetime she will be able to take her children to a dark sky and point to a planet that has an atmosphere like Earth's.

The hunt for exoplanets that can support life was not considered a serious field of academic enquiry when Sara embarked on her research. Part of this scepticism, she tells me, is simply a healthy feature of the scientific method: everything she was theorising went against what had, up until that point, been scientific orthodoxy about the formation of planets. As a lowly PhD student, Sara dared to speculate that what held for our solar system might not hold elsewhere. She has since been vindicated by her later findings (in fact, she says, our solar system is so rare that a copy has yet to be found), and in 2013, Sara was awarded a MacArthur Fellowship, or 'genius grant', worth $625,000. The prize is intended as an investment in someone whose work demonstrates 'originality, insight, and potential', and recipients are free to do whatever they want with the money. Sara chose to spend hers on making sure her domestic duties were discharged, leaving her free to continue to do what she does best: find new ways to search for alien life.

It's something that previously might not have occurred to her. Sara tells me that before her husband died of cancer, she used to play the traditionally male role in her marriage. 'I did nothing, I was oblivious,' she says. 'I mean, I knew my family didn't like it when I was away, but every time I travelled, I had my babysitter stay, to help out my husband. And I would still do five loads of laundry before I went away, you know, I'd still have to do stuff. But it wasn't at the same level as it is now I'm the primary caretaker, and I have to orchestrate. I feel pressure.' Sara wasn't a 'jerk' before; she simply had no idea of how much mind space and energy the role takes up. It's another telling example of how perspective-blindness can play a role in institutional and even individual sexism – like that shown by the men who recently asked her to chair a committee that would involve an amount of travel that is simply not realistic now she is a primary caregiver. (There is evidence that some of the discrimination against female caregivers goes further than simple thoughtlessness, however; a study has found that men who asked for flexible time to enable them to carry out childcare commitments were rated as 'more respectable, likable, committed, and promotionworthy than a woman who made the exact same request'.)

Sara's decision as to how to spend her grant wasn't a deliberate feminist act though. 'It was just an honest answer,' she says, telling me she was surprised by the huge reaction. 'It was wonderful, because women from all over would say "wow, are you even allowed to say that out loud?" and I was like, well I don't know, why not? I mean it just hadn't occurred to me that it was a problem.' She acknowledges that she is extremely lucky to be able to afford help with her childcare and other domestic work – but since she can now afford it, and since her particular talent lies in determining the atmospheric composition of planets that are millions of light years away, rather than in cooking, why should she force herself to do both tasks badly, rather than one task as brilliantly as she does? Somehow, we never seem to ask men why they are outsourcing the majority of their care work to their wives.

While most of us are not going to be awarded genius grants, there is hope that we might be able to cut down our housework time in the future thanks to roboticists like Angelica Lim. Angelica speaks to me from the Honda Research Institute in Japan, the 'birthplace of Asimo, which is a pretty famous humanoid robot'. Robots that undertake housework have not historically been the main focus of robotics, but with the influx of women into the field, Angelica thinks we will start to see more domesticated robots. 'There are a lot of women that could benefit from algorithms being directed toward housework,' says Angelia. She's right: OECD figures from 2012 found that women still do twice the amount of unpaid care work men do per day. 'It would help reduce their stress and it would free their time for other things, but because there are so few women in this field making the technology, we have, you know, military drones as robots.'

Angelica first got into her specific robotics specialism while she was working in her lab in Kyoto on a project to make a robot that would play music. She got the musical robot to work, but then thought: 'Wow this really sucks! You know, it's not expressive, it doesn't express any emotions: it's just not very good. And so that's when I got fascinated with the idea of what would it mean for the robot to express emotional music? Does that mean it has to have emotions to express? If it just plays music that seems emotional but it doesn't actually have emotions, does it count? And that's when I really started looking into what does it mean to feel emotions when you listen to music?'

Angelica now works in the field of affective computing, or emotional robotics. 'It's a very new field,' Angelica tells me – and it's one that has been pioneered by women, and is still dominated by them. 'When I go to a general robotics conference, for example, the biggest one in the world called IROS, the percentage of women will be maybe twenty to thirty per cent, and then when I go to a conference that's particularly about the topic of human–robot interaction, so how to make robots that are more naturally interactive, it jumps to something like forty or fifty per cent.'

I ask her how emotional robotics is regarded within the wider robotics community. 'The field that I'm in, luckily I get to tag on the name "artificial intelligence", which is actually what I'm working on. It's not just making it seem more interactive, but writing algorithms that perform heavy processing and so on. But still, when I say emotion, people are very dismissive. And I'm like, what roboticist do you know that's trying to actually make a robot feel? In reality, that's a very difficult problem.' Not only is it a difficult problem, but there is a growing awareness, in the social sciences and beyond, that humans (yes, men too) are not rational, predictable, emotionless beings. So the tools we design to help us need to account for that, if they are in fact going to help us. This is as true for robots as it has proven to be for predictive economic models, and for safety measures in the aviation and healthcare industries. As Angelica points out, 'they have to be more emotionally intelligent to help us the way that we really want to be helped'.

The developments made by behavioural scientists have yet to fully catch on among what Angelica calls the 'hardcore' robotics set. She tells me about one roboticist who said, '"Oh that's not real robotics." He was working on something like precision manipulators, or something more low-level. So it's really a question of perception, and value-set I guess.' A value-set that, as Felicity Aston discovered, determines that emotion is rubbish, because emotion is for girls.

Even when Angelica wins, she doesn't. 'I once won an award at a robotics conference, and it was a very big thing for me.' The next night, 'I was hanging out with one of the other roboticists and he was like, "You know Angelica, you only got that award because the judges thought you were cute."' She laughs exasperatedly. 'I was like, come *on*, you know?' She tells me about another roboticist at a very prestigious university in Switzerland – 'she is doing an amazing job and she has had the same thing, she has gotten comments just like that'. I am reminded of Candie's experience of so-called positive discrimination – and Sara being told by a less academically successful man that she had got her placement because she was a woman.

The issue of value judgements goes beyond disparagement, however. Angelica mainly works with algorithms which, in simple terms, are the processes by which a decision is taken. So, for example, when you search for something using Google, the algorithm is *how* Google decides which pages to show you. We all use algorithms every day: they are in our computers, in our washing machines, and, of course, on the Internet. They are silently shaping our lives. But while they themselves may seem like harmless processes that help us day to day, they are by no means free from societal baggage, because each algorithm is designed by a human (or a team of humans), meaning that subjective values, interests and biases will inevitably affect the algorithm's design and output.

'In algorithms there are basically three things that the designer takes care of,' Angelica tells me. The first decision, naturally, is to determine what problem is most pressing. What does humanity most need solving? So far, what humanity apparently most needs are more efficient ways to both make money in financial trading and kill each other. But are more drones and super-fast banking algorithms what benefit humanity as a whole, or are they what benefit a select bunch of algorithm designers and their paymasters?

To be fair on roboticists, they have branched out from killing and money-making machines: we also have sexy robots. 'In robotics, I swear, the researchers, who are predominantly male, they're trying to maximise the similarity of humanoid robots to sexy women,' Angelica tells me. 'And there's this one that's just like the icing on the cake. The robot is in a wedding dress, and they're maximising lots of things, they're trying to maximise similarity in the voice, the way she moves, to a sexy woman, the way her skin looks. I guess that's not necessarily what a female engineer would try to optimise, right?' Angelica laughs. And when I look at the robot (sexily named HRP-4C), I can't help laughing too – not least because the dress they've put her in is truly awful.

While there's something incredibly creepy about a 'sexy' robot paraded in a wedding dress, it's not that Angelica minds so much as she simply doesn't find it interesting. 'I just ignore them.' She laughs again. But she tells me that she does find it fascinating that 'the state of the art is a female robot. It looks totally human-like and so forth. But it just doesn't seem to attract as much awe and interest for me as it does my male friends, who are just like, oh my god there's this really hot female robot, and it's like…' She finishes her thought with a dismissive snort.

The contrast between Angelica's response to the HRP-4C robot and the responses of her male friends highlights the issue with the second and third things an algorithm designer 'takes care of', once they've decided on what the problem is (the need for more maiming; more money; more sexy robots). They will decide what parameter to maximise (speed, accuracy, sexiness), and then finally they will run tests to determine the extent to which the algorithm is successful: does it do what they intended it to do? The problems are immediately obvious: even if we accept that 'sexiness' is a useful parameter to maximise, sexiness is in the eye of the beholder.

Angelica broadens out the issues to address web-search algorithms, which, she tells me, are still mainly designed by men. 'It is a bit difficult to say, because what we see is what we get,' Angelica tells me, but what they're doing behind the scenes is 'trying out a whole bunch of these rules, and then they're testing it and they themselves are evaluating how good they think the output is. And so we don't see any of that, we just get the final result.' Angelica's concern is that without a diverse team evaluating the results, some missing results that may not be considered relevant to, let's say, a straight white male audience might be extremely relevant to a black lesbian woman.

Back in robot world, Angelica gives me an example of the perspective-blinkers at work. 'I was at a robotics conference a couple of years ago in Slovenia and there was a company show-casing their robot. It looked really futuristic, really sleek, and it was taller than me. I'm about five foot two, so it was maybe five seven, five eight. Quite tall. And it was on wheels. And so the guys that were showing off this product were like, "Hey try it out, just wave at it, and it will come shake your hand." And so I wave at the robot, and then it kind of turns toward me slowly, puts out its hand, and then comes *barreling* towards me, fast.' Just hearing Angelica's description makes me nervously think of sci-fi robots gone rogue. 'It made me jump backwards, and I made this little shriek.' She laughs. 'It was terrifying! It was like the robot had this hand-seeking missile, you know, it locked onto its target, and it maximised speed and accuracy to come shake my hand, right?'

Like the men who expected more travel from Sara than a primary-caregiver could manage, the members of the all-male team that designed this robot weren't deliberately trying to exclude women from their research. They just had a failure of perspective, being, as men are on average, taller than Angelica. 'For them it probably looked confident, whereas for me, it looked scary,' Angelica explains, pointing out that it would only have needed a single woman testing the robot once to recognise the problem. A robot that inadvertently maximises unease is not the end of the world, but it does highlight yet more flaws in the assumption that value judgements are universal.

But things do slowly seem to be changing. Although women are still in the minority in Angelica's field, their number is increasing, and as it increases, so the direction of robotics is changing: women are deciding that there are different problems we need to solve with algorithms, and the emergence of the female-dominated and -led field of emotional robotics is only the most visible part of this revolution. As for Angelica herself, she, like Sara, feels a sense of wonder that she 'can get paid to do something that I really enjoy'. But it's more than that. Not only does she find her work 'intellectually stimulating', she also, she tells me, feels a sense 'almost like social responsibility: if I don't do this then who will, and how will they do it?'

The exclusion of women from decisions that affect their lives is something that Lučka Kajfež Bogataj encounters in the field of climate change research. 'Impacts will hit women harder,' she tells me, 'but at the same time, when decisions are taken to avoid these impacts, women are not there.' The result, Lučka says, is that when energy policies are set, in large-scale international negotiations on climate change, women are rarely at the top of the agenda, meaning that many solutions, 'even if they are simple or doable', just get missed. It gives the impression that 'no one cares about half of humanity'.

This impression is reinforced by the media's handling of climate change, one of the few phenomena on which they are reluctant to accept expert opinion – a dubious distinction which climate change shares with gender issues. Expert opinion on both climate change and sexism is pretty conclusive: they verifiably exist, they are a problem. Yet, rather than accept this basic tenet and debate potential solutions, the media seem determined to host endless reruns of the same ontological debate, pitting experts against non-expert vested interests, with the implication that the 'opinions' of both 'sides' are equally valid. The fact that the two issues where the media seem to hold the least respect for expert opinion are both deeply gendered is troubling.

Not only will climate change impact on women more than men, Lučka tells me, but the way the impact is divided along gender lines is more dramatic even than the divide between developing and developed countries, or between rich and poor. 'I will start with water,' she says, 'because water is such a clear example. Water and food are always part of women's everyday work.' Climate change means 'less water', meaning that accessing water, carrying water, 'will become an extremely difficult job'. It will also affect food stocks, which will particularly affect countries that are dependent on yearly yields. This means more work for women, who make up the majority of rural smallholder farmers (the United Nations Food and Agriculture Organization estimates this figure at 80%). To give an idea of the scale of smallholder farmers, they are estimated to produce 90% of the food grown in Africa and over 50% of the world's food. This is not a minority issue.

Extreme weather events and negative economic impacts also tend to affect women more, Lučka says, because of women's unequal shouldering of the household care burden. Men are better equipped to cope with the adverse economic impacts of climate change, since it is easier to move away from their home, even their country, in order to find work. In extreme weather events, women have been shown to focus not just on saving their own lives, but also those of their children. 'You can barely take care of yourself,' Lučka says, 'but women are expected to take care of the children as well.'

There is also evidence that the negative impact climate change is having on agricultural yields is causing outbreaks of disease, as humans encroach on bat habitats in an effort to find alternative food sources. This too is an issue that particularly affects women due to their traditional caregiving responsibilities. For example, reports suggest that in the 2014 Ebola epidemic, which is thought to have originated from bat contact, up to 75%

of those who have died are women, purely because it is women who are caring for the sick.

But despite these clear indications of the extent of the impact of climate change on females, it is only very recently that the Intergovernmental Panel on Climate Change (IPCC) has started to even take note of this dimension. This is partly a cultural issue: Lučka explains that some countries did not like the impression that women were being 'pushed forward' by the IPCC high-lighting the particular difficulties faced by women. But it was also a problem of the perspective of the IPCC. When Lučka first joined, it was a 95% male organisation, which, as with the women in the Center for Work-Life Policy report, and as with Sara Seager, led to Lučka being mistaken for a secretary and being approached by men who expected her to handle their expenses and itineraries.

Despite the male-dominated nature of the organisation, Lučka was nevertheless elected to the IPCC – although, as with most successful women, she hadn't felt confident of gaining the position. Once there, her lack of confidence dissipated: 'I am a person that if I am elected, I don't feel any constraints. So I did speak a lot, I decided to make, not a nuisance of *myself*, but of my ideas. After a year or so I think that I did make quite a difference.' Lučka says that there are 'a lot of scientific problems that when you have seven or eight males trying to find a solution, they are, somehow, quite blind. The solution is there in front of their eyes, but because they are male, and not just because they are male, but because they are male in a group, they somehow forget about some solutions.' She tells me that on many occasions when she would propose what were to her blindingly obvious remedies, the male group would look at her amazed that they had never thought of what was clearly the correct solution. 'It is not that they didn't know,' she says, but that 'they did not function in that way'.

And after five years of working in the IPCC, Lučka was one of the recipients of the Nobel Peace Prize. 'I want to stress that this is the Nobel Prize for *Peace*. All other Nobel Prizes are given to the people, to the work of people. But the Nobel Prize for Peace is not of that kind. It is given to a problem. The receivers are not important at all. It is the recognition that climate change is an internationally important issue.' The prize money went to fund young scientists who want to work on climate change.

Lučka is clear that climate change is 'unstoppable. It will go on for maybe five, seven generations. The only question is how much?' The hope is for an international agreement to curb emissions and keep the warming to a minimum – but that still means learning to live in a warmer world. We are going to have to learn very quickly, and it won't be easy, Lučka says, because '[i]t is completely new knowledge. It will lead to a lot of mistakes, because we don't have a historical precedent.' We will need to find new forms of agriculture, of tourism, of governance. And we will have to work together for a solution. 'But,' Lučka cautions, 'not just half of humanity. This is always my message, because the best ideas may come from the other half.' Now, she says, 'it is time for women'.

One of those women might be Polly Apio, a farmer in Uganda. In Uganda, over 80% of the population depend on farming to survive, and most farmers are women – but most of the land is owned and controlled by men. In an interview for the BBC, Polly explains that she has over twenty acres, but works on less than ten of them. 'This year,' she says, 'I think I only worked on two acres, because there was no rain.' It has been unusually arid this year, with over four months of dry weather. Polly is relatively lucky in that she has a tractor, which means she can plough even though the ground is so dry: 'with oxen the land has to be very wet'.

Polly didn't always farm. She started after her husband left the family. 'I found that my husband had a girlfriend,' she says. He worked at Entebbe Airport and used to travel back to the family at the weekends – 'but somehow in the middle he stopped coming home'. Polly was left alone to support their five children, who ranged in age from two to fourteen. She headed back to her home village and took over the land that had belonged to her husband and started farming it. She produces food to eat and to sell, 'but mainly it is for the family's consumption'. What she does manage to produce in excess goes towards her children's education.

Although not all of it does. While pounding millet, Polly explains that 'in the community not all of us have work, so you find some of our women friends or community members have nothing'. Polly gives what she can to these families. Often she will just sense a family's need and offer help; at other times, she pumps the children for information, as the parents will often not own up to their problems – 'but you will find that the children will tell you, "Yes, that day we did not eat, we slept hungry."' She has started up women's groups, 'where we can sit down and share ideas'; the group also functions as a way of knowing who is suffering so that they can be provided for.

Polly has also started agitating for land rights. 'By law women are allowed to own land, but culturally they are not,' she says. Now that she understands her rights, she is able to convince other community members that women can inherit land. The key issue, she says, is education. 'Because most of the village women have not gone to school so they don't know what is happening beyond their villages.' She credits the charity Action Aid with transforming women's sense of what they deserve. It has 'empowered women so much because these women before used to not go to any meetings. But today they talk.' They have even been able to challenge the local authorities. 'There are some problems where they don't consider women, so we normally go and ask, why are we left behind?' Polly says that she has learnt that as a woman she has her own rights – and she is determined to push for change.

Men and women are not born different. But we are treated differently from the moment we are born. And whether we like it or not, this means we experience the world in different ways. This difference can range from our own self-belief, to how others perceive us and what others believe we are suited to and can achieve. All this stereotyping affects women in leadership roles – both their own belief, and that of others, in their ability to lead. There have been numerous variants on a study where CVs are sent out that are identical apart from some having a male name and others having a female name – and those with the male names are far more likely to lead to the person being hired and receiving a higher salary. Cordelia Fine mentions studies where both men and women are found to be slower to associate leadership terms with females than with males. The difference is particularly pronounced for mothers, perhaps because the stereotype that women are caring rather than leading is made particularly salient when a woman is a mother – a dichotomy the Kalashnikov-wielding, baby-suckling fighters of Eritrea might blink at. Fine draws on the experiences of female-to-male transsexuals in the workplace to highlight this phenomenon. Studies show that when they start presenting as men, they experience greater recognition and respect, with perhaps the most stark example being 'Thomas', a lawyer who told the story of how he heard a colleague praise his boss for getting rid of Susan, 'whom he regarded as incompetent. He then added that the "new guy", Thomas, was "just delightful" – not realising that Thomas and Susan were one and the same.' Another telling example is related by Ben Barres, a professor of neurobiology at Stanford, and also a female-to-male transsexual. In an article in *Nature*, Barres relates the story of how, shortly after he had changed sex, a faculty member said, 'Ben Barres gave a great seminar today, but then his work is much better than his sister's'.

The irony is that female leaders have a lot to offer – not least as role models to women. A University of Massachusetts study found that reading short biographies of famous women leaders before taking the word association test improved women's ability to pair leadership terms with females. In a Swiss study it was found that women who gave speeches in rooms where pictures of either Angela Merkel or Hillary Clinton hung on the wall facing them gave longer speeches, and were judged both by themselves and independent observers to have given better speeches. A UK study found that 'the presence of a successful female MP candidate predicts greater campaign volunteerism and turnout for women', while a US study found that the presence of a single female senator or candidate for the Senate raised women's ability to name a senator to 79%, in comparison with 51% in states where there was no female senator or candidate, suggesting that the presence of women in the political arena makes other women feel less alienated, and more like politics is relevant to them. Similarly, the Athena report found that when even as little as 10% of the management are women this has a significant impact on the workforce: 'all of a sudden women feel significantly less isolated, have an easier time accessing role models, and feel that they can talk about work–life issues more readily'. And the more women managers there are, the more dramatic this change is: when 50% or more of the managers are women, 'workplaces are much more comfortable for women'.

The impact also happens because women tend to lead in a different way. Not because we are innately different, but because we have experienced, and continue to experience, the world differently. Think of Sheryl Sandberg and her pregnancy parking, or Sara Seager and the 'old girls' network' she has set up for her female students. Or think of Lučka's focus on how climate change particularly affects women, or Angelica's desire to create robots that address the female experience. Men have been and can be great leaders, and in theory there is no reason they should be any better or worse as leaders for women than women are. One day, we will live in a world where the sex of your manager or your local politician makes no difference to your performance or self-belief. But until that day comes, female leaders will continue to have a dramatic impact on the way the rest of us lead our lives.

4

Advocating Like a Woman

As a child growing up in Iran, Leila Alikarami always questioned
why she was treated differently from her brothers. It was the
little things that niggled and that confused her: the way her
grandmother let her brothers do things she wasn't allowed to
do; why she had to wear a headscarf to school; why she was seen
as different at university. It was only when she studied law that
it all started to come together: she was treated differently because
she was worth less than a man. To be precise, she was worth
exactly half as much.

This was clear from the law that said a mother could not give
permission for her child to undergo necessary surgery – only a
father could. It was clear from the laws that specified crimes to
which a woman cannot testify, and that said that in cases where
a female witness is accepted, her testimony is worth half that of
a man's, so you need two women saying the same thing to add
up to the evidence of one man. It was most baldly clear from the
law that stated that the *diyeh* – 'the amount of money a murderer
or one who has inflicted grievous bodily harm pays the victim
or their family' – for a male victim is twice that for a female
victim: 'If a woman who is five months' pregnant is in an accident and is killed, the amount of money paid for the woman is
half that paid for the male fetus inside her.'

Leila would watch baffled women approach the law over

divorce, custody, *diyeh*, expecting it to help them. She would watch as they were failed by the legal system, and left disappointed and without hope. 'The law was against them and the judge was against them,' Leila tells me. 'And I really wanted to help them.'

At first, Leila didn't aim to change the legal system – she just wanted to exploit every legal tool she had at her disposal to improve the situation for the women who were routinely let down. She began to examine international conventions relating to women's issues, such as the Convention on the Elimination of All Forms of Discrimination against Women (CEDAW), noting where they differed from Iranian law, and asking why.

Leila discovered that she wasn't the only one asking these questions, and she joined a growing group of women – women who were no longer content with their diminished legal status – in calling for the ratification, or official recognition, of the CEDAW. Encouraged by positive noises initially coming from the government, the women decided to take the fight to the streets. They didn't just want support from the elites, Leila says; they wanted 'support from the people', and on 12 June 2006 they held a demonstration in Hafte Tir Square in Tehran. The demonstration was well attended but short-lived: 'Security forces attacked the demonstrators,' Leila tells me. 'Some were arrested, and then charged with being a threat to national security.' Until that point, she hadn't thought that she was putting herself in danger: 'None of us ever thought we would be accused of threatening national security just because we were asking to have better laws for women. I thought I was acting within the legal system. Within the rules.'

The clampdown did not have the intended effect. Fifty women from across Iran decided to collaborate on a campaign called One Million Signatures for the Repeal of Discriminatory Laws. They prepared a booklet, a petition and a campaign plan, and planned to hold a conference in Tehran called 'The Impact of the Law on Women's Lives'. But on 27 August, when they turned up at the location where the conference was to be held, they were faced with closed doors. The security forces had sealed the building off. Undeterred, the women held the conference outside, in front of the sealed-off building. 'Shirin Ebadi [the eminent Iranian human rights lawyer] took the floor and she talked to the crowd,' Leila tells me. 'The campaign actually was born on this day, when we faced the closed door for our conference.'

Since then, Leila and her fellow campaigners have fought for changes in discriminatory laws in the face of a series of closed doors – and locked prison gates. At first, the campaign went well, and received positive coverage within Iran. The signatures on their petition started to grow as the activists went out to villages and small cities to spread their message, to educate Iranian citizens about a legal system they either knew nothing about or thought was the unchallengeable word of God. 'When you are actually describing it to people,' Leila says, 'they really think about it and they get it.' There were, of course, those who challenged her. 'This is from Islam,' they would say. 'We can't challenge it.' In response, the activists would point to the fact that the age of criminal responsibility (eight for girls but fourteen for boys) is not even mentioned in the Qur'an, or point out that the Qur'an actually gave rights to a woman to divorce her husband, and mostly people would listen, would agree, and would add their names to the petition.

The activists were also running training sessions for women who wanted to become part of the campaign, teaching them how these discriminatory laws affect the lives of men and women, and how they could encourage other people to support the initiative. 'But gradually the government realised that we were doing something,' Leila tells me, 'and they tried to stop us from meeting each other, from gathering together. And then they started arresting us.' The women were sentenced to imprisonment for anything between six months and three years. The arrests had their intended consequence: the signatures stopped. Members of the public who had initially been receptive to the campaigners and their aims started to back off. More closed doors.

In 2008, in the face of the hardening attitude of the government, Leila left Iran and moved to the UK to continue her investigation into the compatibility of Iranian law with CEDAW. 'I wanted to analyse two main discourses: one was the process of ratification of CEDAW in the *Majlis* [the Iranian parliament], and the other was the One Million Signatures campaign.' But having completed a PhD, Leila felt unable to return to Iran. I ask if this was because of the threat of arrest. 'I haven't done anything wrong,' she says. 'I'm not sure.' I can't help noticing her note of doubt. But, she insists, the real problem is not the threat of arrest, but the fact that the climate is so hostile to her work. While the Iranian government remains so suspicious of women pushing for gender equality, Leila realised that she could achieve more from outside the country. For now, she remains in semi-voluntary exile: 'I want to continue my study to be able to practise law here in the UK, because I work on Sharia law [the legal system based on Islam].' And there are plenty of women in the UK who find themselves subject to Sharia courts whom she will be able to represent. Eventually, though, Leila wants to go back to Iran.

And she is hopeful that she will get there. She sees an inching open of the political arena in the past few years. 'The number of educated women and men inside Iran make the future much, much better for Iranian women. This is very important.' The changes in legislation will not happen overnight, she tells me – there are too many needed and they are too entrenched. 'But when society changes, when the lifestyle changes, when people's thinking changes', this is when governments start to feel real pressure. And this, Leila says, is already happening. Society has changed and some laws have changed, too: women can now inherit, and men and women are now deemed worthy of equal compensation in car accidents. Leila puts these achievements at least partly down to the One Million Signatures campaign. 'I definitely think Iran will reach equality,' she says, smiling. 'I can't say when, but I think in my lifetime, hopefully, I will see the changes.'

Given the limitations traditionally placed upon women's freedom in other areas of Iranian society, perhaps it is no surprise to find that discrimination has also been enshrined within the law. But what about in a liberal democracy which purports to champion equality, uphold human rights and follow international law? Surely in the West the law serves women as fairly as it does men? If you're one of the millions of women each year who flees persecution in your homeland and puts your faith in the asylum system (according to the United Nations High Commissioner for Refugees [UNHCR], in 2012 the figure was around 7.4 million), don't count on it.

In order to claim asylum, claimants must first escape their own country. This is no mean feat for women. Making up 70% of those globally who live in poverty and two-thirds of those who are illiterate, women usually lack the education, the job and the money required to gain a visa to live anywhere else. They must make the journey illegally, often from countries where travelling without a male guardian is both frowned upon and dangerous. The preparations for their journey must often be made speedily and in secret, in the knowledge that there will be consequences if their plans are discovered. In short, they do not take this step unless they are already desperate and fearing for their lives. They go through the danger and difficulty of the journey – and when they finally get to the country that they hope will offer them protection, they are faced with often poorly trained staff whose main objective seems to be to deny them entry rather than to provide a place of refuge for those in need.

The United States has historically received the largest number of new individual asylum applications, followed by Germany, South Africa and France. But Germany was the only Western country that featured in the top ten countries hosting the most refugees in 2012; the list was headed up by Pakistan and Iran, and included Ethiopia, Chad and Jordan. Germany was third on the list. Developing countries in fact hosted 81% of the world's refugees by 2012 – compared with 70% a decade before.

Those women who make it to the UK will be faced with a series of interviews about their reasons for claiming asylum. Many of them will not speak the language of the country in which they have arrived, nor understand the complexities of its legal system; they will often come from countries where trusting uniformed officials is not a natural response. In the UK since 2007, the verdict is meant to be handed down within a few weeks. The woman seeking asylum may have a chance to appeal (although not always); the decision about that is usually reached within a couple of months. During this time, women can be taken in and out of detention and moved from house to house around the country at the pleasure of Her Majesty's Government.

I get to hear the experiences of some women who have faced this system on a freezing but clear February night in London. A good night for a protest. We are gathered outside the UK Home Office as part of a campaign asking Theresa May, the UK Home Secretary, to stop detaining female asylum seekers. Music blares out of a portable sound system; sparklers weave their spindly lights, illuminating a row of silver balloons that spell out 'SET HER FREE' above our heads.

Over the loud speaker, we hear a woman's voice. She is speaking to us from room 252 at Yarl's Wood Immigration Removal Centre. She is scared for her life, too scared to tell us her name. Her voice keeps being lost in feedback, but occasional words and phrases break through the white noise: 'Can I talk please?'; 'They made me hate myself'; 'I cannot eat.' Then there is respite from the squeals of the technology, and her wavering voice resounds through the amplifier. 'I am very scared for my life in my country. I left everything. My position, my family, money, friends, for save my life. Only to live in peace. Not more.'

She goes on to recount a tale that is mirrored by countless asylum seekers who come to the UK asking for protection. A story of hopes being replaced by fear, disbelief, depression. A story of house raids at 7 a.m. (It's striking how often 7 a.m. emerges in these stories – it seems to be the Home Office's favourite time of day.) A story of indefinite detention.

'Immigration stopped my life since two months… I can't say anything more. I can only say I am completely dead from inside. Not more. My room is 252. Thank you.' The line goes dead. Around me women are silently weeping. They recognise this woman, reduced to a number. They know her story. They remember their own.

It was Meltem Avcil's inability to forget or forgive her experience fighting within the asylum system that started the petition that brought us here tonight. I speak to her a few days after the protest. She told me she felt 'very, very overwhelmed' to see so many people there. 'I'm not alone, we're not alone,' she said.

It all started for Meltem when she was four years old. She fled with her family from the village they lived in in Turkey. 'I remember bits and pieces of village life,' she says. 'Women doing their chores; girls bringing tea.' Her family were Kurds, and they faced persecution as a result. Like many refugees, Meltem and her family first fled to Germany – but they were refused asylum. They arrived in the UK when Meltem was about eight years old, finally being settled in Doncaster as the Home Office reviewed their case. Meltem attended school and dreamed of becoming a doctor.

Officials first arrived to take Meltem and her family from her home when she was eleven. 'I knew what was happening,' she tells me. 'Because I was the only English speaker, so I was always on the phone to the solicitor. I knew what was happening. But, I wasn't really aware... I was in between.'

By the time of their second detention when Meltem was 13, she wasn't in between any more. She was fully aware and knew enough about the system to want to act as her mother's translator. 'The translators are... for some reason, I didn't trust them. And I could translate properly, because I was sharing my mum's pain.' The pain of being blindfolded by Turkish police and being beaten until her ear bled and her eardrum burst, of being taken away from her home by soldiers at six in the morning and driven to a forest, of the 'unsuitable stuff', the 'ugly things' that were done to her in this forest. I ask her about taking on this role when she herself was still so young. Meltem hesitates. 'What else would I do in Yarl's Wood? Go and play badminton? And pretend like everything's OK when I'm locked up? I chose to be in it.' She's fiery now. 'I chose to take my psychology and my mum's psychology on me, so that I could be sure that something good would happen in the end.'

But despite Meltem's translation of their story, they were not believed. They were collected at three in the morning from their cells. 'That's when they pushed my mum onto the ground,' she continues. 'They hit her face with the handcuff, they forced her up the aeroplane steps. They kicked her, they punched her. They kicked me, they punched me, they pinched me, and all the time, the immigration officer was saying to me and, keep in mind I was thirteen, "If you resist, if you shout, if you scream, we will tie your hands and legs, and no one will know." He said this to me five times.' Meltem pauses. 'They handcuffed my mum and they put a towel over the handcuffs, because it's not right to handcuff anyone who hasn't done anything, right? And they kept on blackmailing me all the way [to the airport]. And a female officer said to me, "Oh you have your GCSEs this year, don't you?" And then she started laughing.'

I ask her how she felt. Her answer sounds like calm panic. 'I just had one thing on my mind: what can I do about this? I let them speak, I let them speak into my ear, so many mean things on the way, and I didn't say anything. Because I was busy thinking of what to do, how not to go back to a country I've not grown up in and don't know. I had so many questions going round my head: tomorrow, where am I going to be? What's going to happen?'

As Meltem screamed for help, saying the guards were twisting her hands, her fellow passengers began to record the incident. The pilot stopped the plane and ordered the guards to remove Meltem and her mother, who were taken to the hospital. They were visited by the Children's Commissioner and moved to Newcastle. A new home, a new school. More waiting, more whirling questions.

For six years Meltem was moved unceremoniously around the country, taken in and out of detention. She had to register with the police every week and each time was made to wait. 'For them, it might be that they're short on staff and they need someone to just bring out the paper and say, "OK, sign." But for you, it's a different thing. All the time you're thinking, what's going on, are they going to take me, are they going to deport me…'

Eventually, Meltem and her mother were granted indefinite leave to stay, but she is still haunted by her experience. 'You know, I'm still in fear,' she says. 'When someone bangs on the door very hard, I will just shake.' Meltem has a British passport but, she says, 'I still think, can they take it away from me? Can they lock me up again?' She tells me about a morning not long after they received leave to remain. 'The door knocked really hard, really really hard and I jumped up, and I said, "Mum, is it them."' I can't help noticing it's not a question.

This state of perpetual fear is one that Zrinka Bralo remembers well. She had escaped to the UK from Sarajevo where, one day, she woke up to find her neighbours, her friends, shooting sniper rifles at her house. Playing music outside her window about how she was going to be raped. She went to bed that night clutching a bottle of acid, because it was the only weapon she had. Zrinka is now director and founder of the Migrant and Refugee Communities Forum, but for her first year and a half in the UK, she lived in a state of constant anxiety. 'I went to work every day with a thousand pounds in cash, taped, duct taped, to the bottom of my rucksack, and spare underwear, in case I was picked up and deported.'

Why did it take eighteen months to approve Zrinka's asylum claim? Why did it take six years to approve Meltem and her mother's? When I ask Natasha Walter, founder and director of the charity Women for Refugee Women, she tells me that the length of time it takes from applying for asylum to receiving a verdict still varies. Those on the Detained Fast Track are meant to receive a decision within days (although this is not necessarily a desirable track, with most women on this system being refused on their first application). 'Many women we work with have been here for years and not come to the end of the process,' she says. Asylum Aid reports that 'at the end of 2013 there were 17,180 applicants, including dependants, who had applied since April 2006, and had not received an initial decision, 21% more than at the end of 2012'. Similarly, in America, while the initial process can be quick (initial decisions should be made within the first sixty days after an application has been received), the appeals process can drag on for years. But the reality is that, as a 2012 global report on asylum seekers found, 'little is known about why people are detained and no official statistics on how many asylum seekers are detained or for how long exist'.

'They had disbelief,' says Meltem Avcil, flatly, when she talks about how she was first refused asylum in Germany and then in the UK. She presents the UK Border Agency's attitude as an immutable noun: 'disbelief'. 'We did provide all the evidence. We had newspapers with our family surname on it showing that we had been persecuted.'

Being disbelieved has shaped Meltem's identity. How could

it not when she has been disbelieved since she was four? You can hear it in the way she speaks, often ending her phrases with an upwards inflection, as if she's asking a question – do you believe me?

Disbelief is not only a common theme in these women's stories – it's a common theme in the statistics too. Report after report finds a virulent strain of cynicism within the UK Border Agency (UKBA) that manifests as a 'culture of disbelief'. Things are so bad that an investigation was carried out by Asylum Aid specifically into the quality of decisions made by the Home Office on women asylum seekers. The report found that, on average, 28% of all initial Home Office decisions that went against asylum seekers were ultimately overturned on appeal; when it came to women asylum seekers, this figure shot up to 50%. Clearly, something isn't working. Assessments of the credibility of the women whose applications are initially being turned down are repeatedly found to be inaccurate and ill-informed. Put baldly, the UKBA officials don't believe these women – and the ignorance and callousness displayed in the illustrative cases are shocking.

One case worker had never heard of the term 'female circumcision'. Another decided on the basis of 'an article from the American gossip website www.gawker.com' that a lesbian from Uganda did not have any reason to fear the death penalty if she were returned. A woman who was forced into an abusive marriage at the age of fourteen, and who was abused by her father when she tried to return to her family home, was refused on the basis that she had remained in the marriage for thirteen years. This apparently proved that she was not at risk. A victim of sexual assault was asked if she had tried to stop a man from raping her. As if she had asked for it if she couldn't physically prove that she didn't want it. An Amnesty report found that photos of scars were not being accepted as evidence of torture. What price evidence in the face of this solid entity, 'disbelief'?

Some of the decisions seem to move beyond ignorance to outright deceptive manipulation: one woman who feared 'honour' killing if she were returned to Iraq was refused asylum on the basis of a report that detailed the support available from local police. The very same report also detailed the danger of sexual assault such women faced from the police themselves if they approached them for help. Somehow, that factor was not considered relevant to the case.

Home Office officials have been told to get rid of 70% of these pesky asylum seekers, and these targets are backed up with the reward of shopping vouchers or the threat of being presented with a 'grant monkey', the toy gorilla that is put on the desk of any UKBA official who allows a claim. It is attitudes like these that have led Frances Webber, an immigration barrister, to damningly conclude, 'UKBA officials sometimes give the impression that their purpose is to catch asylum seekers out – they seem to work from the premise that most asylum seekers are opportunistic liars, an attitude strongly fostered by the media and sometimes by government ministers, although it is very far from the truth.' As one female asylum seeker explains, 'They don't believe you. They ask you five hundred questions and they ask the same question in a slightly different way and if you don't answer them all exactly the same, they say that you are lying.'

That doesn't explain why the burden of being disbelieved is falling so disproportionately on the shoulders of women. For the answer to that, we have to look further back, to the wording of another one-size-fits-all solution: the 1951 Convention relating to the Status of Refugees.

The Convention was drawn up in the aftermath of World War II by well-meaning men. The intentions were noble, even beautiful. A person had a right to claim asylum if he or she had a 'well-founded fear of being persecuted for reasons of race, religion, nationality, membership of a particular social group or political opinion'. It's not enough to be persecuted – it has to be for these specific reasons. And we can already see that there is a glaring omission in this list, because a woman may well be persecuted for reasons of race, religion, or indeed any of the reasons for which men are persecuted. But she is most likely to be persecuted for the simple fact that she is a woman.

It is the fact that she is a woman that means her body is most likely to be used as a weapon of war. It is the fact that she is a woman that means that her sexuality is deemed to be dangerous and sinful, and that therefore her genitals, or those of her daughter, must be cut off and sewn up. It is the fact that she is a woman that means she is likely to be raped, beaten, murdered to preserve the 'honour' of her family if she commits the crime of behaving in any way that approximates the behaviour of a free man – and it is the fact that she is a woman that means if she reports this to the police, she is as likely to be attacked again as she is to be protected.

A Women for Refugee Women report found that the number one reason female asylum seekers gave for their persecution was 'because I am a woman'. But only since 1999 has the UK accepted that women can be considered to belong to 'a particular social group', or, sometimes, to hold a 'political opinion', if they have chosen to defy the social norms that restrict so many women's lives. Previously, women did not constitute a social group, and nor did rebelling against limiting female social norms reflect a political opinion. Nevertheless, although we've taken our time to get there, the precedent has finally been set. But most women who claim asylum don't realise that this is the case – and staff at the UKBA seem to be in no hurry to inform them. Indeed, it often seems as if they don't know it themselves.

In 2002, Rose Najjemba was raped by soldiers in Uganda who had come to question her about suspected complicity with rebel groups. And although the Home Office accepted that she was raped, and raped in these circumstances, it denied that this was persecution. In this case, the Court of Appeal judges agreed. Rape, they said, was 'not a matter of persecution', but one of 'simple and dreadful lust'.

The problem facing female asylum seekers is that claiming asylum on the basis of your gender is not straightforward. It often requires complicated legal wrangling in order to make the round peg of women's experience fit the square hole of the refugee convention designed by and around men. These women need lawyers: 'Without lawyers,' Frances Webber says, 'it is virtually impossible for claims based on gender persecution to succeed.' But lawyers are difficult to come by – especially once your claim has been rejected, as happens to 96% of women on the Fast Track system the first time round. And it will soon get harder in the UK, if the 'residence test' for legal aid comes into force. Given that 50% of these rejections are overturned on appeal, given the grant monkey and the shopping vouchers, it's hard to avoid coming to the conclusion that putting this new obstacle in the way is a deliberate and knowing policy by the Home Office.

It's not an easy conclusion to live with. No one wants to feel ashamed of their country. But now the Home Office can no longer rely on the argument that since women's oppression tends to be carried out by private people rather than directly by the state, it needs to refuse these asylum seekers entry to the UK. And in looking for other grounds on which to turn them down, doubting the credibility of their stories is always a good place to start.

For many women, the automatic disbelief with which their stories are met is almost too much to bear. All evening, outside the Home Office, Jade has been dancing and smiling, but as she tells us about her interview with an immigration officer, she wipes away tears as she asks us, 'Can you show somebody like that anything like that? Oh God.' Jade vocally acts this encounter out for us: the 'somebody' she refers to is represented by a deep, aggressive voice and the sharp demand, 'show me how you were raped', in response to a tremulous 'I was raped'.

A woman who was raped by a police officer when she was imprisoned in Ethiopia tells Women for Refugee Women, 'I was afraid of the security guards. The white shirts and the black trousers reminded me of violence.' She says, 'I came because I had to. I would never have chosen to leave my family, everything I love about my country, the sunshine, the music, the food that tastes good in your mouth.' She used to be 'so full of hope', she continues. 'Even when I came to this country I thought I would survive and make a good life for myself. It wasn't what happened to me in my home country which broke me. It was what happened to me here. That was what broke my spirit.' Another woman, who had been imprisoned and repeatedly raped by prison guards in Uganda, said, 'When I was on suicide watch, the door was left open even when I went to the toilet, and a male guard was watching me.'

The lack of sensitivity shown to women who have every reason to fear prisons and male guards is part of a system where a victim of trafficking was expected to provide details of prostitution at her first interview, in front of other strangers and her own children. The fact that she didn't immediately disclose these details in such circumstances was taken as evidence that she was lying. It is part of a system that continues to lock women up indefinitely, in the face of research showing that 85% of female asylum seekers have been raped or tortured, breaching section 9.1 of the United Nations Commission on Human Rights guidelines, which states that 'victims of torture and other serious physical, psychological or sexual violence need special attention and should generally not be detained'. The same research shows that 93% of those detained feel depressed; 85% feel scared; more than half think about killing themselves, and more than one in five have tried.

A 2012 Campbell Collaboration report on the impact of detention on the mental health of asylum seekers around the world finds that the UK is not alone in its questionable treatment of the traumatised. Australia used to be unique in its policy of mandatory and indefinite detention of asylum seekers – but increasingly, other countries are following suit, with a 2010 Council of Europe report finding that this has become the option of first rather than last resort. In the United States, asylum seekers subject to expedited removal are held in mandatory detention until they pass a 'credible fear' interview – and while in detention they can be held in 'pods' for up to twenty-three hours a day, subjected to frequent 'counts', transported in shackles, transferred without explanation and forced to wear prison jumpsuits. The Campbell Collaboration report cites the 'growing evidence' that the detention of asylum seekers 'is associated with substantial mental health problems', pointing to the Bellevue/NYU Program for Survivors of Torture, as well as to the Physicians for Human Rights study, which reported that significant symptoms of depression were present in 86% of detained asylum seekers, anxiety was present in 77% and post-traumatic stress disorder in 50%. It also found that the longer those individuals were in detention, the worse their mental health became.

It is for the women who are still detained, who are still suffering behind barbed wire and eight metal doors, that Meltem continues to fight. This is why she started the petition that had us all gathered outside the Home Office on that February night. 'I said to myself this year, I have two options. Either I pretend like nothing is wrong and create a happy illusion, and just pretend like nothing like this is happening, or, I use my experience for a better future, for those women in there.' She goes on, 'I have one thing in my mind and that is no human being is supposed to be locked up for doing nothing. For committing no crime. If I'm going to be locked up for having been raped and tortured and persecuted, if I'm going to be locked up just for coming here, then I will start questioning the place I came to. My mum, after the flight on the 15th of November, she didn't eat, she didn't sleep, she didn't walk, she didn't talk, she could do nothing at all. And that point, when you realise that the person you love most is like that, it just… really, saddens you and I always had in my mind the feeling that I want do something about it.'

And so she is. At the time of writing, the petition contains over 48,000 signatures. I ask her what she thinks her chances are of succeeding. 'I have no idea. I have no idea whatsoever. All I'm doing is just hoping for people to understand more about detention centres and what it is like. I don't want people to go off the topic. I just want them to understand that the detention centre is a prison and no one deserves to be locked up in there. Oh, and if they want to look at the other side of it, then yes, it's expensive to the UK economy. So, either way, for me it's a win–win. But first, I need more signatures, and we need Theresa May [the British Home Secretary] to notice it.'

The day I interview Noorzia Atmar, the hashtag #FightFor-Yashika is trending on Twitter. Twenty-two thousand people sign a petition, and paper after paper runs the story about a young girl, in the final months of her A levels, being torn apart from her mother and brother and sent back to Mauritius, a country where she has no family other than a drug-dealing cousin who tried to rape her, and who has threatened to be waiting for her as she touches down in the airport. The Home Office releases a statement claiming that 'the UK has a proud history of granting asylum to those who need it'. But when I think about Yashika, not allowed to stay even the two months it would take for her to complete her education; when I think about Meltem, haunted by years growing up in fear of a knock at the door; when I think of the woman in the Women for Refugee Women report, forced to shower in full view of a man who looked so much like her rapists, I don't feel proud. And when I talk to Noorzia, who is crying, and when Mary, my interpreter, begs me to help Noorzia, my lack of pride segues seamlessly into helplessness and shame.

It wasn't long ago that Noorzia didn't need my help. She didn't need anyone's help. She *was* the help. Riding high on a wave of women elected to the Afghan parliament, she helped to pass law after law that would improve the lot of her country-women; one after another, practices that harmed women were banned. Afghanistan signed up without any reservations to the

Convention on the Elimination of all forms of Discrimination Against Women. It seemed like, after years of silence under Taliban rule, women might have a voice again. It even seemed like people might be listening.

'I wanted our motherland to become peaceful and for us to serve our country,' she tells me. 'The day the Taliban came I left Afghanistan and the day they went I returned.' She started working as a journalist, before quitting in 2005 to run for parliament. She wanted to test herself, to see if she had 'the ability to serve my people', she says, 'especially women'. That, she tells me, 'was the courage in me'. She won her seat amid a rush of euphoria: 'everyone was thinking so positive and we were hopeful. People put their hope on their parliamentarians and were listening to us.' Women who 'had courage could raise their voice', Noorzia says.

Not that there were many women who found this courage as quickly as Noorzia. She tells me that during her term in parliament, 'only three women used to speak up. No one else did. We had women who were there for years but never spoke even one word about the discrimination against the women of Afghanistan.' Nonetheless, she says again, 'We had a voice.'

As elsewhere in the Middle East, the situation for Afghan women now seems precarious at best. Fawzia Koofi, a current member of the Afghan parliament, told the *Guardian* that '[t]he leadership cuts our microphones off' when the female members of parliament try to speak. The Afghan parliament tried to pass a law that would have banned victims of domestic violence from testifying against their abusers. After an outcry, Hamid Karzai, the president, ordered 'changes' that, at the time of writing, were unspecified.

The shifts at the top are reverberating through Afghan society,

Noorzia says. 'You can see in the rural area and villages a school-teacher go to work with *Chadari* [burqa],' Noorzia tells me. 'She doesn't have her freedom yet. Because she is scared. You can't see it, but the regime is…' She pauses. 'When we were young, we used to call such a situation *qōdi shani* [let's pretend]. The regime now is the same. People think about their future. And women feel the danger and death.' Every day, she says, 'we are facing threats'. Nose-cutting, ear-cutting – she reels off the mutilations. 'For us, life became unbearable in Afghanistan. Some women, like us [she means her and her interpreter], escape from the country.'

I ask Noorzia why she thinks the tide turned, why, after what she calls ten years of 'good movement', women's rights are now under such renewed attack. 'There are people who don't want peace to come to Afghanistan,' she says. 'They don't want development and freedom. They see their gain in chaos, lack of law enforcement, war and bloodshed.' These, she says, are the 'enemies in white clothes' who fear that female participation in government will result in progress. Who feel that the change effected by the female parliamentarians has moved too far.

Noorzia's own situation mirrors that of her country as a whole. Corruption cost her her seat in the 2010 elections – and her new husband cost her her freedom. Noorzia married Toryalai Malakzai while she was running for re-election; he claimed to be an enlightened man who supported her political ambitions. But as the women of her country were about to begin losing their voices in parliament, so Noorzia was losing her voice at home. Within days of their marriage, the beatings started. The confinement began when Noorzia lost the election; she was not allowed out of the house, she had to wear a burqa. She could not even use her phone. Then he began to rape her. The abuse escalated until one day Malakzai stabbed Noorzia in the neck with a kitchen knife. She decided she had to leave.

She called her brothers to ask for their help – but they told her not to divorce him. 'They saw my face bruised, and scars from the knife, but they told me it was a traditional society, that I would bring shame on the family,' she said in an interview with the *Telegraph*. But for Noorzia, to 'remain subservient' to a man who had abused her body and violated her trust was intolerable. She engaged a lawyer and filed for divorce. Her family abandoned her, and this woman who had once passed laws ended up destitute, hiding from her husband and family in one of Afghanistan's few shelters for women.

Her divorce was hard-won. She had to pay off her husband, which left her in penury. More chillingly, after months of negotiations, she was forced to agree, in a court-sanctioned contract, that if she were ever killed, her husband would not be prosecuted for it. He was later to turn up at her new workplace with a gun. After months of harassment and threats from both her ex-husband and her estranged family, this was the moment Noorzia gave up. She knew she couldn't be safe anywhere in Kabul. She fled again, this time leaving the country altogether.

But she retains her loyalty to Afghanistan. 'I want to serve my country. Serve Afghan women,' she tells me, again and again. 'Even when I was in a shelter,' she says, 'I showed that I want to work for women.' She promises that if she gains her 'social status again, and a safe place, and can return to my country, I can do something'. 'I see the power in me if I am safe. But now there are threats against me. I cannot walk in the street. I cannot live alone. I am in danger. This is the reason I am losing myself. I will become isolated and I will disappear. I don't want to disappear.'

Noorzia understands how easy it is vanish into the impenetrable system of the UNHCR. It is, she says, 'the same as Kabul's
old judicial system'. She says, 'We need to sit with those in charge
and tell them their approach is wrong. It is unfair.' How, she asks,
can these institutions talk 'about human rights, about women's
rights? How can they argue that they are raising the flag for
humanity? What humanity?'

She cannot understand why no one is helping her. 'Everyone
knows about the situation for women in Afghanistan. The whole
world can see the terror we face. It's not hidden from anyone.'
Perhaps the problem is that they know all too well: when
Noorzia approached the British embassy, before she finally left
the country, she was told that she could expect no help, because
to help her would 'open the doors to too many women'.

'Everyone knows why I came here,' Noorzia says, her voice
breaking. 'I wasn't a woman who wanted to leave the country.'
When she was in the shelter, she says, 'I struggled to support
myself. I never asked for people's help. I am suffering if someone
helps me out of pity. Why are they not helping me get my social
status back? I have the courage to fight unjust people.' She's
crying now. 'Why are you are destroying Noorzia? Why? Why?'
I have no answer. If it is this hard for her, a woman who has travelled the world as a representative of her country, what chance
do poor, uneducated women with no documented past have of
securing the help of so-called developed societies?

In the meantime, the situation for women in Afghanistan
continues to worsen. Shelters like the one Noorzia called home
for two years are struggling for funding within a climate where
the justice minister denounced them as 'brothels'. The law that
Noorzia helped to pass, the law that criminalised rape, child marriage, *baad* (the practice of trading a virgin girl to settle a dispute

between families), failed to secure parliamentary approval. It was declared 'un-Islamic'. Noorzia says she 'was very upset at what happened to the law against violence. That law could protect me, not only me, but all other victims. That law was like a mother to me. That law encouraged me to raise my voice and stand.'

Franz-Michael Mellbin, the EU ambassador to Kabul, has particularly highlighted the routine prosecution of rape victims and other abused women for 'moral crimes'. Noorzia tells me that this happens because those who implement the laws that do get passed don't 'have a just and fair attitude. Afghan women are the hostage of years of bad customs, which resulted in women not being able to raise their voices. They cannot ask for justice and stand in front of injustice.' Ironically, tragically, however, prison sometimes seems to be a better option for these women. 'Prison is much better than my own home,' says one woman interviewed for Nima Sarvestani's documentary film *No Burqas Behind Bars*. Another tells him, 'Here you can be yourself. Nobody says anything if you don't wear the burqa. They never ask you, what are you doing? You can even watch the outside from here. When you are out, everybody wants to decide about your life. They just try to control you.'

But despite her exile, despite the corrosion of all she and her fellow female parliamentarians fought for, after all this, Noorzia remains hopeful, for herself and her country. Because women around the world share the same problems, she says, we must stand together and fight for justice. She is confident that this will happen. Problems, she says, come and go. 'It is life.' But 'life goes on', and 'I am not losing my courage'.

Despite clear evidence that all is not well for women in the 'developed world', feminists in the West are often accused of hypocrisy and superficiality. Here in the enlightened West, we are told, feminism's job is done. Equality has been attained. Stop focusing on the decent, enlightened men in our own communities; the Middle East is where it's at. We must turn our attention to the appalling abuse of women in other countries. That's where women are being beaten, raped, and then, to add insult to injury, prosecuted as rape victims for their failures of morality. That doesn't happen here.

Rebecca Solnit begs to differ. 'Here in the United States, where there is a reported rape every 6.2 minutes, and one in five women will be raped in her lifetime, the rape and gruesome murder of a young woman on a bus in New Delhi on December 16, 2012, was treated as an exceptional incident. The story of the sexual assault of an unconscious teenager by members of the Steubenville High School football team was still unfolding, and gang rapes aren't that unusual here either. Take your pick: some of the 20 men who gang-raped an 11-year-old in Cleveland, Texas, were sentenced shortly beforehand, while the instigator of the gang rape of a 16-year-old in Richmond, California, was sentenced in that fall of 2012 too, and four men who gang-raped a 15-year-old near New Orleans were sentenced that April, though the six men who gang-raped a 14-year-old in Chicago that year were still at large. Not that I actually went out looking for incidents: they're everywhere in the news, though no one adds them up and indicates that there might actually be a pattern.'

This is the opening to one of the brilliant essays in Solnit's book *Men Explain Things to Me*. The title of the essay is 'The Longest War', and the war it refers to is a global war of violence against women. But it is war unlike other wars, because its casualties are disowned. They are deemed 'isolated incidents'. Tragic deaths that no one could have foreseen, because they are never counted together as part of a pattern.

But someone has begun to count them, at least in the UK. That someone is Karen Ingala Smith. It started in January 2012, when Karen read about an 'isolated incident': the day after Kirsty Treloar received a text from her boyfriend, Myles Williams, promising not to hit her again, he killed her. He stabbed her twenty-nine times and then dumped her dead body by a wheelie bin two miles from her home. She was twenty.

Karen went on to read about six more 'isolated incidents' in the first three days of the year. And by the seventh, she couldn't leave this unchallenged any longer. 'I just thought, how can we still be talking about isolated incidents? Why aren't people connecting the dots?'

In 2012, 126 women were killed by men. In 2013, that figure rose to 143. To put this in context, that's more women killed in a single year than the number of British troops killed in the past three years in Afghanistan. No one is calling casualties of foreign wars 'isolated incidents'.

Karen brings up the example of Lee Rigby, a soldier butchered in broad daylight on a street in Woolwich. In response, David Cameron convened a meeting of the emergency committee COBRA to discuss security measures. Cameron saw this horrific murder in a wider social context. He did not address it as a 'tragic' and 'isolated' incident, as the weekly butchering of women is often referred to – that is, when it's referred to at all. The murder of women by men is so 'tragically' common, that it's rarely considered newsworthy, certainly not worthy of blanket front-page news coverage for days on end.

In 2013, the World Health Organization called violence against women a 'global health problem of epidemic proportions'. Epidemic is not a term that the WHO uses lightly. Governments have established procedures for dealing with epidemics, with the first step being the methodical gathering and analysis of data. If this were any other kind of epidemic, we'd have found a cure by now. If this were any other kind of epidemic, we'd at least have started counting.

Karen couldn't force the British government to convene an emergency committee meeting. She couldn't force it to stop seeing the weekly murder of women as isolated incidents. But she could herself start doing the job it should have been doing. So, from a room in East London, one woman began a list of dead women, that started with seven names: Kirsty Treloar, Susan McGoldrick, Alison Turnbull, Tanya Turnbull, Claire O'Connor, Marie McGrory and Kathleen Milward. And since then she has continued to search out and count the women who were being killed by men. Between 1 January and 4 September 2014, Karen had counted 100 women killed by men – a rate of one woman murdered every 2.38 days. In London alone, between 11 April and 4 September, three women had been beheaded.

I ask her how she copes. 'I do it all the time,' she says. 'Nearly every day, sometimes several times a day, I Google "dead woman", "woman's body found", "man murders", "man charged", "man arrested".' She rattles this list off in a curiously sing-song manner. When she says, 'Once a month I go through the information en masse,' I wonder if that's the word she uses in her head: 'information'. 'Usually, on the day of the month that I've put it all together I feel quiet, reflective, upset, angry. And just that I need a bit of... coming back down... I've been doing it now for a couple of years, so I'm used to it.' She pauses. 'Sometimes, the cases make me cry, but that's just life.'

Karen has started a petition to ask the government to take over the work she's been doing for two years, on her own, with no practical or psychological support. It's stalled, at the time of writing, at 18,140 signatures. At the time of writing, the government has yet to respond. And why would it, when so comparatively few of us seem to care?

A couple of times, Karen refers to her decision to start counting as 'going off on one'. It's hard to think of a less apt phrase to describe her calm, methodical, almost resigned collection of gruesome, dead numbers. And perhaps this is part of the problem. Unlike consent, data just aren't 'sexy'. If there are few headlines to be garnered from women being killed, how many can the government expect from announcing an exercise in statistics, particularly given that many of those 'statistics' are, Karen tells me, foreign women of colour. It is overwhelmingly these women that Karen doesn't find out about until their killers go to trial (which means that the numbers for 2014, and even for 2013, may yet turn out to be higher than they currently appear). The murders of these dispensable women aren't reported in the media because they are not the type of women we care about. And they don't, Karen tells me, tend to see any justice, for the same reasons. They're 'foreigners'. Not one of us. Not our problem. And so they keep dying, we keep ignoring them, and Karen keeps counting them from her room in Walthamstow.

Karen is the CEO of Nia, 'a skint charity that employs really amazing women' and provides services for vulnerable women and children who have experienced male violence. She spends her whole life immersed in the violent fallout from our society's perception of women and tracks the 'cause and consequence' of women's rapes, beatings and murders back to the myriad ways in which women are marked as different from men.

Anywhere 'inequality is expressed, we've got to get rid of it', Karen argues. We must 'teach young people not to be gendered in the way that they are, to question everything about what they assume being a man is and what they assume being a woman is'. Karen describes 'the pinkification of girlhood' as 'bloody frightening', particularly given the speed with which it has proliferated since the 1970s. 'The more you pinkify girls, the more you create the difference between girls and boys,' Karen says. And the more you encode a gendered hierarchy that puts women below men.

Karen seems to have instinctively recognised this hierarchy as a child and, in a manner that I recognise from my own childhood, tried to emulate the winning side. 'I was what was called a tomboy in those days. I used to hang out with the boys,' she says. 'I felt really comfortable with boys. I might have been one of those women who said, I hang out with men more than women. And that's the opposite of what I am now. I had a newspaper round, I had short hair. If anybody called me "son", as they did once, it made my day – I was really proud.' She laughs, ruefully. 'I tried to walk like a boy when I was a young teenager, the pop stars I wanted to be and identified with were Ian McCulloch and Robert Smith. Women were just not really on my radar.'

Karen and I are not alone in our instinctive recognition that to be identified with femininity is to be identified with the losing side, and our 'solution' of rejecting all things female is not unique. The 2008 Center for Work-Life Policy report found that 53% of women working in the male-dominated fields of science and technology believe that 'behaving like a man improves their prospects for advancement'. The report illustrated how this attitude plays out by reporting the findings from a focus group made up of nine female engineers. All the women had reacted by rejecting the traditional trappings of femininity: make-up, jewellery, heels were out; crumpled jeans, scuffed hiking boots, short hair were in. One woman explained that she had quickly learnt not to wear skirts and make-up 'in order to increase her credibility'. The group revealed that they avoided women's networking events, with one woman stating that if she walked into a room full of women, she would walk straight back out: 'By definition nothing important is going on in this room,' she said. Another study of women engineers found that 'women who attempt to behave like men end up attacking other women, invoking "traditional feminine stereotypes to underscore their shortcomings"'. Again this is illustrated by another focus group, this time made up of senior female computer engineers, which revealed the same dismissive attitudes towards 'women's networks and other women-focused programs'. Many of the women 'voiced negative opinions about women in their field, describing them as "emotional" and "petty"'. Irrational and trivial. Where have we heard those terms before?

Partly because of this instinctive desire to identify the winning sex and to be identified with it, it took Karen a while to come round to feminism. But it was also because of class. She ended up going to a different sixth-form college from most of her friends, one where the majority of the intake were from local private schools. Karen found herself 'just hit in the face by these people who had this self-confidence, that I still really don't understand how it operates'. She tells me about 'going into lessons and there'd be big crowds of louder young women who I just felt really overpowered by, and one of the things I remember, which really seems a weird mark of class to me, was that they said "Hi" and not "Hiya" and I remember thinking

"I'm never going to say 'Hi', this just sounds so phoney"'. She laughs before explaining how this resulted in an instinctive reaction against feminism when she first learnt about it in her sociology A level.

'I was talking to my best friend, who had also come from the other school, after one of the first lessons [in feminism] and I really remember saying to her, it's just ridiculous, there's no way that I've got more in common with them lot than I have with working people. And it was the time of the miner's strikes as well. The town I grew up in wasn't a mining town, it was a mill town, but all the mills were closing at the same time and it just very much felt like there was a threat against ordinary working people who were working in factories, mills, from the government. I guess it felt like we were being trampled on.'

It didn't help that 'feminism was something that happened in books, it wasn't around me'. This is something that Karen feels hasn't much improved within feminism. She tells me about a recent seminar she attended at the British Library, a retrospective on feminism's past and how it compares with the present day. 'Class was one of the issues that was discussed as a topic and one of the questions from the audience was "why haven't we got a working-class woman talking about class?"' Karen noticed that the next time she saw a poster advertising an event held by the same organisation the issue was no longer class, but income inequality.

'I think there is a lack of understanding of the disadvantage that being working class brings,' Karen tells me. It's about lack of expectations and exposure to ideas, she says. While she was 'lucky enough to have been fed as a family around a kitchen table', there 'never was political debate about ideas around it'. She wasn't expected to study A levels, to go to university. No one was interested in what subjects she was taking. 'I always went along day by day and did OK because I was doing all right, but there was no direction. I had no ambition, there was no sense of anything other than living a small life.'

Karen can hardly be described as without ambition now. Having single-handedly embarked upon such a huge project as counting all the women killed through male violence in the UK, her impact is about to get even bigger. In June 2013, a year and a half after she first started counting murdered women, she received a phone call. It was from a lawyer who worked at Freshfields Bruckhaus Deringer. They had heard of the work Karen was doing and they wanted to help her. They brought in a corporate sponsor to fund a purpose-built database that will hold five years' worth of information about women killed through male violence – and, most importantly, they wrote to every police force in the UK with a freedom of information request for the names of all women killed by men since 2009. Karen had been working with media reports, which are patchy, unreliable, and, crucially, cannot release certain information until after a trial.

Freshfields currently have the police information uploaded into huge Excel spreadsheets, and will transfer it over to the data-base before it goes live in 2015. Since Freshfields got involved, so has Women's Aid, one of the UK's largest providers of specialist domestic violence services. Women's Aid's involvement will mean they have access to more detailed information about the abuse leading up to the murder of many of the women on the database. Karen hopes that the database, which will be approved-access only, will be used by academics, journalists and policy-makers, and that it can form the basis for a revolution in government policy to address these murders – so many of which, if we acknowledge the pattern that there is to them, could be preventable. In September 2014, Karen was honoured for this work when she won the Positive Role Model Award for Gender at the National Diversity Awards. Not a bad achievement for a working-class girl from Yorkshire whose parents believed she was destined to lead a small life.

By the time a woman is murdered by a man, she has usually been failed by the justice system on a chronic scale. In the UK, domestic homicide reviews (investigations that take place after a woman has been killed as a result of domestic violence) repeatedly conclude that signs were missed. In those cases, the opportunity had been there for the now-dead woman to have been protected. If only the dots had been joined up. There are always *if only*'s. In the case of Natalie Esack, for example, who was stabbed eleven times by her former police detective ex-husband in her hair salon in Kent, if only police had heeded what the homicide review into her death called 'evidence of escalating abuse towards [Natalie Esack] in the six months before her death and risk factors in [Ivan Esack's] behaviour'. If only, she might still be alive.

A preventable murder such as this is a grave injustice. But what about after that? Where does the justice system leave these victims then? The most recent figures for England and Wales (2009–10) are currently incomplete, as there are still cases pending. But if those are excluded from the data, the percentage of recorded homicides which result in a conviction is 67%. For 2008 the figure is 72%, and for 2007 the figure is 70%. More recent statistics are available from Karen, who has also been keeping track of the trial outcomes of the men who murdered the women she has counted. Her figures for 2012 currently present a conviction rate of 85% (it might have been higher had a further 10% not been murder-suicides, where the murderer then killed himself). Natalie Esack should not have been murdered. But her husband has been sentenced to prison for life.

In England and Wales the comparable conviction rate for rape is only 6.5%. The Crown Prosecution Service likes to bandy about the much higher figure of around 63% – but that figure relates only to those cases which have been brought to trial (the percentage of *trials* resulting in convictions for homicide was 79% in England and Wales from 2009 to 2012). You might notice that the percentage change when we consider the conviction rate in the case of trials rather than recorded incidents is much higher for rape than for homicide. There is a very simple reason for this: rapes are far less likely to be prosecuted than murders. So when we compare conviction rates based only on trials, we are not comparing like for like. There is something else going on when we look at the rape figures.

A Ministry of Justice report released in 2013 found that over the previous three years in England and Wales, an average of 85,000 women had been raped every year. Only 15% reported the attack. Of those 15%, 10.8% were 'no-crimed' (which means that the police decided that there was no rape to investigate), which is more than triple the 3.4% 'no-crime' rate for crime overall. In 2012, only 2,822 defendants were tried for rape. With an average of 85,000 rapes a year, that means that, in 2012, 97% of rapists got away with it.

It gets worse. In 2013 an internal investigation found that a number of police units in London were persuading women to drop their reports of rape. It was a deliberate policy, intended to boost their performance figures. One woman who reported a rape in 2008 did not, as a result, have her case investigated. Her rapist went on to murder his two children, aged eight and ten, with a carving knife. The report found that the officers who should have been disciplined had in fact been promoted.

And what happens to the women who are persuaded to withdraw their allegations? Well, they can be prosecuted. In an article for *openDemocracy*, Lisa Longstaff, spokesperson for Women Against Rape, told the story of two women in the United States who had been pressured to retract their allegations of rape, only to find themselves charged with lying. Both women's rapists were later caught raping again more than once – rapes that could have been prevented had the women been believed in the first place. Again, the police involved faced no disciplinary procedures. Back in the UK, a teenager faced prosecution for lying because forensic tests did not corroborate her testimony; when her case was reinvestigated, new tests found semen where the original police team had claimed there was none. And all this despite studies showing that only 2% of all reported rapes are false, making rape reports less likely to be false than any other crime. Furthermore, of those false rape reports, a high percentage 'involved young, often vulnerable people', some with mental health difficulties. About half of the cases involved someone who 'had undoubtedly been the victim of some kind of offence', even if not the one which had been reported. So, not quite the vindictive regretful response to a one-night stand the media leads us to imagine.

This seems to be a global problem. In Australia, 60% of sexual assault investigations are marked as unresolved after thirty days, and only one in six rape cases makes it to court. In South Africa, which a United Nations report found to have the highest number of rapes per capita, an estimated 500,000 rapes take place every year, with someone being raped every 17 seconds. Rape Crisis South Africa reports a conviction rate of between 4 and 7%. And in the United States, where the Rape, Abuse & Incest National Network (RAINN) estimates that a victim is raped every two minutes, for every 100 rapes, forty are reported, ten result in an arrest, eight in a prosecution, and four in a felony conviction – and only three perpetrators will spend any time at all in jail. A CBS report from 2009 found that the arrest rate in 2008 was 25% – compared with 79% for murder and 51% for aggravated assault. It told the story of Valerie Neumann, who reported that she was raped on her twenty-first birthday. The suspect denied the charge, but an exam revealed 'evidence of forced sexual penetration', and semen was found on her underwear. A nurse took a rape kit (swabs and clothes to provide DNA evidence). The kit was never tested, and the man Valerie says raped her is still at large.

The issue of untested rape kits looms large across America. The CBS report revealed that '[a]t least twelve major American cities: Anchorage, Baltimore, Birmingham, Chicago, Cincinnati, Cleveland, Columbus, Indianapolis, Jacksonville, Oakland, Phoenix, San Diego said they have no idea how many of the rape kits in storage are untested'. But one woman is set to change this. Her name is Kym Worthy and she is the prosecutor of Wayne County, Michigan.

In 2009, Kym was informed that a police evidence storage warehouse contained a stash of abandoned rape kits. The Michigan state police had taken over the Detroit police department crime lab and were doing an inventory that included 'a building where none of us who had been in criminal justice in this town even knew the police were keeping evidence'. Inside, they found 11,341 rape kits: unsorted, uninvestigated. 'Not much surprises me any more, but I was shocked,' Kym tells me. 'I was outraged that eleven thousand victims, because each kit represents a potential victim, had their lives sitting on hold on a shelf for years.'

Some of them went back decades, to the 1980s. 'At that time [the kits] went back twenty-five years. Now they go back over thirty years in time. So we basically had, no, we *did* have over 11,000 victims who had not only been sexually assaulted, but had gone through the process of a rape-kit exam which can be anywhere from four to ten hours of poking and prodding and looking at and examining every orifice of a woman's body to try to find any evidence that they can use to find the perpetrator. So even after they were sexually assaulted, they reported it, which a lot of women do not do, *and* they went to have a sexual assault kit done... Over eleven thousand lives sitting on shelves and nobody was doing anything about it. It was a *tragic* situation.'

Kym is clear that this is a gender issue. 'No question about it,' she tells me firmly. 'If men were the ones that were primarily being raped there would never be backlogged kits or abandoned kits. It's just a fact.' Kym describes sexual assault as 'the stepchild of violent crime. It's the crime within violent crime that gets the least attention, the least resources.' Sexual assault victims 'are among the only victims that are treated like defendants when they first enter the system. They are among the only victims where they are actually talked out of prosecuting their cases. [We] start by not believing them. And for instance if your house is broken into, or your car is stolen, or you are robbed, you don't walk into the police station and some police officers automatically think you're lying about it. That *is* the case with sexual assault, so of course it has to do with gender. Of course it has to do with the fact that mainly women are raped. And of course it has to do with the fact that no one really paid attention and gave the due toward sexual assault. [Otherwise] you wouldn't have sexual assault cases thrown into police warehouses across the country ignored.'

But once Kym had heard about them, they would be ignored no longer. 'That's not justice, that's a huge injustice, that had to be immediately dealt with,' she says of the lives that were simply 'dumped in these big bins'. She was determined that the kits would be organised, categorised, tested – and if perpetrators were found, they would be prosecuted. 'I'm going to see it to the end,' Kym tells me.

Beyond prosecuting cases, Kym has also thrown her effort into publicising this as a nationwide, even an international, problem, and into drawing up a blueprint for other jurisdictions to address it. Her help has been accepted. 'I think that [other jurisdictions] realise that rapists don't stop at 8 Mile Road [a road that marks a major racial and class dividing line in Detroit], they don't stop at the city line, they don't stop at the county line, they don't stop at the state line.' She is also addressing prevention, by taking 'a look at how sexual assault victims are treated from the moment they come into the criminal justice system, until they are done with the criminal justice system. It's astounding how badly they are treated at times.' Sadly, she says, 'even women fail to understand the sexual assault victim and are hard on the sexual assault victim. Even women. Women jurists for example.'

So far, Kym's team has tested 1,500 of the 11,341 rape kits, with tests underway on another 8,000 and results expected any day. Fourteen cases have been tried, and 'hundreds of cases are in the queue to be investigated'. Kym anticipates that 'if the hits keep coming the way they have been coming, we will have over three thousand prosecutable cases'. And, likely, more serial rapists than the 127 they have found so far. 'We know that these rapists… had gone on to rape in twenty-four jurisdictions total – that's almost half of the states in the United States,' Kym tells me.

I ask Kym how she felt about the fact that so many of these rapes could have been prevented had the kits been tested, had rape been treated as a serious crime worth investigating. 'This is a travesty of justice,' she tells me. They are working as fast as they can to right this wrong, but still struggle with 'a huge manpower issue' that means 'we're not going as fast as we could be'. But thanks to her leadership they are, at least, going. As a result of the systems she has put in place to 'make sure that this doesn't happen again', Kym firmly believes that this episode marks a watershed. 'I do, yes,' she tells me. 'Yes, I do absolutely.'

The failure to investigate over eleven thousand rape kits is shocking. A conviction rate for rape of 4% is shocking. Women being unfairly prosecuted for lying about their rape is shocking. But still, despite the incompetence, despite the routine disbelief victims suffer at the hands of our civilian police forces, at least they are a nominally independent and impartial service. The person to whom you have to report your rape is unlikely himself to be your rapist, or a friend of your rapist. But for women who work in the United States military, the odds are less in their favour. In 2012, through the testimony of numerous service-women, interviews with former and current military leaders, and analysis of the military's own data, a documentary called *The Invisible War* uncovered not only a pattern of rape and sexual assault within the US military but a total absence of justice.

Servicewomen in the United States military have to report their rape to their commander. And, as the husband of one of the rape victims interviewed for *The Invisible War* put it, commanders in the US military have 'an unbelievable amount of power'. He tells the documentary makers that he experienced this himself when he was a lieutenant in Iraq. 'It's scary. You appoint the prosecution, you appoint the defence, you appoint the investigator, you're in charge of the police force, you're in charge of the community. You own everything. You are judge, you are jury, you are executioner.' And, as Staff Sergeant Stace Nelson of the US Marine Corps explains, most of these all-powerful beings 'don't have the training or the education to determine what's appropriate in serious felony criminal investigations'. Worse, rape is viewed as a failure to command whoever perpetrated the crime, and that will adversely affect a commander's career, so that he (and it usually is a he) has a vested interest in not escalating rape allegations.

'I have heard the accusations as well that commanders are sweeping this under the carpet,' admits Major General Mary Kay Hertog, Director of the US Military's Sexual Assault and Prevention Office. Her advice for victims who feel that their case has not been properly investigated is for them to approach the Department of Defense Inspector General – who, according to a recent report cited by Congresswoman Jackie Speier, declined to review even a single case out of 2,500. He had, he explained, 'higher priorities'. Still, as Hertog cheerfully explains, at least the commanders overlooking the initial investigation are paragons of impartial virtue: 'There is absolutely no conflict of interest.' That must explain why, according to figures cited in *The Invisible War*, 33% of servicewomen didn't report their rape because the person to report to was a friend of the rapist, and why 25% didn't report because the person to report to was the rapist himself.

At a screening of *The Invisible War* in London, Emma Norton, a solicitor for the human rights organisation Liberty, explains that the situation in the UK is marginally better. But only very marginally. Emma has been working with Sharon Hardy, sister of Anne-Marie Ellement, who was allegedly raped by two of her Royal Military Police colleagues. The investigation into Ellement's alleged rape was conducted by the Royal Military Police, and, Sharon explained, it was overseen by an army prosecutor 'who had not done the basic rape training that all CPS lawyers do'. No charges were brought, and Ellement then faced eighteen months of relentless bullying. Eventually she killed herself.

In the UK, the commanding officer is required in nearly all cases to refer serious offences to the service police. The 2006 Armed Forces Act only excludes three offences from this requirement, and all three are sexual in nature: voyeurism, exposure and sexual assault. In February 2014, Shami Chakrabarti, Director of Liberty, wrote to the Secretary of State for Defence, Philip Hammond, pointing out that this discrepancy led to 'an obvious and unacceptable risk of injustice', and asking him to address it. By September of the same year she had yet to receive an answer.

Lisa Longstaff of Women Against Rape is also on the panel, and she reveals that in the UK military the conviction rate for reported rapes is 1% (remember that the civilian rate is 6.5%). Even if we look at the conviction rates for cases that actually make it to court, while the civilian rate is 63%, the conviction rate in courts martial is 16%. The figures for 2007–9 seem actually to have been worse than that: the Ministry of Defence took two months to reply to a simple request from Channel 4 News about the military's conviction rate for rape. Eventually, it reluctantly revealed that the Armed Forces investigated seventy-six allegations of rape over those two years, resulting in two convictions. A rate of 2.6%.

The US Department of Defense estimates that there are about 19,000 sexual assaults in the military every year – although it estimates a figure of 26,000 for 2012. And yet in 2011, only 1,108 investigations were filed, only 575 cases processed, and only 96 went to court martial. In *The Invisible War*, Susan Burke, a lawyer who has specialised in cases against the US military, explains: 'When you look at prosecution rates in the 2010 Department of Defense reports you begin with 2,410 unrestricted reports and 748 restricted. What that means is they've already funnelled 748 sexual assault victims into a system that has absolutely no adjudication whatsoever. Then you take the 2,410 that have been reported. Of those, they identify 3,223 perpetrators. Now what happens once you send a perpetrator over to command? Well, the command has just completely unfettered discretion to do whatever it is they want. And what is it that they do do? First off, they drop 910 of them. They just don't do anything. Then of the 1,025 where they actually take some action, do they court-martial them? No. Only half of them, 529, actually got court-martialled. The rest, 256, were subjected to article 15 punishments, 109 to administrative discharges, and then 131 to "other adverse administrative actions", whatever the heck that means. And then of the convictions where they actually get jail time, when you work your way all the way through the numbers, what you're looking at is that out of 3,223 perpetrators, only 175 end up doing any jail time whatsoever.' So that's a conviction rate of 5% – although if we take the department's average estimated figure of 19,000, that would work out at less than 1%.

Emma Norton explains that the military is 'a very different environment [from civilian life], because you're living with people, you're working with people, you're socialising with people, and if something like [rape] happens to you and it's the people who you trusted who do it to you, the effects can be devastating'. This analysis is echoed in *The Invisible War* by Brigadier General Loree Sutton, a psychiatrist in the US Army, who reports that the effect on raped servicewomen is 'akin to what happens with a family with incest'. When these women report, it is they, rather than the men who raped them, who are framed as the aggressor who has split up the family. The only explanation for seeing a rape victim as an aggressor is if you think that she is lying.

'They took me before my Lieutenant Commander, he says "D'you think this is funny?"; I was like, "What do you mean?"; he's like, "Is this all a joke to you?"; I was like, "What do you mean?"; and he goes, "You're the third girl to report rape this week; are you guys like all in cahoots, you think this is a game?"' This episode is reported in *The Invisible War* by Tia Christopher of the US Navy. Rather than prompting commanding officers to think the military might have a rape problem, the sheer volume of sexual assaults in the military leads them to think that the women who report it must be lying. Indeed, the level of disbelief is so high that Christina Jones of the US Army reports that '[e]ven with the rape kit and everything, and my friend catching him raping me, they still didn't believe me'. The level of disbelief is so high that the women themselves sometimes end up facing charges.

Andrea Warner of the US Army: 'They actually did charge me with adultery. I wasn't married. He was.'

An anonymous female marine: 'I got called up to a major's

office and he charged me with fraternisation and adultery. He was married, I wasn't.'

Lieutenant Elle Helmer of the US Marine Corps: 'The colonel at one point said, you know, Lieutenant Helmer… we'll never really know what happened inside that office. Only you and the major know and he's not talking. So at this point, the investigation is closed for lack of evidence and we have reopened a new investigation, against you, for conduct unbecoming an officer, and public intoxication.'

Sergeant Myla Haider of the US Army Criminal Investigation Division: 'I was told to advise a victim of her rights for false statement when I knew that she wasn't lying. I was asked to bring her in and advise her of her rights, like a criminal, and interrogate her for false statement "until I got the truth out of her".'

Given the serious repercussions servicewomen face for reporting, it is no surprise that many decide not to. Myla didn't. She wanted to keep her job. In an interview with America's National Public Radio (NPR), Myla explained, 'I've never met one victim who was able to report the crime and still retain their military career. Not one.' So when she herself was raped, she kept quiet. But one day, she received a phone call. Her rapist was being investigated for a stream of other rapes, all of which had happened after hers. 'I thought the only right thing for me to do was to be involved,' Myla says. And with all the evidence that had mounted up against him, she thought, 'there was no way that, you know, he wouldn't be convicted'.

But the military found a way. Although Myla and his other victims testified against him, the charges were reduced, and, as a result, he never even made it onto the national registry of sex offenders. This, says Stace Nelson, is a favoured tactic of the military: they only have to report crimes to outside bodies when they have decided that they are felonies. 'The military doesn't like to prosecute people and keep them as felony convictions', so many cases 'are pled down'.

But while her rapist evaded any repercussions for his actions, Myla wasn't so lucky. On the night she received the phone call about her own rapist, she also received another call – about another rape victim. In her role as an army investigator, she went on to give professional testimony at this victim's trial, she told NPR, when the defense attorney asked her, 'Isn't it true that you're a rape victim yourself?' She was 'appalled, because as an investigator [I knew that] it had nothing to do with the case'. But it had everything to do with her career. 'When I reported [the rape], it was a very small part of my life. But by making that choice, my reporting of it took over my life, ruined my career and wound up, ultimately, getting me kicked out of the army,' she says. 'I was administratively discharged with no benefits after nine and a half years of service.' It is this, Myla says, that most hurts. 'I had an almost ten-year career, which I was very invested in, and I gave that up to report a sex offender who was not even put to justice or put on the registry' – and, she adds, who is 'probably doing the same thing right now'.

Major General Hertog's next piece of advice for women who do not feel their case has 'been taken care of adequately' within the justice system is to approach their 'congressman or congresswoman'. But Susan Burke gives this suggestion short shrift. 'You cannot go to your *congressman* to obtain justice for being raped! I mean, imagine how silly that is. Imagine if you told civilians that, "Oh, gee, sorry you were raped, go talk to your congressman"?!'

Susan wanted to do something, and the only thing she knows

how to do to help people, she told the *Washington Post*, 'is to sue'. So that's what she did: she gathered sixteen servicemen and women, including Myla, and together they took former US Secretaries of Defense Donald Rumsfeld and Robert M. Gates to court for their respective roles in the military's 'systemic failure to stop rape and sexual assault'.

The First Amended Complaint she prepared is relentlessly detailed – and damning. It claims that Rumsfeld and Gates 'violated Plaintiffs' Constitutional rights' by failing to: 'investigate rapes and sexual assaults', 'prosecute perpetrators', 'provide an adequate judicial system as required by the Uniform Military Justice Act', and 'abide by Congressional deadlines to implement Congressionally-ordered institutional reforms to stop rapes and other sexual assaults'. Instead, the document continues, 'Defendants ran institutions in which perpetrators were pro-moted and where military personnel openly mocked and flouted the modest Congressionally-mandated institutional reforms. Defendants ran institutions in which Plaintiffs and other victims were openly subjected to retaliation, were encouraged to refrain from reporting rapes and sexual assaults in a manner that would have permitted prosecution, and were ordered to keep quiet and refrain from telling anyone about the criminal acts of their work colleagues. Defendants lack any legal justification for their failures to remedy such a flawed system. Defendants' failures to act violated Plaintiffs' individual Constitutional rights.'

But thorough as the complaint was, there is no legislating for the establishment's determination to protect its own, and in December 2011, the court delivered its verdict: the suit was dismissed.

Susan appealed against the decision in this case – but her

appeal was dismissed in 2013. Since launching the original case, she has continued to represent for free numerous other victims of sexual assault who have been failed by the US military. So far, these cases and their subsequent appeals have all been dismissed too. When I contacted Susan in April 2014, her spokesperson informed me: 'The Government successfully argued that rape is an occupational hazard of military service and that it cannot be held civilly liable.'

But Susan isn't giving up – and she's started something big. A banner at the bottom of her practice website reads, 'Due to the volume of inquiries, Burke PLLC is no longer able to respond individually to all military rape and sexual assault survivors who contact us. We have developed a collaborative relationship with Protect Our Defenders to locate "pro bono" (free) legal counsel for those who need assistance. Please go to their website and fill out this form.' We can choose to be disheartened by the volume of rape victims who need Susan's help and we can choose to be outraged by the grounds on which the cases so far have been dismissed. But we can also choose to rejoice at the volume of women who had been suffering in silence but who now feel some chance of being heard, of being believed. Of eventually receiving justice.

The law when it comes to servicewomen is muddled, to say the least. But it's even worse when it comes to women who sell sex. Against Violence & Abuse, a UK charity concerned with violence against women, cites a Home Office report from 2004 which found that '[m]ore than half of women in prostitution have been raped and or seriously assaulted and at least 75% have been physically assaulted at the hands of the pimps and punters'. A report from 2009 found that '[w]omen in prostitution are 18

times more likely to be murdered than the general population',
while a 2007 report found that '[w]omen in street prostitution
are 12 times more likely to be murdered than the rate for all
women in the same age group in the UK'. But while women
who sell sex are more likely to be murdered, their murderers are
less likely to be convicted. According to a 2006 report, the
average conviction rate drops from 75% for the general population to 26% if the victim worked in prostitution. A June 2013
report into policing in London found that some boroughs had
'a history of naming and shaming the women involved in street
prostitution in the borough, including publicising women with
ASBOs on the council's website and putting photographs of the
women in residents' letter boxes'.

When Ruth was raped in her flat, she tried to report it. 'I
was given a number of one of the officers who was meant to be
nice to working girls.' This nice officer neither returned her call
nor referred it to anyone else. On another occasion, other nice
officers who'd visited her flat left all her work gear laid out on
the bed, she tells me, 'my underwear and, you know, vibrators
and whatever, like as if to say we know what you're doing'. She
didn't report her second rape.

Ruth first started selling sex when she was twenty-one. She
grew up in a violent household, where she was called a 'whore'
from the age of ten, given the nickname 'Jam, meaning tart', and
subjected to sexual and physical abuse. Having left home at
seventeen, she got on to a training scheme at a department store
and worked there for four years, 'running on anger', until she
suddenly had a breakdown. It was her first hospitalisation. 'When
I came out, I got a telemarketing job,' she tells me. 'But I think
I just couldn't deal with life and I had started self-medicating
with drugs. At the time, I was thinking, I'm having sex with

men, and being promiscuous and acting out… I may as well get paid for it, because men are all c★★ts anyway. I think as well, though, I was probably finding it very hard to go to work every day, and function.'

Ruth kept up her telemarketing job for a while after starting to sell sex. 'I didn't really need the job', she says, 'but I think I kept it going for a while, because… I don't know why. I can only imagine, maybe I wanted to think that I wasn't just a hooker.'

I know Ruth doesn't routinely use the term 'hooker' – so I'm struck that she keeps referring to herself that way. When I ask her why, she says, 'I would never call myself a prostitute, I say hooker. But I don't want anyone else calling me a hooker.' It is, she says, 'an offensive word' and she'd never use it to refer to someone else, but when she uses it of herself, she says, 'I think maybe it takes away, like maybe making it kind of a bit lighter.' For women who want to call themselves sex workers, she respects that choice, and 'I think it's very important that the word is used, because people deserve a way to earn money, but "sex worker" for me doesn't fit what I did, because I ended up sticking needles in my arms and I was killing myself, and crying and feeling repulsed by being touched. It was very traumatic for me.'

Ruth is matter of fact as she tells me about the men who attacked her during the five years or so that she sold sex around the world. There were the men who kidnapped her when she was in Miami and threatened to kill her. There was the man who thought she was sixteen years old, and who forced her to act things out that took her back to the experience of being abused as a child. There was the man in Australia to whom she'd agreed to give either a blow job or a hand job (she can't remember which) in return for heroin. 'He drove me out into the outback,' she tells me. 'I kept asking him to stop, and we just kept going, out into the middle of nowhere, and then he raped me. I thought I was going to die.'

And there was the man, 'a punter', who raped her in her flat in London. 'The whole time he was raping me, I was thinking, I'm gonna kill him. I'm gonna kill him.' She didn't kill him, but she did fantasise about exacting her revenge. A year later, he called out of the blue ('he obviously had forgotten that he'd raped me'), and she wondered if the time had come, but he never ended up phoning back. 'He must have realised, oh no, I've done her already.'

It was getting clean that ended Ruth's days of selling sex. She says it would have been impossible to stay off drugs otherwise. 'I find life hard enough anyway, but to go through that... no. I couldn't do it. Maybe I could have managed for a few months, even a year, but I imagine for me that it would probably have been a few punters and I'd have thought, I've got to have a hit and just get my head out of this.'

Ruth went into sales and tried to put her experience behind her. But then an anonymous 'call girl' started blogging under the pseudonym Belle de Jour and the blog ended up being turned into a book. The book became a popular TV show, and it presented a life as a call girl that Ruth just didn't recognise. Ruth stresses that she and Brooke Magnanti (the woman behind Belle de Jour) actually now agree on their approaches to helping women in the sex trade, but at the time, she found herself thinking, 'It's just not like this. I don't want young women saying, look how easy it is, and how much fun, to be a call girl. I wanted to show what really happened.' She started writing a series of books called *Soul Destruction*, about the life of a 'drug-addicted call girl'.

That was all she thought she could do. 'I never planned to do any activism at all. I always used to say though, what I'd really love to do is work with women in the sex trade.' She tells me in a somewhat conspiratorial voice about her dreams of winning the lottery and being able to set up a centre in London that would connect all the services that women in prostitution need. But she never thought she'd be able to do it – she points out that 'it's nearly impossible to pay for childcare and do everything else, and do that kind of job' (she has two young children).

In 2013 Ruth heard about the Merseyside model. She tells me she cried when she read about the results achieved with this model of policing the sex trade. At the time, everyone was talking about the Nordic model (where buying sex is criminalised, but selling sex is decriminalised). She couldn't understand why more people weren't raving about this new miracle approach.

The difference between Merseyside and the rest of the country is that in Merseyside the police have made a choice. They have decided that getting violent men off the streets and into prison is more important than getting women selling sex off the streets and into prison. Their new priority, as Detective Superintendent Tim Keelan told the *Guardian*, is to protect the women rather than to prosecute them. Crimes against women selling sex in Merseyside are now treated as hate crimes. 'It's a kind of unofficial decriminalisation, really,' says Ruth. It means that when women in Merseyside report a rape or an attack, 'they *know* that they're going to be treated like any other victim of crime. They're not going to be charged with running a brothel because they live with another woman or stand on the street.' By focusing instead on violent men, the police in Merseyside have managed to 'build trusting relationships with the women, so the women report on crime'.

This approach has had a dramatic effect: in the five years before the model was introduced in 2007, there was, according to the *Guardian*, 'just one conviction for a series of assaults against sex workers'. By 2010, while conviction rates for rape languished at 6.5% nationwide, convictions for the rape of women in prostitution in Merseyside had risen dramatically to 67%. If you're selling sex in Merseyside and get raped, Ruth says, 'they are ten times more likely to catch the rapist than anywhere else in the country'.

Given these remarkable figures, you can understand why Ruth was perplexed that the model hadn't already been adopted throughout the UK. 'Everyone was going on about the Nordic model, and yet here's something that works, immediately, right now, and the results are amazing,' she says. 'If we were talking about conviction rates for the rape of women in general, do you think we would have been waiting eight years to have made it policy? People would be going crazy ages ago. It's because it's women in the sex trade.' When I asked her why she thought this was, the word she uses is 'sacrifice'. She feels that people are putting ideology above women's lives – that the lives of women like her are too easily abstracted away into expendability, for the sake of the greater good.

'The focus has not been on the Merseyside model because the focus isn't actually on protecting people in the sex trade at all,' she says. 'For moral reasons or reasons of radical feminism, it is always about *ending* the sex trade, rather than protecting the women who are in it.' But, she says, the Merseyside model also has better results on helping women to leave the sex trade than the Nordic model. 'Isn't it insane?' she asks me. 'People say they don't want harm reduction, they want harm elimination. But harm elimination actually means the elimination of the people who are getting harmed. That's what it means. You're eliminating real people.'

'It's all about how it looks, about sending a message to men,' Ruth concludes. 'Well, what about the women who are dying when that message goes out?' As it happens, I think sending a message to men that women's bodies are not theirs to buy and sell – or even to rent for half an hour – is no bad thing. But I can't help agreeing with Ruth that, as a society, we've got our 'focus' wrong here: a 2012 study on women who wanted to leave prostitution in the UK found that 49% of them had a criminal record directly relating to prostitution. And anyway, by the time a man is habituated enough, cynical enough and entitled enough to start complaining, 'Sorry, what do you mean NO, this is what I paid for', or moaning about a woman making it 'glumly obvious that my visit was just a chore', or gleefully recounting how after a disappointing visit to a sex worker he went home and 'gave the missus a good seeing to, so not a complete loss' (all direct quotes from punternet.com, a website where men 'review' women), it may be all but impossible to convince him that women do not exist purely for his sexual gratification. The focus on men has to begin far earlier, Ruth says, when they're still boys at school. 'I think education needs to start teaching men about objectifying women, that it's not OK. You're not going get that kind of a change from a law.'

I think the issue here is one of desperation. It is not fair or accurate to accuse feminists who want to end the sex trade of not caring about the women in it; but it might be fair to question how realistic we are being. The desire of feminists is to protect women – all women, including those who sell sex – from male violence. And they want that violence to end now, today.

While no feminist would disagree that education is a vital step towards ending that violence, it's a step that will take decades to move us forward. That, many feminists would argue, is just too damn far into the future. We need results now. We need the raping and the beating and the killing to stop now.

To achieve this, Ruth says, we also need to focus on the women and why they're choosing to sell sex in the first place. 'It's not about men,' she insists. 'In so many of these conversations, it's always about the men. Not about the women who are trying to pay their rent so they don't get evicted. Who are skipping meals, who can't pay the bedroom tax, who can't give their children anything else but baked beans on toast for two weeks. But, they're not talking about that, they're focusing on the men! They've got their focus wrong.' She would sell sex again if she had to, she tells me. 'And it would be different for me now, being much older – I wouldn't get so much money for it! But, however traumatic it is, I have to keep a roof over my children's head.' Ruth tells me that she doesn't 'promote prostitution', but she is very clear that there is a fine balance between showing young women that 'this is not easy money' and increasing the stigma for people who are already dangerously marginalised. 'I don't believe that there should be any shame in it.'

She points out that the vast majority (70%) of those who sell sex are single mothers living in poverty. 'I think because so many people can't put themselves in that situation, they just think everyone's got parents who are going to bail them out. They think, how can you not have enough money to put your heating on when it's freezing and get hot water? How can you not have enough money to buy food? But when you've got absolutely nothing in your purse, you're going to go out and...' She trails off. 'Well, I've got huge respect for women that go out and sell sex so that they can provide for their children if there's no other way.'

Ruth is right to highlight the often stark choices facing women who end up selling sex. In a 2014 article in *The Times*, the journalist Janice Turner writes that in France, 85% 'of prostitutes are immigrants, many without papers, vulnerable to exploitation. In Germany, with its legal super-brothels, it is about two thirds.' A 2010 UK study into the trafficking of migrant women in off-street prostitution found that 96.4% were migrants. Nationally, the report estimated that 2,600 women had been trafficked, with a further 9,600 considered to be 'vulnerable'. These are not people we should be criminalising.

When Ruth heard about the Merseyside model, she didn't just cry. She decided she had to take action. She had made her life about trying to protect women who, like her, had turned to prostitution out of desperation. And here was a model that was proven to work. Here was something positive she could fight for. So, together with Jackie Summerford, the mother of Bonnie Barratt, who was murdered by a punter well known by the women of East London to be violent, Ruth set up a petition asking the Home Secretary to roll this policing model out across the country. Ruth also delivers talks and workshops, has given evidence to Parliament, and made a BBC documentary about the model.

There is still some way to go, but people are starting to listen. 'Before this, I thought that most people in society don't care about women in the sex trade,' she says. 'But I'm really shocked that we're doing so well.' They've recently had their first comment from a government minister. 'You know, it's just the standard kind of line, but still, we've had a comment and he knows about it. And the petition has already got *sixty-seven and a half thousand* signatures,' she tells me, beaming. 'To think how many people do care is *amazing*.'

Anyone who has taken more than a passing interest in prostitution will know how hard it is to come by reliable studies on the topic, especially when so many of the initiatives are still so new. The evidence is mounting that decriminalisation increases trafficking (often of underage and migrant women), and that criminalising demand lowers it. Janice Turner points out that Sweden, which criminalised demand in 1999, found that demand decreased, the number of women in prostitution declined, 'with no spike in sexual violence', and the country had 'only one quarter of the trafficking cases of next-door Denmark', which decriminalised prostitution in the same year. Nevertheless, there are credible studies that claim to demonstrate the opposite.

But while we continue to disagree over which model best protects women who sell sex, one issue on which everyone can agree is that the commodification of women is a global industry. As a result, models instituted in a single country can have an effect around the world. Ruchira Gupta, co-founder of a group that advocates for Indian women in prostitution, explains: 'Today, pornography is often made in one country and exported to another country; sex tourists are travelling from place to place; websites auctioning girls are accessed from anywhere in the world; the cult of masculinity which drives demand is everywhere; prostitution, if it's normalised in one place, will get normalised somewhere else, because people will say, this is what men do, or it's as old as the hills, or whatever. Cultures affect each other, so we need a global consensus on certain things and we need global laws.'

But, she cautions, we also need localised solutions, not just for different countries, but for different regions within each country: 'context is so important'. India, Ruchira tells me, would need specific 'planning and investment' to account for its largely agricultural economy. Better to train many of the girls in agriculture and financial literacy than in computers, as you would in the big cities. (And they are girls: Ruchira tells me that the average age of entry into prostitution in India is between nine and thirteen.)

Ruchira gives me a particularly troubling example of an insensitive local solution, instigated with the best of intentions by a global foundation (an unfortunate pattern in what Teju Cole has dubbed 'The White Savior Industrial-Complex'). Fifteen years ago, the World Health Organization had come out with a report saying that India would be the epicentre of the AIDS pandemic in the world. On the basis of this report (which later turned out to be based on inaccurate data), the Bill & Melinda Gates Foundation decided to pour millions of dollars (over $500 million) into India to prevent the spread of AIDS. A laudable aim.

To get a programme for tackling the problem designed, the foundation hired an employee from the marketing company McKinsey, Ruchira tells me. 'They began to think about what could they market as the solution, and they focused on the condom, because that was a good product to market.' This new employee identified the red light areas in India as 'the place where the highest number of sexual transactions happened', so they targeted their condom distribution programme there. The Bill & Melinda Gates Foundation funded 'twenty-three global NGOs' to carry out this programme, and also funded 'UNAIDS and other international UN bodies and organisations' to 'do similar advocacy for their programmes by publishing in journals, documenting it as best practice'. The whole programme, Ruchira says, 'was geared to protect male buyers from disease, rather than protecting the women and girls from the male buyers. It was a completely gender-insensitive programme. And it had an absolutely disastrous impact inside the red light areas where I work.'

The problem, Ruchira says, was that the focus was on simply getting 'condoms out of the door'. NGOs knew that the way to continue to receive funding was to make sure they distributed a certain number of condoms, so to achieve that they outsourced the distribution within brothels to pimps and brothel managers. 'And *that* became an end in itself,' she says. 'So if *I* went to the police station to complain about a pimp or a brothel manager holding a girl hostage or beating her, or controlling her, and [said] what about her human rights, I was told, this is NGO rivalry, because that pimp or that brothel manager is a peer educator, or the staff of such and such NGO.'

The rabbit hole gets deeper. 'To make this programme even more "efficient",' Ruchira says, 'NGOs began to organise the pimps and brothel managers to form associations. And these associations then began to demand the legalisation of sex work. But they were basically led by pimps and brothel managers, not by the fourteen-year-old locked up inside the brothel, because she had no voice. She would have to support what the brothel manager was telling her. So it had *huge* unintended consequences because it effectively legitimised the pimps and the brothel managers, as peer educators. It entrenched the sex industry, which grew by seventeen times.'

And deeper: 'It also created a false notion of "ethical demand" because people began to believe that it was all right to buy sex if you used a condom. There were actually ads by Gates–

funded organisations which said, "it does not matter which sex worker you choose, but choose the right condom"' – women reduced to the level of objects without self-determination, like so many items off a shelf. Ruchira accuses these organisations of 'invisibilising and sterilising the exploitation out of the industry' – and when she tells me about a report brought out in 2012 by UNAIDS and the United Nations Population Fund (UNFPA) which recommends that 'pimps and brothel managers should not be punished', it's hard to disagree with her. Ruchira says that when she went to the head of NACO (the Department of AIDS Control in India) to complain about the increase in trafficking as a result of the legitimisation of the brothels, she was told that she could go after the 'big picture' if she wanted, but that NACO's remit was to run an AIDS programme. If the brothels did not exist, she was asked, where would they distribute the condoms?

And deeper: Ruchira tells me about the Sonagachi model, which is run by an NGO called DNSC, and which promotes the hiring of pimps and brothel managers to distribute condoms. The model was started, Ruchira says, by a forty-five-year-old male doctor who wrote about the programme for a healthcare journal. Ruchira tells me that the doctor advocated turning a blind eye 'if you see a girl being abused inside the brothel', on the grounds that 'you don't want to upset the status quo inside the brothel, because we have to continue with our condom distribution programme'.

I am reminded, as Ruchira lays out this litany of unintended and uncared-for consequences, of the Contagious Diseases Act of the Victorian era. That too was a programme designed to protect men against diseases they picked up when they visited prostitutes. But unlike the Sonagachi model, there was no pretence that it had anything to do with the women's welfare. The act gave the police the right to arrest prostitutes, subject them to compulsory checks for venereal disease and, if they were found to be infected, lock them up for three months, while the unexamined men were free to continue infecting prostitutes and their unwitting wives.

Ruchira first started working with women in prostitution after she visited some remote villages in Nepal while researching an article on how they managed their natural resources. In these villages, girls and young women were all but non-existent. Ruchira started to ask why, and was met with evasiveness, shame, even outright hostility from the local men. But a few of them spoke to her – some of them giggling – and told her that the girls were all in Mumbai. This confused Ruchira – these villages were two to three hours from the nearest highway and Mumbai was 14,000 kilometres away. Why were so many of these Nepalese village girls ending up in the Indian captial? Ruchira's questions led her to uncover what she describes as shockingly well-organised criminal networks. 'I found, to my horror, that the flesh trade existed, in my lifetime, in my generation.'

This is how it works. 'A local village procurer offers poor, starving and isolated farmers $50, $100, maybe $300 even, for their daughters.' They tell them they will get their daughter a job in the city, or they'll get her married – some of them even admit they will sell her into prostitution. But, they assure her family, the child will have a bed and food, and will be able to send money back home. The farmers are too poor to refuse. The girls are then handed over to transporters, who smuggle them over the border into India, via the time-honoured method of a lucrative handshake with the border guards. Once safely across the borders, what is called the 'seasoning' begins.

The girls are kept locked up in 'shabby lodges made of corrugated cement and plastic sheets'. They are beaten, starved and drugged. They are told there is no going back. This goes on for two or three days, before the girls are picked up by another set of transporters, who put them on buses or trains, straight into the brothels of Mumbai, Kolkata, Delhi. And now they start the negotiations over the price of a child as young as nine: fair skin, docility and youth fetch a premium price in these flesh markets. Once the pimps have claimed their prizes, the girls are handed over to the respective brothel managers, who again lock the girls up in small rooms with iron bars on the window 'and trot them out for eight or ten customers a night, every night, for the next five to seven years' for little more than 'loose change per rape'. Many of the women Ruchira has met have not even seen the street that they lived on. They have not been allowed outside, even for medical check-ups, in half a decade.

Beyond subjecting their captives to multiple rapes every night (no matter what your feelings are on prostitution, trafficked girls kept captive cannot be considered to have consented to what is done to them), the brothel managers work hard to break the girls' spirits. As soon as they start working, they are told that they are now sexually used, devalued. No one will marry them, their families will not want to know them. If the girls cry, they are beaten until they learn to stop. The pimps ply them with alcohol and drugs, which the girls accept only too keenly: it helps them pretend that the repeated bodily invasions are not real. And these people, these traders in stolen bodies, are the very same people the UN says we should be careful not to offend, for fear of disrupting programmes to protect the health of the men who rape their captives.

Having witnessed such a sophisticated level of coordinated

inhumanity, Ruchira couldn't let it go. In her fourteen years as a journalist, she'd covered war, ethnic conflict, caste conflict, famine – but she'd 'never seen this kind of deliberate exploitation of one human being by another'. It was 'modern day slavery' and she wanted to do something about it. She spent eighteen months working on a documentary about the lives of these women: she wanted to give them a voice, to force the world to contemplate the nature of their existence. *The Selling of Innocents* won an Emmy – and a stream of offers of work for Ruchira.

But Ruchira didn't want these offers. She had 'made eye contact with the women and got to know them as human beings' over the months she had spent with them. 'So I quit journalism,' she says. 'I didn't have a job, I didn't know what I was going to do *exactly* at that time.' But the twenty-two women about whom Ruchira had made the documentary had ideas. After the Emmy, they said to Ruchira, 'now that's done, but what about us?' They asked Ruchira to help them.

Ruchira was flummoxed – what more could she do? She had done what she could by giving them a voice in the film. And in any case, she couldn't help them unless they were willing to help themselves. They were willing, they said, but they needed support. This was something Ruchira felt she could offer – so, together with these twenty-two women, Ruchira set up Apne Aap, which literally means 'self-empowerment'.

They set about achieving the 'four dreams' Ruchira tells me they had, which have formed the 'Four Essential Rights' around which Apne Aap is based. One of these rights is so basic it really brings home the reality of the women's lives. These women, who had never even heard of Virginia Woolf, told Ruchira that they wanted 'a room of their own'. They wanted somewhere they could sleep when they wanted, where their children could play, where 'no one can walk in and out as it pleases them'. These women wanted the most basic of human freedoms: a right to privacy, and to 'peace'. They wanted what is now enshrined as the Right to Safe and Independent Housing.

The Indian government runs a programme called Below the Poverty Line, which will cover the cost of building a home for people in poverty. Most of the women Ruchira works with are eligible for the programme – but most of them are not aware of its existence, and Ruchira says there is a deliberate effort to deprive people of information about their entitlements. Together with a toxic combination of complicated local politics and corruption, this has meant that most of those who benefit from the programme are not those who actually need it. Apne Aap not only makes women aware of the existence of the programme, it also helps them take advantage of it by helping them with paperwork and with tackling intransigent local officials. Thus supported, the women have gone on to petition local authorities, organise rallies and stage sit-ins at government offices.

'The second thing they said they wanted was a job in an office – what has become in Apne Aap's manifesto the Right to A Dignified Livelihood. And I asked them, "What do you mean by a job in an office?" and they said, "Well, where we can have fixed working hours, where nobody dominates our time, where we have old-age pension, where nobody shouts and beats and abuses us."' But how could they achieve this with no education, no training, no access to finance? They act collectively. The first step is to start saving. Each group sets a monthly savings goal to which each woman contributes, and every month they give over a portion of the pooled money to whichever member of the group's need is most urgent – usually it goes to pay for a child's food or school fees. After about six months, the group will have saved up enough money together to be able to open a bank account. And at this point, once they have access to financial services, they can begin entrepreneurial projects based on their skills. Apne Aap also offers various courses such as English language, computer skills and tailoring.

The third dream was the Right to Education for their daughters. 'As the women grew older in the brothels,' Ruchira says, 'and by older I mean in their late twenties, the brothel managers saw that they were not commercially viable, because customers wanted younger girls. So they would put pressure on them to replace themselves with their daughters.' The women did not want their daughters to inherit their lack of choices. And so, in spite of resistance from the principal of the local school who didn't want to admit daughters of prostitutes on the basis that other parents would complain, this was the first campaign they launched – and won.

After this success, the women moved on to their next dream and set about tackling a more dangerous enemy: the police. The Right to Legal Protection. Before I interviewed Ruchira, I read about a woman who was bleeding from her vagina. The hospital refused to treat her because, they said, she was a 'whore'. I wondered how common this was. 'Extremely common,' Ruchira tells me. She has great difficulty finding doctors to treat the women she works with, or lawyers to take their cases on. Apne Aap itself suffers from high staff turnover, because 'the stigma means it's impossible to find good staff'.

Nevertheless, Ruchira says, it is not always down to prejudice that a hospital may refuse to treat a woman – it could equally be a result of the hospital's fear of having any dealings with the police. She tells me that 'people will leave a body by the side of the road' rather than escort a victim to the police station and risk being accused of the crime. 'The police are known for having done that.'

Police corruption does not only result indirectly in women being denied vital treatment; police are also directly involved in, and financially benefiting from, prostitution. The women with whom Ruchira founded Apne Aap told her that they wanted *nyaya* – that is, justice. They wanted those who had bought and sold them to be punished: 'they contracted away our dreams', they told her. Most police officers would not even register a complaint from a woman in prostitution – and all too often, if a woman managed to escape from a brothel, the police would bring her back.

'The police are part of the problem,' says Ruchira. At best, she tells me, 'they are simply patriarchal or sexist, and elitist as well'. She has been told by them that 'if prostitutes don't exist, girls from good families will be raped' – the subtext being that 'poor and low-caste women have to be sexually available, to spare upper-caste and upper-class women' and that 'this is what [women from low-caste communities] do and this is what they should do. And nothing is going to change that.' That's the police attitude 'at best', Ruchira says.

At worst, well, there are grades. Police own brothels anonymously, she tells me. 'They are part of trafficking rings' and they 'extort money from the women in prostitution and from the brothel manager and the pimps', in a system known as *hasta*, which literally means 'weekly', but which in slang means the weekly collection, by police, of money from brothels. They also, of course, afford themselves free services from the women and girls – and are renowned as some of the most violent of all the clients.

But the women of Apne Aap didn't want to put up with police brutality any more. Newly emboldened by their triumph at the local school, they took on the police officer who had tried to extort money from one of them, and who had beaten her so badly he broke her jaw. They marched en masse to the police station – and because there were so many of them, they had the unprecedented satisfaction of forcing the police to register their complaint.

This was a huge victory for the women – practically and psychologically – but it hasn't endeared Apne Aap to the police. Ruchira tells me of continual police harassment and intimidation of her activists, including filing cases against them for trafficking. On one occasion, they took away the fourteen-year-old daughter of one of Apne Aap's activists – a woman who had formerly been in prostitution. They kept the child in the police station overnight, denied her mother access, gave her no blanket, no food, and administered 'the two-finger test', claiming they had to check that the girl was a virgin to make sure she herself was not trafficked.

And Ruchira herself has been attacked. She tells me about having had knives pulled on her, of being stalked, of having traffickers walk into her house to threaten her. She laughs ruefully when she tells me about the 'pornographic phone calls' that come in 'all the time', especially when she's 'in the middle of a case against traffickers'. She is less sanguine, however, about attacks – less threatening though they may be – from academics, or from women who angrily tell her they have personally chosen to sell sex. 'I find it so frustrating,' she says. 'I'm working [in the] real world and [with] real women who are going through this experience and you know the horror of their lives, the exploitation, the sheer dead end. And then to have people legitimising it, and saying this is what girls and women want, because I know they don't.'

Calling it 'selling sex' is a misnomer, as Ruchira explains to me with brutal precision. For the first five years, this job is in fact 'debt bondage'. The girls are working off the amount paid to their families when they were first sold off – only, the girls have no idea how much this actually was, and even if they did know, they are kept too drugged to keep track. For the next five years, a girl is normally allowed to keep half of what she earns. But by then her earning capacity will have come down (they really like them young), and in addition, 'she has to pay for the drugs and the alcohol that she has become dependent on, she has to pay for the upkeep of her children. She has medical issues by then ranging from tuberculosis, to jaundice, to STDs, psycho-social trauma, repeated suicide attempts on her body, repeated abortions…' She also has to pay 'for the pimps and the musclemen who protect her from the client brutality, or the police who come and take weekly and monthly pay-offs. She has to pay for the bed that she sleeps on, the food that she eats, the make-up she is forced to wear.' All this, and she doesn't know how to count.

'The earnings are all going into the prostitution system,' Ruchira tells me. 'It's not like a win–win where a poor woman is earning an income and the poor migrant worker is getting sex in exchange. There are people controlling this poor woman who are actually earning off her while she's just getting deeper into debt. And she doesn't even know that.' The amount of money paid to the women also depends on the time of day, Ruchira tells me. Unless a woman has earned her contracted daily amount, her brothel manager will not feed her, so as the night goes on, she gets more desperate: 'there is no such thing as minimum wages'. The price also depends on her age: 'this is an occupation where you earn less as you grow older. You don't earn more with more experience,' Ruchira points out. Finally, after her tenth year, the girl, who will now probably be in her early-to-mid-twenties, can keep what she earns. Only, she can't stay in the brothel unless she pays rent, because she is no longer commercially viable. And the rent charged for these tiny, dirty rooms is extortionate – deliberately so. So now the woman is homeless, undocumented, uneducated, illiterate, with no transferable skills, reduced to trying to eke out an existence begging on the street, along with all the other people never given a chance in life and dismissed as unsightly undesirables, surplus to society's requirements. Meanwhile, her daughters are being lined up to take over her duties.

The August 2014 edition of *Red Light Dispatch*, the monthly Apne Aap newsletter, contains an account from Shilpa, who is sixteen years old. She comes from the Perna caste – which practises intergenerational prostitution ('pimping passed down from father to son and prostitution from mother to daughter, or mother-in-law to daughter', explains Ruchira). Shilpa has been involved with Apne Aap since 2011. 'The day I received my first stipend from Apne Aap, I was overwhelmed and it made me more determine[d] to fight against exploitation against girls and women… I have to walk a long way ahead. Eventually, I hope each and every girl from my community should come out of this hell, where no women and girls will be branded as a "prostitute", which really hampers the dignity of women in society.'

Of course, not all women have managed to escape. Only one of the original Apne Aap women is still alive – 'the others have all passed away, some from AIDS-related complications, one from suicide, one from murder. But their daughters *have* turned their lives around.' Ruchira tells me proudly about the daughter of one of the original co-founders of Apne Aap who has become an animation artist – and about another who is currently studying at a university in the United States. Ruchira won't tell me which one, though, as 'she wants it to be kept a secret'. As Ruchira says, 'life has moved on'.

5

Choosing Like a Woman

What does choice mean for a woman? We are told that feminism is about acknowledging the agency and empowerment of strong women and celebrating their free, independent choices. But is it really so simple? In her essay 'Taming the Shrew? Choice Feminism and the Fear of Politics', Michaele L. Ferguson criticises a feminism that uncritically celebrates 'choice'. Such a feminism, she writes, fails to 'differentiate between those who can choose and those who cannot; analysis of how class, race, sexuality, and power affect women's choices is often missing'. For example, we are told that we cannot question an industry where women are trafficked and raped and beaten, because women have made the choice to engage in it, and we should respect that. But, as Catharine MacKinnon wrote in her 1993 paper 'Prostitution and Civil Rights', '[i]f prostitution is a free choice, why are the women with the fewest choices the ones most often found doing it?' What price freedom if it simply means the freedom to 'choose' to continue to be oppressed?

In her 1993 book *Fire with Fire*, Naomi Wolf criticised what she called 'victim feminism' for being 'judgmental of other women's sexuality and appearance'. She advocated instead 'power feminism', which acknowledges women's 'right to determine their lives'. But what does power look like when 70% of the two billion people who live in poverty around the world are women, and when women make up two-thirds of the global illiterate? They may have the right, but do they have the power to exercise it? What does choice look like for them?

No feminist denies that women have a right to choose. But some feminists refuse to pretend that right is already being exercised. To refuse to analyse the structures that force women into very particular choices for fear of seeming like we are condemning the women rather than the structures is to give up the fight in the face of wilful misunderstanding. Criticising a society in which so many women feel compelled to radically alter their bodies with surgery is not the same as criticising the women themselves. Feminism is about freedom and liberation. Is this what we really think it looks like? Don't we want more?

Humaira Bachal did. It was Humaira's mother who made sure she was educated. In defiance of her husband, who protested about their daughter being educated even to primary level, Humaira's mother smuggled her out to secondary school from their village in Pakistan. Every day, for three years, they managed to keep up the ruse – but then, just before Humaira was about to sit her ninth-grade exams, her father found out. 'He beat my mother and beat me too,' she tells me. Her brother didn't approve either, and nor did her father's family – or the community at large. Because Humaira wanted to be educated, they thought she was 'not a good girl, not a good woman, not a good child, not a good daughter', Humaira says. 'They really don't like me. They use really cheap and bad words for me.' Eventually, Humaira and her mother convinced her father at least to let her sit her exams. When she aced them, he relented, and allowed her to finish her schooling.

But this wasn't enough for Humaira. She had seen from an early age how devastating illiteracy could be. She tells me how, when she was ten, her father had taken the family on their usual summer visit to their ancestral village. 'In my village we have a strong tradition,' says Humaira. 'We don't allow women to go to school and we don't allow them to go to hospital when they are ill.' Her father's older brother is 'a community elder' and 'decision maker', Humaira tells me. 'So he took all the decisions away from the community women' – including his own daughter, twenty-six-year-old Shabana.

Shabana had a six-year-old son, with whom Humaira used to play. One evening, Humaira tells me, she came back to the house and everyone was crying. She asked her mother what had happened, and was told that Shabana's son was dead: 'this mother killed her child'. Humaira tells me, 'My younger brain could not accept that a mother is able to kill her child. How is it possible? Mothers love little kids. Mothers care for us, give us food, they give us shelter. How can a mother possibly kill her own child?' It soon transpired that Shabana had given her child expired medication – and as the news of this shamefully inadequate mother spread around the village, Humaira found out why she had done this terrible thing. 'Just a date,' Humaira says. An expiration date, that the mother had not been able to read, and which had caused her to kill her own son. Humaira tells me that her heart was broken and that she marks that day as when she 'committed in [her] heart' to find a solution to these problems. The solution she found was education. And so she set about building a school for her community, in a country where female literacy stands at about 40%, and where two-thirds of those who aren't enrolled in school are female. It was to become her life's work.

On the day I speak to Humaira, the battle she fought for female education is brought into sharp clarity by a story that is unfolding in the news: over two hundred girls have been kidnapped from their school in Chibok, Nigeria, by the extremist group Boko Haram. The fact that this story has made the headlines is itself the work of a single woman who started the #BringBackOurGirls campaign that forced the issue into the media and celebrity spotlight and, as a result, onto the agenda of world leaders. The media now overruns with speculation about what will happen to these girls – the general consensus seems to be that they will be sold into (probably sexual) slavery. Their sexual exploitation and violation is, under Boko Haram ideology, apparently preferable to their being educated. Little more than a year earlier, the world was horrified with reports that Malala Yousafzai, a fifteen-year-old girl, had been shot at point-blank range for the crime of advocating for female education. Like Humaira, she was from Pakistan – but that doesn't put Humaira off.

'Just the opposite,' she told an NPR journalist who asked her if the shooting made her scared for her safety. 'I am not worried about this any more. Now I'm not afraid. It is not just one Malala or one Humaira who has raised a voice to change this situation. There are a lot of other girls who are trying to change things. Even if they kill one hundred Humairas, they won't be able to stop us.' Her optimism seems entirely genuine; I have never known anyone who smiles as much as Humaira. When she talks about the school she built, she beams.

'It is a really long fight in my life,' Humaira tells me. She spent eight years simply explaining to people why this mattered, trying to explain to them 'why I am crazy'. Humaira laughs when she says this. They would tell her, 'it is not our culture, it is not our religion'. Humaira has little patience with this argument – and in fact spent four years at a madrasa (an Islamic educational institution) specifically so that she would have the knowledge to counter it. She did not complete the five-year degree – 'I am really a questionable student', she says laughing again, and explaining the differences of opinion she had with her teacher. The books said one thing, but the teachers said another. And of course, Humaira wouldn't let it lie. She challenged her teachers' interpretations – and eventually left. But not, she tells me, before accumulating 'solid information regarding women's rights in Islam'. Contrary to what she had been told about Islam 'restricting women's lives', Humaira discovered that Islam had a history of respecting and empowering women and of allowing them to be educated.

'We don't have a culture of sending daughters anywhere, not just to school,' Humaira tells me. 'We don't allow them to market, to hospital. They are taught it is not our tradition or culture. They are taught it is totally shameless, a shameful thing when there are females out of the home.' Armed with her new knowledge, Humaira set about trying to re-educate her community.

'Initially we just went door to door campaigning,' says Humaira. It was a slow process in a community she describes as 'strong, traditional, backward-minded', but some parents were eventually convinced, and agreed to send their daughters to Humaira's school. 'And now these girls, now they have graduated,' she says. 'Then [the other parents] saw the change. I have another thirty-three Humairas like me now in my community. This is a big achievement in my life,' she beams. 'Now I am not alone. I have so many like-minded like me, powerful, strong girls in my community. I am not the only role model.'

While Humaira may have won people over on primary education, she still has a way to go on convincing parents of the necessity of educating girls past the age of thirteen. This is a problem throughout Pakistan: while 54% of girls are enrolled in primary education, only 30% are enrolled in secondary education. And in rural areas like the one in which Humaira works, the figures are even worse: 50% and 24% respectively. But, naturally, Humaira has developed a plan to deal with this reticence. Her 'small plan' starts with the mothers. Humaira invites them to the school, and talks to them about their lives – and asks them if they want the same for their daughters. It usually transpires that they don't, but for the occasions that technique doesn't work, Humaira has a trump card: for every girl who is educated beyond the age of thirteen, two sons will be educated for free. And, Humaira assures me, jubilantly, 'It is working! It is really working!'

And it is working not least on her own family. Her mother, of course, has always been 'my big supporter... She gives me strength to fight against the restricted cultural norms and the bounded thoughts of people about education, especially girls' education,' Humaira says, explaining how her mother always taught her to believe in her ability to achieve whatever she set out to achieve. But even her father is now 'a big supporter' and, more than that, an advocate: 'he is convincing other parents to send their daughter to school'. Even those members of her family who won't speak to her are educating their girls. She tells me about one of her stepbrothers: 'He don't talk to me. Not in a good sense or a bad sense, but he is silent. He is a bit against my life, but I don't know the reason. But the good thing is, he sends his thirteen-year-old daughter into my school.' So she is getting an education anyway, I point out. 'Yes,' she says, grinning.

Ouyang Le, from Guangzhou in China, is also receiving an education, although not quite the education she wanted. Ouyang had always planned to study international relations in

Beijing. If she had been a man, she could have: her score of 614 on her entrance test was more than the 609 points required for male applicants. Unfortunately for Le, as a woman, she was required to have scored 628.

This disparity in entrance requirements is, according to a 2012 *New York Times* report, a 'growing trend' in China. Because most women tend to keep quiet about the problem for fear of 'making trouble', it is hard to know how many are affected by this illegal practice (the Education Law forbids discrimination on gender), but according to Xiong Jin, another woman affected by such a policy, the number could run into the thousands on a yearly basis. And because it is all unofficial, no one really knows how long this has been going on – but it began at least as early as 2005, in direct response to the increasing number of women getting into universities. According to Ministry of Education figures reported in the *New York Times*, in 2004, women made up 43.8% of undergraduate students, a figure that had risen to 49.6% by 2012. By 2010, women made up 50.3% of master's students – a rise of 6.2% since 2004.

By 2012, unofficial gender quotas were 'deeply entrenched', with the problem particularly acute in language courses and at military or police-affiliated universities, and with some courses, such as tunnel engineering and navigation, being closed to women altogether. A 2013 report released by an NGO called Women's Media Monitor Network found that among the 112 top universities in China, 81 practised gender discrimination, and 34 broke the Ministry of Education's rules, including new regulations from May 2013, which read, 'Except majors of military affairs, national defense and public security in some special schools, unequal female–male enrolment rates are not allowed in institutions of higher education.'

In 2012, Lu Pin, a programme manager at the Women's Media Monitor Network, and Huang Yizhi, a lawyer, filed an 'open information' request with the Ministry of Education. The *New York Times* reports the bafflingly enthusiastic reply they received: 'Comrade Lu Pin,... In view of considerations of national interest... a few colleges may appropriately adjust the enrolment ratios of men and women... Thank you for your support of the open government information work of the Education Ministry!' Lu Pin and Huang Yizhi were unimpressed by this 'very vague' response and have filed another request, asking the ministry to define 'national interest'. *China Daily* reports that the Ministry of Education 'did not respond directly'.

The disparity in entrance requirements is a clear indication of the relative worth ascribed to the sexes in China. It is not considered vital that a woman should receive a higher education or that the choices opened up by such an education should be equally available to her. Conversely, it is imperative that men receive help in the form of lower standards, to ensure they get a place. It is positive discrimination in favour of those who already benefit from positive discrimination. And this level of discrimination goes all the way down to which children are even allowed to be born.

The average global birth sex ratio is about 105 boys for every 100 girls. According to figures collated by All Girls Allowed, a Christian women's charity, by 2010, the average birth sex ratio in China was 118:100 – and in some provinces it was even higher, with six regions recording a ratio of 130:100. Two provinces had a ratio of over 140:100. By 2012, there were over 18 million more boys than girls under the age of fifteen in China, and 40 million more males than females overall. There are over 100 million 'missing girls' in the world, of which about half would have been born in China.

That this is down to China's one-child policy is indicated by the fact that the only areas in China where the birth sex ratio coincides with the global average are the two regions inhabited mainly by minority ethnic groups, which therefore have not practised the one-child policy. That the ratio is being skewed by gender-selective abortion, despite the fact that birth scans are illegal, is suggested by the finding that if a second child is male, he will arrive on average four months later than a second-born female – indicating that there is a likelihood of a female baby having been terminated previously. No woman should be forced to carry a child to term if she does not want it – but when such a high number of girls are being aborted, the relative value of women becomes clear.

And the after-effects of such a gender imbalance are not good news for women either. A 2007 discussion paper on China's one-child policy found that a 0.01% increase in the sex ratio led to a 5–6% rise in violent crime. An MIT study found that China's increased sex ratio correlated with increased bride abduction, trafficking of women, rape, and prostitution. And a CNN report linked the steep rise in the trafficking of women in China to an over-abundance of men. Although there is no research showing a direct correlation with China's uneven sex birth ratio, there is evidence that the country is becoming more sexist in its attitudes: a 2011 survey released by the All-China Women's Federation found that 61.6% of men and 54.6% of women agreed that 'the field for men is in public and the domain for women is within the household'. This compares with 53.9% and 50.2% respectively in 2000.

The Chinese government is aware of the crime issues associated with too many men – as well as of the issues posed by an ageing population. They want women to have more children. The problem is many men are not keen to marry the new breed of successful, highly educated women that China is now producing. The Chinese government's solution to this problem has been to shame these dreaded career women. Since 2007, state media outlets have been reporting on the phenomenon of *sheng nu*, or China's 'leftover women' still left on the shelf by the ancient age of twenty-seven. In a 2011 post on a government-run website, *sheng nu* are described as 'old – like yellowed pearls'. The gender pay gap has also been widening in China in recent years. In urban areas, women were paid 78% as much as men in 1990; by 2010 this had fallen to 67%. In rural areas the situation is worse, with the figures dropping from 79% to 56%. Women's leadership in business is also falling: in 2005, they made up 43% of com- panies' boards of directors; in 2011, they made up just 32%. A dramatic drop. And then, of course, there's the trend to deny them entry to university at all.

Ouyang is now at Guangdong University completing a degree in foreign studies, but she has not accepted the injustice with the meek submission expected of a well-behaved woman. In a country where public protest is strictly forbidden unless it has government approval, she has stood up to that government to demand what is rightfully hers. Along with three other women at her university, and up to twenty more across the country, she staged a public head shaving, all the while singing, 'I am as strong as you are, and I am putting all I have into chasing my dream.' Her message is clear: she will carry on fighting until she has forced an end to discrimination.

And she is not alone. In August 2013, five female students sent a letter to the Ministry of Education reporting eleven top

Chinese universities for gender discrimination against women. On the same day, eleven female lawyers 'requested an explanation from the Ministry of Education on the enrollment practices of these universities'. On 1 September 2014, '25 female college students nationwide sent a letter to 25 universities respectively, to request recruiting information, in a bid to eliminate gender discrimination in college recruiting'. In June 2014, the Ministry of Education released new regulations banning universities from recruiting students based on gender. According to the website *Women of China*, '[t]his was the first time the ministry addressed gender in its regulations'.

Fereshteh Khosroujerdy was born in Gonbad-i Gh boos, a city in the far north of Iran, into a culture in which she not only had her gender held against her, but also her blindness. The fact that she wasn't a boy was an immediate blow to her parents; her other disability took a while to be discovered. But as she continued to bump into things and fail to grasp hold of toys on her first attempt, Fereshteh was taken to a doctor, who pronounced her blind. 'My parents were very religious and they think when you get an ill or disabled child it's God's punishment, to show you are not a good person. They didn't know what they should do with me.' They feared their double disgrace would stigmatise them in their small community, where 'everybody thought like them'.

Fereshteh's childhood was 'very hard', she says. 'They hit me a lot, and all the time my mom would say, "One day I will kill you and put you in a hole and nobody will know where you are", and always I was very scared.' She had a recurrent 'bad nightmare that my mom would hold my neck and in the other hand had the knife and tried to take my eyes out and I was shouting and nobody could help me'. A routine punishment for her blindness was to be sent out of the house for the whole night. 'I remember one time there was a very big dog, or maybe it only seemed very big because I was very small, and it came to smell me.' She touched and then hugged the dog – 'and my mum hit me and said, you see you are dirty and you touch and hug the dirty, the same as yourself'. When the dog gave birth to puppies and the puppies were buried alive, Fereshteh broke down in tears and was jeered at, she tells me. The villagers said, 'Look at the dirty person crying for another dirty. We can't get rid of you but we are able to get rid of the other dirty animals.'

In spite of the cruelty of her childhood, Fereshteh was not entirely without joy. She loved the neighbourhood dogs she befriended – and she loved to sing. She doesn't know where the singing came from. It was certainly not encouraged by her parents, who beat her for it, telling her to shut up and that only prostitutes soliciting for business sang in public. Perhaps because it was all she had, perhaps because others in her community told her she had a beautiful voice – the only compliments she would hear as a child – Fereshteh did not shut up. At school in Tehran, away from her parents, she was praised for her strong voice and joined the choir. 'I remember one day, they asked me to sing on the TV.' Her parents responded to her excitement with a threat to 'bring some petrol and put it on you and make a big fire of you'. Not to be deterred, Fereshteh continued singing at school and while she was studying sociology at university.

When her course ended, she was forced to return home and marry a man who already had two wives. For marrying 'the blind woman', this man was lauded as an 'angel' – an angel who subjected her to constant physical abuse. He was always careful to leave no marks on her body, usually favouring the method of twisting parts of it, 'but one day he kicked me a lot in my leg' and she went to her father to show him the bruises. Her husband denied the abuse and claimed never to have seen the marks. Fereshteh's father told her husband he should beat her for lying. Eventually, she filed for divorce. But like everyone else, the judge believed the pious act her husband put on. 'He started swearing at me,' Fereshteh tells me, 'saying, this blind person doesn't know the difference between an angel and Satan.'

The angel didn't only abuse Fereshteh, he also used her to abuse others. Fereshteh tells me he would lure unprotected women who had escaped from abusive homes back to their house, saying, 'I am married to the blind lady, but she is educated and she is very responsible and I am sure she can help you.' He then either convinced them to sleep with him or raped them in front of Fereshteh, who was powerless to act. There was no point getting the police involved, she says, as they would only blame the women. And so, Fereshteh says, 'this crazy life' went on for eight years.

But it was during this time that Fereshteh found her means of escape. Withdrawing back into her studies, she started to research how computers could aid blind people to be independent. She emailed the Royal National Institute of the Blind about her research, and was invited over to the UK to deliver a workshop. A friend convinced her husband to allow her to travel, and Fereshteh found herself in the United Kingdom. Her first experience was having her bag stolen. It held all her papers and her passport. Her friends encouraged her to apply for asylum rather than go to the Iranian embassy, as they said if she went there, she would be sent home.

Unfortunately, in Britain, Fereshteh found herself being abused for being an asylum seeker, and a Muslim in a headscarf, as well as for being blind – while the assistance offered by the various social services was neglectful at best. Yet despite this treatment, Fereshteh knew that she would never be going back home. Having made her escape, she was determined to make it work. She rang her husband and informed him she would not be returning. He responded with a promise to track her down and kill her, while telling her parents she had run off with another man, ensuring that if she ever did return to Iran, she risked being stoned to death for her dissolute ways.

Still, Fereshteh did not give in – and slowly, she found people and organisations who would help her. She was given a guide dog, Bruce. 'I love him and I hug him because there is nobody to hit me and say that we are dirty. I love my boy,' she tells me. Fereshteh keeps Bruce's lead under the radiator, 'and every time when I want to take him out, I need to take the lead, and always when I touch the radiator I remember when my father tried to hit me with his belt. I have this past,' she says. 'Sometimes you still carry the past.'

As was now a theme in her life, she began to educate herself. Settling in London, Fereshteh started to learn English at college and became a member of the Islington talking newspaper. It was there that she met Baluji Shrivastav, the founder of the Inner Vision Orchestra, a group formed exclusively of blind musicians. These musicians were, she says, 'one of my first and one of my best friends'. Fereshteh tells me about how embarrassed she was at the first show she sang at with them, but 'if you see our shows now, I can talk to people and communicate with them'. She has toured with the orchestra across the country, making her own choices and living the life she wants to lead.

In October 2013, Fereshteh was one of 100 women from around the world selected by the BBC as inspirational role models. One of her friends called her parents to say she would be on TV; they hung up. 'They didn't want to listen.' They had always seen her disability, not her abilities, she tells me. 'I was thinking if I show my abilities definitely my parents will love me. I tried to learn everything.' But while Fereshteh's perpetual learning may not have won her parents round, it nevertheless proved her escape route from a life of abuse. Without her education she would never have escaped her 'angelic' husband, who has now finally divorced her: 'I am a free lady, which is very good really.' And through her singing she has found happiness. 'I think I did manage very well. I had a lot of problems, but I settled. I started helping other blind people and I am happy to help them. And I am happy.'

As we have seen, access to education is by no means a given for women. Almost universally, women are less likely to be literate than men and 53% of the world's out-of-school children are girls. The UN reports that poverty, gender, and place of residence 'are key factors keeping children out of school' and that 'even in the richest households, girls are more likely to be out of school than boys'. In *The Equality Illusion*, Kat Banyard quotes a Childline report that found that in South Africa a girl has a higher chance of being raped than of learning to read. And although women in developed countries are much more likely to be literate than those in developing countries, we are by no means shining beacons of gender equality when it comes to educating our girls.

In 2005, Lawrence Summers, the then president of Harvard University, made a bizarre speech about how girls are just intrinsically worse at maths than boys, and that issues such as 'socialisation and continuing discrimination' are in fact secondary to this 'variability of aptitude'. If this is the case, how then to explain that it is Anglo-Americans who show the most marked sex difference in maths performance – and Anglo-American women who respond most dramatically to having stereotype threat removed (specifically, their scores leapt from 19% to 30%, meaning they outperformed every other group in the study, including both groups of men)?

It might have something to do with the way girls are penalised when they don't conform to stereotypical gender behaviour. In *The Equality Illusion*, Kat Banyard cites a 2003 study of teachers which found that the same behaviours that led boys to be indulgently labelled as 'just mucking about' led girls to be called 'bad influences', 'spiteful', and 'scheming little madams'. Unsurprisingly, girls in general 'get progressively more silent in class and experience an associated drop in self-esteem' – and a lack of self-esteem is at the heart of the stereotype threat effect. Interestingly, a 2007 US study found that African-American girls 'tend to maintain their assertiveness and self-esteem into adolescence'. This gender-variant behaviour did not go unpunished: the girls were labelled as 'loudies, not ladies', and one after-school club, 'The Proper Ladies', 'instructed its members to spend a week not speaking in class until spoken to first'. So in the developed world we think educating our girls is important enough to send them to school – but not so important that we actually want them to contribute at an equal level to the boys.

Perhaps this can explain the UN's rather lackadaisical approach to its second Millennium Development Goal: universal primary school education. While good strides were being made (the UN reports that the number of out-of-school children dropped from 102 million to 57 million from 2000 to 2011), by 2011 progress came to 'a standstill' when, for the first time since 2002, international aid to basic education fell. Indeed, in 2014, the *Guardian* quoted a UNESCO report which found that progress in this area had in fact been slackening since 2007. The same article pointed out that when 'the former British prime minister Gordon Brown, now UN special envoy for global education, made a plea for $6bn to achieve universal primary-school education, he was met with only weak applause'.

This is a shame, because it has been well established that education is a crucial factor in women's empowerment. Women with a primary school education are less likely to contract HIV/AIDS. Women who have been educated are less likely to live in poverty, and more likely to be able to escape abusive domestic situations. They are also less likely to be forced into underage 'marriage' (the quote marks because a forced underage marriage is nothing less than child sexual abuse), with girls with no education being three times more likely to be married before the age of eighteen than those with secondary education. Educated women are more likely to have fewer children (and are therefore less likely to die in childbirth – although this is also because of marrying later and therefore having developed bodies capable of giving birth by the time they do). And the daughters of these educated women also fare better, being less likely to drop out of school and be married early themselves. In essence, education is the key to providing generations of women with the *power* to exercise their *right* to choose.

Shada Nasser, a Yemeni lawyer, argues that 'the best cure for the child bride epidemic is education'. On the issue of underage marriage in Yemen, Tavaana, 'an e-learning institute for Iranian civic activists', explains that with 'nearly 75% of Yemeni women illiterate and many too poor to go to school, families feel forced to marry their daughters to older men who many hope will raise the girls'. The result? A total of 52.1% of brides in Yemen are still children at the time of marriage, resulting in one of the highest maternal mortality rates in the world (370 per 100,000), since the bodies of young girls are simply not equipped to push out a baby.

According to the global children's charity Plan, fourteen million girls every year face early and forced marriage worldwide, with one in three girls in the developing world married by their eighteenth birthday. Some girls are married by the time they are five years old. In developing countries, childbirth is the leading cause of death among girls aged fifteen to nineteen. Girls of this age are twice as likely to die in labour as a woman over twenty, and approximately 70,000 girls die in labour every year. They are also more likely to have HIV (Kenyan research found that the HIV rate in adolescent married girls was double that of the national average) and, according to the World Health Organization, to experience domestic violence. The issues of education and early forced marriage are linked in a vicious cycle, with girls being married off because in low-income families they may be viewed as an economic burden due to their perceived lack of earning potential. As a result, girls from the poorest 20% of households globally are three times more likely than their richer sisters to be married off early and against their will – and, as we have seen, less likely to educate their own daughters.

Nujood Ali, from Yemen, was nine years old when her father married her off, for the princely sum of $750. 'When I got married, I was scared,' Nujood told CNN. 'I didn't want to leave my house. I didn't want to leave my family and siblings.' Her new husband was not meant to sleep with her before her first period (although there is no age limit on marriage, it is against Yemeni law for a marriage to be consummated before the bride reaches puberty), but, like so many other husbands, thirty-year-old Faez Ali Thamer had no intention of waiting. He insisted, and when Nujood resisted, he beat her, and then he raped her.

After two months Nujood managed to escape. Shortly afterwards she stormed into a courthouse in Sana'a, the capital of Yemen, and filed for divorce. She did not accept the judge's initial proposal that she live apart from her husband for a few years until she was old enough to cope with his tender affections. She would accept nothing but divorce – and, faced with her intransigence, this was what the judge ultimately granted her. 'I'm a simple village girl whose family had to move to the capital, and I have always obeyed the orders of my fathers and brothers,' she said. 'Since forever, I have learned to say yes to everything. Today I have decided to say no.'

And since Nujood said no, other Yemeni girls have started saying no too. In an interview with Delphine Minoui, Nujood's lawyer said that since Nujood's case she has handled 'nine more divorces of young girls married to older men who sexually abused them'. She has 'won favourable settlements for at least three'.

But saying 'no' is a dangerous business for women, particularly when that 'no' is to a man who has decided he deserves to marry you. According to a 2013 BBC report, 1,500 acid attacks are recorded globally every year, although the Acid Survivors Trust International says the figure is probably much higher, since '[m]ost victims are fearful to report [an attack] to the police for fear of reprisal'. The most common motives are rejected marriage proposals and sexual advances, and women and girls are the victims in up to 80% of cases.

In the UK, where this form of attack is relatively rare, the most famous victim is Katie Piper, a former model who in 2008 suffered an acid attack orchestrated by her jealous boyfriend. She has had 100 operations since then. In 2013, seven acid attacks were reported in Italy alone. And in Colombia between 2004 and 2014, the Institute for Legal Medicine estimates that over 900 acid attacks have been carried out. But it is in South Asia that the problem is particularly acute – in large part because of the accessibility of acid, which can be sold for as little as thirty cents a litre in any store. Indian women are perhaps the most likely victims of acid attacks, with an estimated 1,000 attacks taking place there every year.

When I speak to Laxmi Aggarwal, an acid-attack survivor from Delhi, she tells me that the vast majority of acid attacks are by men who have been turned down by a woman. These men target a woman's face, she tells me, because 'they want to destroy her life… and all her dreams'.

Laxmi's attack happened on 2 April 2005, when she was fifteen years old. A man of thirty-two, more than twice her age, had been pursuing her relentlessly, demanding that she marry him. He continually called and texted, telling her he loved her. After refusing his proposals a few times, Laxmi stopped answering. She ignored his calls, she didn't reply to his texts. But he refused to accept her decision. One day, while she was waiting for a bus, he tried to ensure that if he couldn't have her, no one would want her. He rode up on a motorbike with an accomplice who pushed her to the ground and poured acid on her face, chest, back and hands. The whole thing took less than a minute. Laxmi was left writhing on the ground as her attackers sped off through the crowded streets. She cried out as the acid melted her skin, but no one helped. Unable to see, she stumbled through the traffic trying to wave down cars that did not stop. Some nearly ran her over.

Laxmi woke up in the hospital bed that would be her home

for the next two and a half months, with her face bandaged. She told me that one of the hardest things was not being allowed to see her face the whole time she was in hospital. Her family and the doctors were trying to protect her, but Laxmi was tormented by the thought of what she looked like. And the thought of what she no longer looked like. She was tormented by not knowing.

Eventually she was allowed to go home, where she remained for three years, suffering from severe depression and unable to walk. 'Please kill me,' she begged her mother, 'and give birth to me again.' Such a life as she was now forced to live was unbearable, she said. 'Nobody should have to live like this.' If she woke and couldn't see her mother, Laxmi would crawl around the house on her knees, searching desperately for her. She had become dependent on her again – 'like a small child'.

Down a crackling Skype connection which keeps cutting in and out, Laxmi tells me that the three years she spent at home were 'very difficult'. Although her parents were supportive, there were neighbours and relatives who blamed her for the attack. After seven long reconstructive surgeries, Laxmi still cannot see properly. She can't stretch out her right arm. Her face still needs more surgeries. And she is still in pain. Her right hand and the left side of her face have suffered a lot of nerve damage, and they don't just hurt, they itch. When Laxmi eventually left the house and tried to find work, employers who sounded keen on the phone lost interest at the face-to-face interview.

Laxmi describes these three years as a time of abject misery. But despite this, her sense of justice, and her bravery and determination in seeking it, never seem to have wavered. In 2006, she filed a case against her attacker – a rare step for a survivor to take in a society where the shame of an acid attack still too often falls on the victim rather than the attacker. In the same year, she became involved in a case filed in the Supreme Court of India by Stop Acid Attacks, requesting a ban on the sale of acid. It was only a year after the attack. In 2013, having spent eight years hiding behind her veil, she became the face of the Stop Acid Attacks campaign. One day, she tells me, she simply decided that she 'didn't want to hide anymore'.

In July 2013, Laxmi went public with her story and fronted a petition calling on the Indian government to regulate the sale of acid. Within a week, just under 30,000 people signed and she and a fellow survivor delivered the petition to the Home Minister. A day later, the government announced that it would regulate the sale of acid in the open market. In her victory message on the petition website, Laxmi wrote, 'If the proposed guidelines are implemented, shopkeepers will need a valid license to sell acid, and the buyer should produce a valid identity card and address proof.'

This has been a victory, but the fight is not over yet. The moral argument may have been won, but Laxmi tells me that the guidelines have not yet been implemented or enforced. Laxmi and her fellow activists have a tactic to address this discrepancy, in the form of a campaign called 'Shoot Acid'. Activists go into shops with hidden cameras and attempt to buy acid. Their results, they hope, will force the government into translating its promising words into tangible changes that defend a woman's right to choose, and to choose to say no.

Laxmi is confident that they will win a concrete expression of this right, but she cautions that it is not just about changing the law and stopping the sale of acid. It's not just about fine words and top-down policy. It's about societal change from the ground up. It's about women and their place in the world. It's about 'trying to make a society in which people don't have acid in their heart'.

In an article on radical feminism and women-only spaces, Marina Strinkovsky, a UK writer and activist, describes a woman who says 'no' as 'uncanny'. The woman who insists that she has 'a border, a definition, a limit to [her] physical and psychic self which you are not allowed to enter', the woman who insists that she is a person, and demands that her personhood be respected by respecting her right to set boundaries, this woman, Strinkovsky writes, 'is a monster of sorts, an aberration for which we have no language. She is uncanny; she is neither a man nor fully a woman, for to be a woman is to be the opposite of all of the above. To be a woman is to be permeable, accommodating, open, inclusive. Femininity is inclusion. The aggressive hand raised in a gesture of prohibition is the antithesis of femininity, and to see someone like me, who for all other intents and purposes looks and acts like a woman, enact that transgression, is disorienting and potentially frightening. All the more fright-ening when many women, whole groups of them, communities of women, stand up and say: no more. We shall not contain. This is our space and we get to say who comes and goes here.'

If a woman who demands the right to say no, to define her own boundaries, is a 'monster', what does this mean for women's choice? What does it mean for perhaps the most fraught choice of all – the right to choose whether or not to carry a foetus to term?

These are the global facts on abortion. Nearly half of all abor-tions worldwide are unsafe – a term which the World Health Organization defines as 'a procedure for terminating a pregnancy that is performed by an individual lacking the necessary skills, or in an environment that does not conform to minimal medical standards, or both'. Of these unsafe abortions, 98% take place in the developing world. According to the Guttmacher Institute, a sexual and reproductive health charity, '[h]ighly restrictive abortion laws are not associated with lower abortion rates'. For example, in Latin America, where 'abortion is illegal under most circumstances in the majority of countries', the abortion rate is '29 per 1000 women of childbearing age'; in Western Europe, where 'abortion is generally permitted on broad grounds', the figure is 12 (a notable exception being Ireland, where recently a rape victim who had been prevented from having an abortion had a forced Caesarean). The reality is that anti-abortion laws don't save foetuses – they just kill women.

The Guttmacher Institute reports that 'estimates for 2005 indicate that 8.5 million women annually experience complications from unsafe abortion that require medical attention, and three million do not receive the care they need'. Unsafe abortion is 'a significant cause of ill-health among women in the developing world'. In the United States, legal abortion results in 0.6 deaths per 100,000 procedures. The worldwide figure for deaths from unsafe abortions is 350 times higher, at 220 per 100,000, and in sub-Saharan Africa, the rate is 800 times higher, at 460 per 100,000. Almost all abortion-related deaths occur in developing countries, with the highest number occurring in Africa. But in South Africa, after abortion laws were liberalised in 1997, the annual number of abortion-related deaths fell by 91%.

In December 2013, Spain's Cabinet approved a draft bill that would have made abortion illegal in all circumstances other than rape, or if there was a serious health risk to the mother or foetus. Polls showed that up to 80% of Spain's population opposed the move, and tens of thousands of Spaniards poured onto the streets to protest it, rallying under the social-media-driven banner of *#mibomboesmio* (my belly is mine). By September 2014 the government had given in and the justice minister, Alberto Ruiz-Gallardón, had resigned. The law was abandoned – although the government still intends to force girls under the age of seventeen to seek parental approval. But why was the bill introduced in the first place, in the face of majority opposition and the facts? Why is abortion illegal anywhere, when it is repeatedly shown that, if anything, that increases abortions, and most certainly results in a huge number of female deaths? It is hard to come to any conclusion other than an aversion to women enforcing their own bodily boundaries. To women insisting on their right to choose, and to choose to say no.

When Ana Luisa was sixteen, her no was ignored. She was raped. And because she lives in El Salvador, where abortion is banned under all circumstances, including rape, including if the foetus is deformed, including if the foetus will kill the woman, she was faced with the choice between bringing her rapist to justice and having to raise the baby he had forced upon her. 'I didn't want to have an abortion. I didn't want to be pregnant. I didn't want to be raped. I was 16 years old, and I didn't want to be alive,' she told Eleanor Klibanoff for the Pulitzer Centre on Crisis Reporting.

Ana Luisa calls herself 'lucky'. She does so in spite of the rape, in spite of the fact that she has never been able to receive help to cope with her trauma for fear of being prosecuted for her abortion, and has carried her past in silence. But she is lucky, relatively speaking. She managed to have an abortion and she has not been prosecuted for 'aggravated murder' and sentenced to prison for upwards of twenty years.

Other women have been less fortunate. Women like Glenda
Xiomara Cruz, who at the age of nineteen went to hospital
suffering from abdominal pain and heavy bleeding. There she
not only found out that she had been pregnant, but that she
had lost the baby. Four days later, reports Nina Lakhani for the
BBC, she was charged with aggravated murder on the word of
the partner who had been violently abusing her for years. He
claimed her miscarriage was intentional. She was sentenced to
ten years at a court hearing she was too sick to attend. Eighteen
year-old Cristina Quintanilla was seven months' pregnant with
her second child when she too felt intense abdominal pain. She
woke up handcuffed to a hospital bed, and was sentenced to
thirty years in jail. 'I will never understand why they did this
to me,' she told Lakhani. 'I lost four years of my life and still don't
know why I lost my baby.'

As ever in countries where abortions are illegal, abortion in
El Salvador has not decreased; it has merely become more deadly.
A report by the Centre for Reproductive Law and Policy found
that women were resorting to 'clothes hangers, metal rods, high
doses of contraceptives, fertilisers, gastritis remedies, soapy water
and caustic fluids such as battery acid' in order to deal with unwanted pregnancies. Another method, one which Ana Luisa
considered, is suicide, which has become the third most common cause of maternal mortality, Lakhani reports. In 2011, it was
also the 'most common cause of death among 10-to-19-year-
old girls, half of whom were pregnant, according to Health
Ministry figures'.

The 2011 figures do not specify the socio-economic background of these dead young women and girls, but it is likely that
most of them lived in rural areas and had received little education. That, according to the Centre for Reproductive Law and

Policy report, is the profile of the vast majority of the women who are prosecuted for miscarriages and abortions in El Salvador. These women have 'inadequate' access to both contraception and prenatal monitoring, meaning they are more likely both to get pregnant in the first place, and then to suffer from the complications that could land them in prison. These women are the ones who are killing themselves rather than bring up their rapist's baby; who resort to battery acid and metal rods; who are reported by workers at public hospitals. Those who can afford private healthcare can miscarry without fear of being reported for murder; indeed, it is estimated that thousands of abortions take place every year in private hospitals.

This mirrors the finding of a study into the 413 women who have been arrested in the United States between 1973 and 2005 because they 'miscarried or were perceived as risking harm to fertilized eggs, embryos, or foetuses'. Low-income women and women of colour, especially African-American women, were 'overrepresented'. One of these women was Regina McKnight, who in 2001 was charged with homicide and sentenced to twelve years in jail after she miscarried; her conviction was overturned in 2008, when her miscarriage was found to be the result of an infection.

There are currently seventeen women in El Salvadorian jails serving sentences for abortion or miscarriage (their lawyer says only one of them actually aborted her baby), for whom all legal avenues of reprieve have been exhausted. Their only hope now is a presidential pardon – and a campaign started by local women's groups has grown up around them called 'We are all the 17', demanding their release. Speaking on BBC Radio 4's *Woman's Hour*, Nina Lakhani didn't hold out much hope for their release: to pardon them would not be 'seen as a politically smart move', she said. One of the women has already been in prison for thirteen years.

It is for women like this that Rebecca Gomperts first set up Women on Waves, an organisation that sails around the world and transports women who live in countries where abortion is illegal to international waters in order to provide them with safe abortions. 'Abortion is about everything,' Rebecca tells me, amid interruptions from her young son who is not keen to go to bed. 'It is about huge social injustice. It is always the women that have no money and no access to information that are suffering from these laws.'

The problem, Rebecca says, is one of 'public perception'. When people think about abortion, 'they think about a teenager that didn't pay attention, that was stupid and had unprotected sex for the first time. They think about women that are totally out of control that have sex with everybody and don't care.' The other perception, she says, is, 'Oh, it is these selfish, nasty women that just think about their careers and want to go on holiday and a baby doesn't fit in.' These, Rebecca says, 'are not realities', and for this discrepancy between perception and reality, she in part blames the media. 'There is no film where a woman needing an abortion is portrayed as anything other than a victim or a stupid woman or a bitch,' she points out. Such a woman is never represented sympathetically, as an autonomous individual making a difficult, but carefully considered, decision. Rebecca's insights are borne out by a 2013 University of California study into the fictional representation of abortion over the past decade. It found that in 9% of the stories the mother dies from legal abortion – versus a real-life statistical likelihood of 0% in America; it also found that 9% of mothers had the baby, versus a real-life 1%. There is also a theme where women considering abortions are murdered or commit suicide.

The reality, Rebecca says, is that 'more than half of the women who have abortions are women that already have children. They are mothers.' The vast majority of the remaining women have used contraceptives that have failed. 'Also, late abortions, that is what people think about,' Rebecca says. 'Like a foetus that is coming out like, you know, a big doll. Well most abortions, ninety-five per cent, take place in the first trimester, the first twelve weeks, when there isn't a doll or anything that looks like a human being.' As for the idea that abortion is dangerous, that it will make you infertile or depressed, that women who have abortions feel guilty and eternally regret it, Rebecca has little time for this stereotype. 'Eighty-nine per cent of women who have an abortion are actually OK with the decision. They might be sad, they might grieve for a while, but they are fine, they are not depressed, not suicidal and not regretting their decision.'

Fighting these 'myths and preconceptions' is 'still ongoing work in every country around the world', Rebecca tells me, not least in her native Netherlands, as she discovered when she gave up a 'position where [she] could become a radiologist, which is a very well respected medical profession' and began to work at an abortion clinic. She had left her original post because it hadn't given her 'the satisfaction that [she] needed to get from doing work', but started at the abortion clinic for the rather more prosaic reason of it being 'close by and [she] was just looking for some work'. But she was shocked by the reaction to her choice.

The Netherlands has one of the lowest abortion rates in the world, mainly down to its excellent sex education, but anti-abortion groups are nevertheless very active. 'In the Netherlands, abortion still is a taboo,' Rebecca says. It is rarely discussed, and when it is mentioned, it is in a negative context. 'People still think you are really stupid when you need an abortion.' They couldn't understand why she would choose to work at the clinic.

Shortly afterwards, Rebecca was working as a ship's doctor with Greenpeace, sailing around Mexico, a country where over half of its thirty-one states have a law stating that legally protected life begins at the moment of conception. Rebecca hadn't realised that Mexico restricted abortion, but she was soon learning 'about the enormous impact illegality has on people's lives. For example, some of the girls I met there talked about their own experiences or [those of their] friends and how hard it has been with an unwanted pregnancy in a country where [abortion] is illegal.' One of the girls was bringing up her own siblings after their mother had died during an abortion that went wrong. These conversations, the contrast between the lives of women here and in the Netherlands, the 'judgemental' attitudes she had encountered while working at the abortion clinic back home, all conspired to set Rebecca thinking seriously about the issue for the first time: 'I don't think I found it,' she says, 'it found me.'

While Rebecca was discussing the ordeal of Mexican women with the captain and others on the boat, someone suggested taking a Dutch ship outside Mexican territorial waters and doing a legal abortion there, because it is Dutch law that applies on board a Dutch ship in international waters. 'I thought that this idea was actually quite fascinating. I decided that it had to be investigated, to see if it was feasible.'

At first, Rebecca's focus was on surgical abortions, and the cost was going to be 'pretty extensive'. You would need to either buy or rent a large boat, 'not huge, but big enough to be safe', and that would come with high maintenance costs. And, of course, there was the problem of performing surgery on a boat. However, Rebecca managed to get hold of arts grant funding for a pilot project, and, together with artist Joep van Lieshout, a friend from art school, she created a mobile surgical clinic. 'The mobile clinic is in a shipping container so that it can easily be put onto the ship for two weeks without having to change the whole ship into a clinic.' Rebecca was ready for her maiden voyage.

Ireland was the first destination for Women on Waves. 'Like anything you try for the first time, everything that can go wrong does go wrong,' Rebecca laughs. But, ultimately, it didn't matter because people 'don't remember those things. What they remember is that there is a ship that does abortions at high seas.' Rebecca had started a conversation, and she began to receive emails from women all around the world who needed help.

Her second trip was to Poland. 'Of course we were investigated by the police and by the judiciary in Poland and every time we sailed out into international waters we had to go back to the police station afterwards to declare what we had been doing. It was a real hassle, but we were able to help a few women,' Rebecca says.

It was in Portugal, the third country she visited, that she faced the first real opposition. Rebecca was unable to help any women at all – at least initially. Having heard of this travelling abortionist, the Portuguese government 'decided we were a threat to national security and they sent two warships to block our entry to national waters. So the ship never actually entered Portugal.' Rebecca took the Portuguese government to court; she lost the case, but later won on appeal in the European Court of Human Rights. By then, it was of course too late to help the women who had hoped to be treated. But not all was lost: 'there was such an enormous amount of press, debate, outrage, awareness, discussion within Portugal' that, Rebecca says, the fall of the government two months later was in part attributed to the scandal. 'The party that supported legalisation of abortion won overwhelmingly and abortions were legalised two years later. So I think that we contributed to that.'

Learning from their experience in Portugal, when they sailed to Morocco in 2012, they were already in Smir harbour before they announced their intentions: they didn't want to risk being denied entry again. Within two hours, they had been escorted out by the Moroccan marines. 'They sealed off the whole harbour with a cordon of police so no one could enter, no press, nobody.' It was, Rebecca says, 'much scarier' than what had happened in Portugal. Although Portugal deployed its warships against Rebecca's mobile clinic, at least they were accompanied by an official legal letter, which meant there was something tangible they could fight against. 'Being blocked by warships is an outrageous act,' she says. 'But you do have the ability to fight it within a relatively independent legal system – at least that's what you assume. But if you don't even have the possibility to fight this kind of decision, that's a totally different situation. That is really a lack of any human rights, of the right to due process or the rule of law.' And that, she says 'was what we encountered in Morocco'.

Rebecca's experience in Portugal was also what prompted her to start thinking beyond the floating clinic. 'In the end, you can only help a few women' by offering abortion at sea, Rebecca says. 'We cannot solve the problem for women in that short period. Because when we leave there are another hundred thousand women who need that service. So after Portugal, when we couldn't sail in, we started getting all these desperate phone calls from women in Portugal that needed help.' So they deployed new tactics. They got the message out in Portugal that women could buy Artotec in pharmacies that they 'could use themselves to induce abortion' – an abortion that is indistinguishable from a miscarriage. 'This totally changed the whole strategy. When we started publishing this information on our website, we got hundreds of thousands of visitors,' and so Women on Web, a 'service that makes sure that women can access medical abortions wherever they are', was born.

Rebecca has been accused of cultural imperialism for the work she has been doing. 'When we started there was an idea that we were imposing our moral values,' she says. But she points out that Women on Waves doesn't 'go somewhere and say, "Here we are!"' They only go where they are invited by local women's groups, with whom they always work very closely 'to put the issue of unsafe abortion on the political agenda', and figure out the costs and benefits, what can realistically be achieved with a campaign. 'It's not like we can just go anywhere,' she says. But in any case, Rebecca says, 'abortion is a reality wherever you are'. 'Women need abortions. It doesn't matter where they live. The only difference is whether they have access to a safe abortion.' Women on Waves doesn't force anyone to have an abortion. 'We are just offering the option to women who need it and in that sense that is actually where we differ fundamentally from anti-abortion-rights groups or from the governments that are prohibiting abortions. They're the people who want to impose their values on others.' By contrast, since 2001, across five physical campaigns, and through thousands of emails to desperate women around the world, Rebecca has been providing women with the gift of choice.

★

Abortion is a clear feminist issue. To force a woman to carry to term a foetus she does not want is a flagrant violation of her body. The principle of abortion is one that affects all women in so far as a society that rejects abortion is a society that rejects women's personhood. As one famous slogan has it, since an organ donor must consent to save a life, a woman forced to carry a foetus to term has fewer rights than a corpse. Of course, not all women will face this choice, or need an abortion. But there are other choices that affect all people on a daily basis. These choices are some of the most basic imaginable: the right to free movement, and the right to determine how she clothes her own body. And they are denied to women all over the world.

In a powerful paper called 'Foucault, Rape and the Construction of the Feminine Body', Ann J. Cahill writes about the 'invisible wall' a woman throws up around her to ensure her safety. This, Cahill writes, is represented by 'the smallness of a woman's step, the gathering of her sitting body, and the daintiness of her gestures', which she contrasts to the expansive body posture of men, most often found sitting with legs splayed apart. Anyone who has perused the Tumblr *Move The Fuck Over, Bro*, with its parade of men with their legs sprawled across seats and women with their legs tightly crossed, will recognise this juxtaposition. These gestures and postures, Cahill writes, 'mirror the larger hampering of her mobility'. The 'travelable world' for a woman is 'a small space. Entire portions of each 24-hour period are deemed unsafe, and unless accompanied by a man… these hours should be spent in the safety of one's own home. Geographical areas which may be completely accessible to men are, for women, sites of possible (even likely) harassment, molestation, or rape.' So women 'choose' to limit their own movements. Is this freedom? No one is putting a gun to our heads.

What about the body modifications we choose to perform on ourselves? Again, no one is explicitly forcing us to do these things. But when a 2012 US study found that two-thirds of eighteen-to-twenty-four-year-old women regularly go through the expensive and painful procedure of waxing their pubic hair, with a fifth removing it completely, what does choice mean? What does choice mean when in the UK in 2013, women made up 90.5% of all cosmetic-surgery patients? And when in the United States in the same year, women made up 91%? What does choice mean when how we look is considered so important in Brazil that cosmetic surgery is offered to low-income families for free – with breast enlargement being the number one procedure performed? What does choice mean when we all make the same choice?

Similarly, when it comes to dress, we are supposedly free to wear whatever we want – but if this is the case, why do we wear such similar clothes? Why are we choosing to wear shoes that are almost perfectly designed to make walking as difficult as possible? Why is what a rape victim was wearing when she was raped considered relevant to whether or not she is telling the truth? She was wearing a mini-skirt, Your Honour, she was asking for it. She looked like a 'slut', Your Honour, she wanted it really. Or, in some countries, she wasn't wearing a headscarf – so she can't have been raped.

One day in spring 2014, Masih Alinejad, an Iranian journalist, decided to post a picture of herself on her Facebook page. She was running through a London street 'full of blossoms' and 'feeling the wind through [her] hair'. She was not wearing the hijab, as she had been forced to do back home.

'Growing up in Iran,' Masih tells me, 'they tell you these things like, hijab protects your virtue and all Islamic countries have hijab. But in Turkey or Lebanon, it is not mandatory.' In Iran, she tells me, 'you learn to rebel, to push your scarf back to show a few strands of hair'. When Masih left Iran to live in exile in England, she initially wore a hat. 'It was my version of hijab,' she says, 'not quite strict, but western too. It was a sign that even though I was out of Iran, I respected its traditions and honoured my family.' She wore the hat for three years, 'but one day I had enough and stopped. Just like that. No big deal. It was my choice. I let others make their own decisions.'

The reaction to Masih's Facebook picture suggested it was a very big deal indeed. She was flooded with messages from other women, many of them back in Iran, envying her freedom to walk down the street, her hair no longer 'a hostage in the hands of the Iranian government'. Spurred on by the response, Masih posted another picture, this time of her in Iran, driving at the wheel of her car without a headscarf, accompanied by the phrase 'My Stealthy Freedom'. Masih's inbox exploded. Thousands of women started to send her pictures of themselves, walking down streets, running through fields, sheltering by mountains, all without the hijab. Messages accompanied the pictures.

'I am 68 years old. I hope you do not laugh at me and do not tell me that my time has passed. I am a human too and like to be comfortable. I want to go to hell and it is none of anyone's business. I don't want to go to heaven forcibly.'

'What I fear is living under the shadow of this compulsion forever! not their finding out that I have uncovered my hair.'

'This is Iran… The feeling of the wind blowing through every strand of hair, is a girl's biggest dream.'

'My problem is not having to wear the headscarf. My problem is not having a choice.'

It is the lack of choice that bothers Masih, too. 'I am for choice and not for mandatory actions. I am against mandatory removal of hijab or mandatory enforcement of hijab,' she tells me.

Masih was two at the time of the 1979 Iranian Revolution, and grew up in a traditional family. 'My father was a farmer and religious. Hijab was part of my life. But no one asked me if I wanted to wear the hijab. Before the revolution women in Iran could choose whether to wear the hijab or not. Some families did, others didn't. When the revolution was happening, the clerics said the hijab would *not* be mandatory, but once they gained power, they changed their minds and made it compulsory.' Women in Iran, Masih says, 'want the choice, the freedom, to choose hijab or not'. It's a matter of 'basic human rights', she tells me.

But not all Iranians agree. Since Masih posted her first picture, she has also been receiving messages of a less supportive kind. 'Hate messages, insults and threats,' Masih says, from 'men associated with the clerics, fearful of change and equality'. She has been threatened with having her head chopped off in front of her children. Her family in Iran have been threatened. The state media tried to discredit her, claiming she had taken drugs, removed her hijab, and subsequently been raped by three men in front of her son. It was 'a complete lie, to embarrass me, to make me feel scared that this might happen, but also to denigrate me and give the impression that I am a loose woman. And to suggest that this is what happens to women who take their hijab off… In effect, I was asking for it.' One prominent Iranian commentator called her 'a whore', but she was pleased that seventy Iranian journalists, 'many of whom are in Iran, signed a letter of protest against the fake news story'.

At the time of writing, Masih's My Stealthy Freedom Facebook page has over 485,000 likes. The pictures and messages it holds are of 'ordinary women', Masih says. 'These are just young girls, sometimes they are mothers and grandmothers', who share a desire to experience 'the feel of the sun and the wind on [their] hair'. Is this, one woman asks, 'a big sin?'

This was a question Nervana Mahmoud, a doctor and political blogger now living in England, found herself asking when she was a student at university in Cairo. Out of about 280 Muslim girls in her year, about twenty or so were what she calls 'elite' – that is, the 'daughter of a rich businessman, daughter of a rich professor, daughter of a politician… and nobody dared to challenge them'. But as for the rest, 'there was a massive campaign for us to conform to the Islamic dress code', Nervana says. 'I was one of four who refused that. Absolutely refused.' But no didn't seem to be an option. She had to defend her choice to 'flaunt' herself.

Nervana re-enacts the conversation for me:

'"I'm not going to cover my hair."

"Why?"

"Because I don't want to."

"Why?"

"Because I don't believe God judges us with pieces of cloth."

"But your hair is frizzy."

"Fine."

"So why do you want to show it?"

"I don't want to show it, I just don't want to cover it!"

And that was the conversation going on and on every year.'

Nervana interprets this prohibition on women's hair as 'a form of control'. Once you control women, she says, 'you control half the society. You will control the way they raise their kids and you will control the way the future generations behave. So that's why for them, covering the hair is very important. It means submission. But not to God. It means submission to their ideology.'

In Haifaa al-Mansour's debut film, its ten-year-old eponymous heroine Wadjda wants to be allowed to buy a bike and race it against her friend, Abdullah, while her mother battles with her driver in an effort to get to work on time (women are not allowed to drive in Saudi Arabia). This was the first feature-length film made by a female Saudi director, and it shone a rare spotlight on the lives of Saudi women.

In an interview with US political blog *Think Progress*, Haifaa explains that the 'relationship between drivers and women [is] very funny. It is very funny because it is a power struggle all the time. [W]omen think they are the boss since they are paying, [but] the drivers know that women cannot go anywhere without them, so they know that they are ultimately the boss.' When Haifaa first moved away from her parents' house (in itself a taboo-busting move), she was forced to employ a driver in order to get to work and drew on the absurdity of that relationship for the film. 'Every day I would wake up in the morning and try to find him like Wadjda. [I'd k]nock on the doors and be like, Where is he? Where are you? And all the time I'd go late… I bought him one day an alarm clock, like, "Alright, you don't wake up? This will." And he was happy, and we went to the place and bought him it, and I'm like, "Yeah maybe he will wake up tomorrow morning." He took the clock and sold it!'

It's a stalemate that Manal al-Sharif recognises well. In the video she made that launched her as the 'villain back in my home country, and the hero outside', Manal and her friend Mrs

Wajeha Al-Huwaider discuss the various difficulties caused by the Saudi driving ban. Manal talks about Farah, who works for CNN and has to pay two-thirds of her salary to her driver so she can get to work. 'She says, Manal, I wake up at 5 a.m. and I start at 7 a.m. He comes and picks me up and goes around and picks up other ladies. She told me, I finish work at 3 p.m. and get home at 5 p.m. If I had a car, my house wouldn't be even ten minutes from my work.' And of course, as Manal points out, not all women can afford a driver and have to depend on unreliable taxis which are like gold dust during rush hour, since every other woman who can't afford a driver is trying to get one too. 'It's humiliating,' she says. 'There's no way I'd humiliate myself by begging someone, for what? A taxi.'

Sometimes it goes beyond the problem of getting to work. Manal recounts how the first driver she had as a young woman used to sexually harass her and 'adjust the rear-view mirror to see what I was wearing'. Standing on the street trying to hail a taxi also leaves women open to street harassment. At a Women in the World event, Manal revealed that she 'almost got kidnapped... walking at 9 p.m. trying to find a taxi for a ride home, and someone followed me and I had to throw a stone at this guy to protect myself. That was very defining for me.' And yet, the cultural proscription against women driving is often justified as a way of defending women's 'virtue'. Just as Wadjda is told in Haifaa al-Mansour's film that riding a bike will threaten her virginity, so the notion of women driving has been associated with a whole range of ills, with one Saudi academic linking it to 'rape, adultery, illegitimate children, even drug abuse, prostitution', according to Manal. But, as she points out, when she drives herself 'there is nobody getting in my way and nobody harassing me because I'm in my own car with the doors locked'.

The odd thing is, driving is not actually illegal for women in Saudi Arabia. 'The Saudi government has never issued a royal decree stipulating the ban, nor even imposed a system,' Manal wrote in an article for the political Islam analysis website *Islamist Gate*. But 'on the occasions that I and many others have tried to obtain a driver's licence from the traffic department, we have been surprised, upon entering our identification numbers into the relevant system, to find an error message appearing on the screen: "The ID number entered belongs to a woman, it is not possible for a woman to obtain a driving licence".' So Manal filed the first lawsuit against the general directorate of traffic police 'for not issuing me a driver's licence'. Her case has been referred to a special committee at the Ministry of Interior. 'In other words, to the very party I wished to prosecute.' She adds, 'When you hear the words "special committee" in Saudi Arabia, you know your case has been relegated to oblivion. And this has remained my fate until today.'

Although not quite, because going via the legal system is not the only tactic Manal has up her sleeve: she also films herself driving – and encourages other women to do the same. 'It was May 2011,' she says, 'and I was complaining to a work colleague about the harassment I had to face trying to find a ride back home, although I have a car, and [an] international driver's licence. As long as I know women in Saudi Arabia have been always complaining about the ban. But it's been twenty years since anyone tried to do anything about it. A whole generation ago.' It was this colleague who first alerted her to the fact that there was no actual law banning women from driving in Saudi. 'It was just a custom.'

Armed with the knowledge that she was breaking no law by driving, Manal videoed herself driving and uploaded it to

YouTube. It went viral that same day. Unexpectedly, the authorities 'remained very quiet', which 'really creeped us out'. Manal decided to give them a shove. She deliberately drove with her brother in front of a police car. They were arrested and forced to sign a pledge that Manal would not drive again before being released – or at least, Manal's brother was forced to sign a pledge, since Manal's signature, being that of a woman, would not be worth the paper it was written on ('We are minors until the day we die,' Manal says). But that was just as well, given that Manal had no intention of complying. Upon her release she was back on the roads again in a matter of days – and was again arrested. This time she was sent to jail.

'I wasn't sure why I was sent there, because I didn't face any charges in the interrogation,' Manal says. 'But I was sure […] of my innocence. I didn't break a law.' She was so convinced she would be released that same day, she refused to remove her *abaya* (the loose garment that covers her from head to toe while she is out in public), despite the advice of her fellow prisoners to do so. Manal was kept in jail for nine days.

Undaunted, once out she continued organising for the first mass demonstration of women driving she had planned. On 17 June 2011, '[t]he streets were packed with police cars and religious police cars. But some one hundred brave Saudi women broke the ban and drove that day. None were arrested. We broke the taboo.'

Manal says that many people support her within Saudi Arabia: 3,000 signed a petition demanding her release from prison; 3,500 signed a petition asking the Shura Council to lift the ban on women driving. But, inevitably, there has also been a substantial backlash. Immediately after uploading her video, she 'started receiving threats to be killed, raped, just to stop this campaign'; a cleric demanded that she be flogged. When she gave a talk at the Oslo Freedom Forum, 'they hated that speech so much, they call it a betrayal to the Saudi country and the Saudi people, and started a hashtag called #oslotraitor on Twitter. They even [ran] a poll asking, "Will you thank Manal al-Sharif after her speech in Oslo, or do you consider her speech a betrayal?" More than 13,000 voters answered this poll. 90% said yes, she's a traitor.'

Manal rejects the traitor label. 'I'm a proud Saudi woman and I do love my country, and because I love my country, I'm doing this. Because I believe a society will not be free, if women of that society are not free.' But first Manal must convince women who 'believe in their inferiority' to question the oppressive rules by which they are forced to live, rather than fight 'those who try to question' them.

The extent to which women internalise their own oppression and repackage it as chosen freedom is something that feminists have been writing about for a long time. 'Considering the length of time that women have been dependent, is it surprising that some of them hug their chains, and fawn like the spaniel?' Mary Wollstonecraft wrote in 1792. She quoted 'a naturalist' who had observed how trained dogs at first displayed signs of unease and 'kept their ears erect; but custom has superseded nature, and a token of fear is become a beauty'.

It is as tokens of fear, of oppression, rather than as marks of respect, that Manal views the labelling of women as 'queens' or 'jewels' that must be protected. It may seem as if we honour women when we describe them in such elevated metaphorical language, but as Wollstonecraft asked, 'why are girls to be told that they resemble angels, but to sink them below women?' She asked this question in the same chapter in which she dissected the representation of 'woman' as a being that which exists purely for the pleasure of man. To exist merely as a foil to another, Wollstonecraft declared, is to deny women humanity. It is to deny them an autonomous existence. It is little more than a devious ploy to deny them their freedom. In the same vein, Manal describes women in Saudia Arabia as being like a pistachio nut. 'Like something that is protected. So even if you have a very good education, restraints are put on women. It's like saying, I know you have feet, God gave you feet, but I'm going to cut them off and put you in a wheelchair – and wherever you want to go, I will take you.'

'In my opinion', Manal says, 'freedom is a personal decision, not a political one. When the Saudi woman realises this fact, she will get in her car and drive it as many times as it takes for it to become a common sight, forcing the authorities to regulate the phenomenon rather than prosecute it. And when she learns that rights are seized rather than granted, she will recognise how to eliminate the male dominion that has been imposed on her and cast her as a minor her whole life.' If 'we keep quiet, nothing will change', Manal says, pointing out that 'usually the regimes are very comfortable unless you shake the ground under them. What you do is keep shaking the ground.'

Manal is often asked how long she thinks it will take for the situation in Saudi Arabia to change. But she points out that this is the wrong question. Change will happen, she says, 'only if women stop asking *when*, and take action to make it *now*. So it's not only about the system, it's also about us, women: to drive our own lives.'

Afterword

'"The female is female by virtue of a certain *lack* of qualities,"
said Aristotle, "we should regard the female nature as afflicted
with a natural defectiveness." And St Thomas for his part
pronounced woman to be "an imperfect man", an "incidental"
being. This is symbolised in Genesis where Eve is depicted as
made from what Bossuet called "a supernumerary bone" of
Adam.' These men were quoted in the introduction to Simone
de Beauvoir's classic feminist book, *The Second Sex*. Along with
the insights of some French Enlightenment thinkers, these views
led de Beauvoir to write that 'humanity is male', and woman is
not 'an autonomous being', but relative to man. 'She is defined
and differentiated with reference to man and not he with reference to her.'

It is unlikely that many men would confidently sign up to
such assertions today. Indeed, most men would find such a
description of womanhood to be ludicrous. And yet, as we have
seen in the stories of this book, so much about how the world
is constructed, so much about how women are limited, shows
that while we may not consciously evince these views, they are
still there, barely concealed under the surface of a supposedly
more progressive society.

They are there when Candie and Dana McKeon (and Jane
Austen) are considered incapable of producing true art, when

Latifa Nabizada and Victoria Henry don't have access to uniforms for their body – and when women die because drugs and pacemakers are designed for men. They are there when our lives are not reported in the news media. They are there when women who have fought for their freedom are told to take a step back, because they can be represented adequately by men (although the same is never assumed for men). They are there when a woman's life is worth exactly half that of a man's. They are there when women do not even have the most basic degree of autonomy over their own bodies and movement.

In a blog post called 'Decent of you to allow that I may be a real person after all', journalist Sarah Ditum uses this line, spoken in a children's book called *Marianne Dreams*, by a young boy outraged to find himself a bit-part player in a girl's dream, as a jumping-off point to explore how women are treated, both as writers and as characters in literature. Our writing, she points out, has historically been dismissed as trivial, while female characters in books by Great Male Writers (she particularly highlights Nabokov and Dickens as chief culprits) are almost laughably insipid. 'If we want to know our own selves, women will have to tell our own stories, listen to our own oracles. We must ignore the voices of the men who declaim our triviality, remembering that for those who would control us, our humanity is the most dangerous thing about us,' she says. Rather than 'working for a place in this man's world', she challenges women to 'illustrate our own dreams, write to invent new worlds altogether'. There, she writes, 'on a windy ridge at the top of a trackless slope, we will find our sisters and embrace'.

This is what the women in this book do. When Felicity Aston crosses a continent twice the size of Australia, she pours scorn on the idea that a woman is inherently frail and weak.

When women in Afghanistan risk their lives to write scorchingly personal and political poetry, they ridicule the concept of public speech being a male preserve. When women stand up in unison to decry the sexual harassment they face on a daily basis just for leaving the house, they assert their right to occupy public space and to have their own personal space respected. When Sara Seager and Polly Apio model an alternative to traditional leadership, one that is more generous and collaborative, they show that our historical concept of power has been hopelessly constrained. When Karen Ingala Smith refuses to let us forget murdered women, when Kym Worthy and Leila Alikarami refuse to allow the justice system to systemically exclude women, they are demanding that women be recognised as human beings. And when Humaira Bachal builds schools in Pakistan, when Fereshteh Khosroujerdy asserts her right to escape an abusive husband and sing, when Rebecca Gomperts fights for the most fundamental right of having women's bodily boundaries respected, they are refusing to be told what to do. They are saying women are not children. They are saying women are in full possession of all the faculties available to humanity – and they deserve the right to exercise those faculties to determine their own lives. They are showing us all what it means to do it, and to do it like a woman.

Acknowledgements

My first thanks of course go to all the amazing women who feature in this book – first for having been brave and brilliant on behalf of us all, and then for sparing time out of their busy lives to speak to me so honestly about their work, their challenges, their victories. This book would not exist without them – and the world would be a lot poorer. Special thanks to Karen Ingala Smith and Helen Lewis, who not only gave up their time to be interviewed but who were also kind enough to cast their expert eyes over parts of my first draft.

I am also hugely grateful to my wonderful (and feminist!) agent Hellie Ogden at Janklow & Nesbit. This book would never have progressed past a vague idea in my head without her, and her patience and advice as I stressed over how on earth to write a proposal were invaluable, as were her insightful comments and calm presence at the end of the phone throughout this process. She has taken amazing care of me, and I can't thank her enough. Thanks, too, to all at Janklow & Nesbit for taking a chance on an unknown quantity.

Another brilliant feminist woman is Laura Barber, my editor at Granta. Working with Laura has been an absolute joy. Bouncing off from her incisive comments and judicious editing made producing my second draft a deeply exciting experience. I'm so grateful to her for putting so much thought and effort into helping me create something I can feel proud of. I'd also like to thank all the team at Granta for making me feel so welcome – it's been wonderful working with them all.

No feminist work is ever truly original (except perhaps for Mary Wollstonecraft's *A Vindication of the Rights of Woman*, from which I quote liberally). I have all the feminists who came before me, and on whose work I have built, to thank for the ideas and insights developed in this book. I also have my feminist contemporaries to thank, with whom I have debated and from whom I have learnt so much (and am still learning).

I'd particularly like to thank the wonderful women of my online discussion group, who have not only spent many hours discussing some of the most thorny of feminist issues with me, but also held my hand and kept me going when I felt I was falling apart. They have also been there for me during what has been a difficult year, as I recovered from months of abuse, got used to having a public persona, and went through two stressful court trials. You know who you are – and I couldn't have done any of this without you, as you very well know. Particular thanks to Gia Milinovich for introducing me to the massively stress-busting art of boxing – this made all the difference in the final weeks of writing – and to Juliet Oosthuysen for being a protective mumbloc who never fails to make me laugh. Also huge thanks to Alice Ford for providing vachechats and much-needed escapes from London along the way.

I am particularly indebted to Sharon Sperling, who in the final months of my first draft helped me to transcribe several interviews – I hit my deadline in the end, but I wouldn't have been able to do it without her. I'd also like to thank Hannah Curtis and Catherine Brockhurst, who never failed to take over the reins at the Women's Room for me when I was tearing my hair out. Huge thanks also to Rebecca Reilly-Cooper, Sarah Ditum and Michelle Belden for casting their eyes over various bits and pieces all along the way.

Biggest thanks of all, however, have to go to Matthew and Poppy, for putting up with my slovenly and stressed ways as I got increasingly desperate about ever getting it finished. Poppy has sat on my lap providing moral support for pretty much the entire writing of this book, only occasionally being difficult by putting her head on my keyboard. Matthew has been the most patient, supportive and caring partner I could ever ask for. He's read pretty much every draft and provided comments and thoughts all along the way – and never wavered in assuring me I would eventually finish. If there's one person I could never have done this without, it's him.

Notes

Foreword

p.9   *not that all the people who wrote it were rapists, but that they are a member of the group who do* – http://www.theguardian.com/world/2006/ apr/12/gender.politicsphilosophyandsociety

1. Doing It Like a Woman

p.18   *And so I'd get the strength to carry on, to get up and go* – http://www.theguardian.com/lifeandstyle/2012/sep/17/i-skied-solo-across-antarctica

p.22   '*Weeping Her Way Across Antarctica*' – http://www.dailymail.co.uk/home/books/article-2387073/Weeping-Way-Antarctic-Alone-In-Antarctica-By-Felicity-Aston.html

p.34   *In a 2014 interview with the* Guardian *to mark the release of her new album* – http://www.theguardian.com/music/2014/aug/23/taylor-swift-shake-it-off

p.34   *Living art, but art that says nothing* – http://www.independent.co.uk/voices/why-beyonc-shouldnt-inspire-feminists-despite-her-vmas-performance-9689938.html?lsdjfkl

p.38   *Steel gets harder with hammering* – http://www.npr.org/2011/09/15/140147424/for-afghan-female-pilot-a-long-turbulent-journey

p.38   *You don't get your wish if you don't take the risk* – http://www.thedailybeast.com/witw/articles/2013/08/13/latifa-nabizada-afghanistan-s-first-female-pilot.html

p.38   *I wondered if it was also possible for me to fly some day* – http://www.abc.net.au/news/2013-02-12/latifa-nabizada-mama-asia-afghanistan/4489756

p.38–9   *We spoke about how the aeroplanes were made and how it feels to be a pilot* – http://www.bbc.co.uk/programmes/p017k0cj

p.39   *Eventually, a civilian doctor certified them fit* – http://www.bbc.
        co.uk/news/magazine-22943454

p.42   *Who only uniforms designed for their bodies in 2014* – http://
        usatoday30.usatoday.com/news/military/2011-04-22-women-
        soldiers-uniforms_n.htm

p.47   *The (usually) male partner earned enough for his wife to remain at
        home, doing, well, wife-work* – Susan Maushart, *Wifework*
        (Bloomsbury, 2003).

p.49   *Greenpeace released a video* – https://www.youtube.com/watch?
        v= BNwX8LYT9aQ

p.52   *"Angry Women Get to the Point"* – http://www.thetimes.co.uk/
        tto/news/uk/article3813752.ece

p.53   *'Warsi flounces out in a fit of righteous fury over Gaza'* – http://
        www.dailymail.co.uk/news/article-2716356/Foreign-Office-
        minister-BaronssWarsi-quits-protest-government-policy-Gaza.
        html

p.54   *Both in the early eighteenth century* – Oxford English Dictionary

p.54   *The* Daily Mail *issued a very sober rendering of Cook's resignation* –
        http://www.dailymail.co.uk/news/article-172253/Robin-
        Cook-resigns-Cabinet.html

p.54   *Compare this with how the same paper reported Clare Short's resig-
        nation less than two months later* – http://www.dailymail.co.uk/
        news/article-180386/Clare-Short-quits-Cabinet.html

p.56   *Shortly before flashing his penis live on air in front of a scantily dressed
        nurse (and a 1,000-strong audience)* – http://www.dailytelegraph.
        com.au/ sport/afl/will-the-afl-footy-shows-sexist-drivel-ever-
        stop-sam-newman-thinks-nothing-of-objectifying-and-
        degrading-women/story-fni5ezdn-1227017671765?nk=
        ac42aa27c6c5e11550db20c6f0c1d686

p.58   *One female football journalist working in North America told Women
        in Football* – Women in Football survey march 2014

p.59   *There may be legitimate reasons for not allowing women into an area
        where men may be naked* – http://www.dailymail.co.uk/news/
        article-1356474/Sir-Alex-Ferguson-sexism-football-row-
        Woman-physio-My-lads-wont-like-that.html

p.59   *This is an industry that welcomes a convicted rapist back into the fold
        with open arms* – http://t.co/VcHgQi9r5G

p.60   *There was not even one security guard to be seen* – http://www.
        theherald.com.au/story/443698/abuse-yelled-at-female-
        referee-at-cessnock-game/

p.60   *Summoned before a disciplinary tribunal for abusing a female referee during and after a junior boys' soccer match* – http://www.theage. com.au/victoria/soccer-official-faces-charges-of-abusing-female-referee-20140516-38fhh.html

p.62   *The media and football world erupted with outrage* – http://www. theguardian.com/sport/2007/apr/19/football.media

p.62   *Far better to leave commentating to serious journalists who complain about female lineswomen* – http://www.dailymail.co.uk/news/ article-1349729/Sky-Sports-presenters-sexist-diatribe-female-linesman-Apprentice-star-Karren-Brady.html

p.62   *Joke that a striker who missed a shot at goal should have put a skirt on* – http://www.independent.co.uk/sport/football/worldcup/ world-cup-2014-bbc-receive-172-complaints-after-mark-lawrenson-made-a-sexist-comment-during-argentina-vs-switze rland-9583926.html

p.62   *SB Nation, a sports news website, reported that they also read the following email from a listener* – http://www.sbnation.com/2013/ 4/24/4261288/sexism-female-sports-reporters-duncan-keith

p.63   *Men are novelists, women are women novelists – at least on Wikipedia they are* – http://www.independent.co.uk/news/uk/home-news/wikipedia-in-sexism-row-after-labelling-harper-lee-and-others-women-novelists-while-men-are-american-novelists-8590632.html

p.64   *The equivalent publications aimed at men, such as GQ, appear under 'Lifestyle'* – http://thesocietypages.org/socimages/2013/02/16/ male-as-the-neutral-default

p.64   *Rendering the unmarked version the de facto 'For Him'* – http:// www.amazon.co.uk/product-reviews/B004FTGJUW

p.64   *A Berlin-based blogger called Sophia Gubb wrote a post* – http:// www.sophiagubb.com/sexism-in-our-culture-male-as-default/

p.65   *Only in a society that considers the female body to be an anomaly could this rationale, reported by the* New York Times, *have been acceptable* – http://www.nytimes.com/2014/05/15/health/nih-tells-researchers-to-end-sex-bias-in-early-studies.html?_r=1

p.66   *It is in fact male bodies that are more variable* – http://www.ncbi. nlm.nih.gov/pubmed/24456941

p.67   *Heart disease is the leading cause of death for women in the United States* – http://motherboard.vice.com/read/technology-isnt-designed-to-fit-women

2. Speaking Like a Woman

p.69   *She was dead* – http://pulitzercenter.org/reporting/afghanistan-pashtun-poetry-landai-women-rights-war-exile-independence

p.69   *Her family thought she had taken a lover* – http://pulitzercenter.org/projects/afghanistan-landai-pashtu-poems-women-expression-society-war

p.70   *The word literally means 'short, poisonous snake' in Pashto* – http://pulitzercenter.org/reporting/afghanistan-pashtun-poetry-landai-women-rights-war-exile-independence

p.70   *Most women have experienced enough dominance from men – control, violence, insult, contempt – that no threat seems empty* – Andrea Dworkin, *Intercourse* (20th Anniversary edition) (Basic Books, 2011)

p.71   *In mixed groups women speak much less than the men in the group* – https://journals.cambridge.org/action/displayAbstract;jsessionid=854F1E16E7AD36D8269E

p.71   *May God destroy the Taliban and end their wars. / They've made Afghan women widows and whores* – Eliza Griswold (Trans.), *I Am the Beggar of the World: Landays from Contemporary Afghanistan* (Farrar Straus Giroux, 2014)

p.71   *That's why we started a poetry club: to encourage women to grow* – https://www.youtube.com/watch?v=dHBlshuNULY

p.72   *Female poets who, as three-quarters of the Afghan population do, live in rural areas* – Isobel Coleman, *Paradise Beneath Her Feet: How Women Are Transforming the Middle East* (Random House, 2010)

p.72   *Nadia Anjuman, a well-known poet and journalist who was murdered by her husband in 2005* – http://www.englishpen.org/the-erotic-and-revolutionary-poetry-of-afghanistan/

p.72   *In 2012, she published a book of her poetry,* Beyond Infamy – http://www.khaama.com/a-young-poet-exiled-from-her-village-9887

p.72   *They said I should be got rid of. They meant I should be killed* – http://www.bbc.co.uk/news/world-asia-24608666

p.73   *And you will give me refuge in your shivering red body* – http://www.bbc.co.uk/news/world-asia-24608666

p.73   *To a life lived as a hostage, in silence, I prefer a dignified death* – http://www.bbc.co.uk/news/world-asia-24608666

p.73   *Eliza Griswold* – http://www.nytimes.com/2012/04/29/magazine/why-afghan-women-risk-death-to-write-poetry.html?pagewanted =all&_r=0

p.74   *May God destroy your home, I was your daughter* – http://www. poetryfoundation.org/media/landays.html

p.74   *When we recite our poems, we remove our pain* – http://www.bbc. co.uk/news/world-asia-24608666

p.75   *Someday, we hope we will win* – http://www.bbc.co.uk/news/ world-asia-24608666

p.77   *Globally, it is estimated that more than 125 million women have been mutilated* – http://www.who.int/mediacentre/factsheets/fs241/ en/

p.77   *Over 90% of girls will have experienced this trauma* – http://www. who.int/reproductivehealth/topics/fgm/prevalence/en/

p.77   *In Mae's home country of Liberia, it is a practice that is carried out by ten out of Liberia's sixteen tribes* – http://www.newnarratives. org/stories/mae-azango/sande-tradition-of-genital-cutting- threatens-health-of-liberian-women/

p.77   *A 2007 Department of Health Services study* – http://www. newnarratives.org/stories/mae-azango/sande-tradition-of- genital-cutting-threatens-health-of-liberian-women/

p.78   *This same attitude was expressed in a baffled response by the UK media to 2014 research* – http://www.demos.co.uk/publications/ misogyny

p.79   *She had been forced into the Sande bush for a crime her mother committed in her village in 1976* – http://www.newnarratives.org/ stories/mae-azango/sande-tradition-of-genital-cutting- threatens-health-of-liberian-women/

p.83   *The immediate effects of FGM include tetanus, HIV, hepatitis B & C, inability to urinate and damage to nearby organs* – http:// www.nspcc.org.uk/inform/resourcesforprofessionals/minori- tyethnic/female-genital-mutilation_wda96841.html

p.84   *A man threw liquid in her face as he screamed that she was a slag and needed to learn some shame* – http://www.theguardian.com/ society/2013/may/08/female-genital-mutilation-death- intimidation

p.85   *With two suspects being formally charged and entering pleas in court* – http://www.theguardian.com/society/2014/apr/15/fgm- first-suspects-charged-court

p.85   *David Cameron, Britain's Prime Minister, announced that parents who fail to prevent their daughter from being cut will be prosecuted* – http://www. theguardian.com/society/2014/jul/22/parents- allow-female-genital-mutilation-prosecuted-cameron-law

p.86   *The privilege of education, of work, of being able to travel freely 'obliges*

me to fight ten times as hard as women who don't have that privilege,'
she says – http://www.aljazeera.com/programmes/headtohead/
2014/02/do-arab-men-hate-women-201421282224596667.
html

p.87   *'Why Do They Hate Us?'* – http://www.foreignpolicy.com/
articles/2012/04/23/why_do_they_hate_us

p.88   *'Women and girls are the vulnerable group in society,'* Mae says –
https://www.internews.org/our-stories/profiles/liberian-
journalist-mae-azango

p.88   *The 2010 report by the Global Media Monitoring Project (GMMP)* –
http://www.genderclearinghouse.org/upload/Assets/Docume
nts/pdf/gmmp_global_report_en.pdf

p.89   *Only 12% of those who spoke in the US media on abortion were
female, according to research by 4th Estate* – http://www.4thestate.
net/female-voices-in-media-infographic/

p.90   *A topic that 'occupies the least space on the news agenda when compared
to the other major topics', such as the economy or the government*
–   http://www.genderclearinghouse.org/upload/Assets/
Documents/pdf/gmmp_global_report_en.pdf

p.90   *'Epidemic' is the World Health Organization's word, not mine*
–   http://www.who.int/mediacentre/news/releases/2013/
violence_against_ women_20130620/en/

p.93   *There has been limited coverage of the way in which the government has
focused its budget cuts disproportionately on women's services* – http://
library.fes.de/pdf-files/id/10526.pdf

p.93   *On a single day in 2012, 180 women were turned away from refuges,
because there was no space* – http://www.theguardian.com/
society/2013/nov/16/domestic-violence-survivors-
abandoned-budget-cuts

p.93   *When the media notices at all, it blames the women for staying with
those abusive partners* – http://www.birminghammail.co.uk/
news/news-opinion/maureen-messent-domestic-abuse-
against-6918862

p.94   *A US study by Name It. Change It.* – http://www.
nameitchangeit.org/blog/entry/Name-It-Change-Its-New-
Research-Explained-By-Stick-Figures

p.99   *Pyotr was surprised at what Nadya described as her 'fit of absolutism'*
– Masha Gessen, *Words Will Break Cement: The Passion of Pussy
Riot*, p. 273 (Granta, 2014)

p.99   *The truth is not a political concept at all* – Gessen, p. 273

p.99   *I could have used constructions from contemporary philosophy that are better suited to describing this precisely, but I wanted to be understood* – Gessen, p. 273

p.101 *Pussy Riot's appearance [...] 'disturbed the integrity of this media image, created by the authorities over time, and exposed its falsehood'* – Gessen, p. 218

p.102 *It's not the three Pussy Riot singers* – Gessen, pp. 194–200

p.104 *We will see this yet* – Gessen, pp. 215–216

p.104 *There have always been witches who don't repent* – all quotes from the documentary *Pussy Riot: A Punk Prayer*, dir. Mike Lerner and Maxim Pozdorovkin (Roast Beef Productions, HBO Documentary Films, 2013)

p.119 *A unique and rare opportunity to promote awareness of our nation's history and acknowledge the life and work of great Britons* – http://www.bankofengland.co.uk/publications/Documents/speeches/2013/ speech652.pdf

p.119 *Even their ability to give good speeches* – Pippa Norris, Joni Lovenduski and Rosie Campbell, *Gender and Political Participation* (The Electoral Commission, 2004); Nancy Burns, Kay Lehman Schlozman and Sydney Verba, *The Private Roots of Public Action: Gender, Equality, and Political Participation*, (Harvard University Press, 2001); Eric P. Bettinger and Bridget Terry Long, 'Do Faculty Serve as Role Models? The Impact of Instructor Gender on Female Students', *American Economic Review*, vol. 95, no. 2 (May 2005), pp. 152–157; David M. Marx and Jasmin S. Roman, 'Female Role Models: Protecting Women's Math Test Performance', *Personality and Social Psychology Bulletin*, vol. 28, no. 9 (2002), pp. 1183–1193; Ioana M. Latu, Marianne Schmid Mast, Joris Lammers, Dario Bombari, 'Successful Female Leaders Empower Women's Behavior in Leadership Tasks', *Journal of Experimental Social Psychology*, vol. 49, no. 3 (May 2013), pp. 444–448

p.119 *But Mummy, spies are men* – Email to Caroline Criado-Perez from Women on Banknotes campaign supporter, 3 July 2013

p.119 *Mummy, can a woman be Prime Minister?* – Interview with Eleanor Mills, 3 February 2014

p.119 *As Cordelia Fine reports in* Delusions of Gender – Cordelia Fine, *Delusions of Gender: The Real Science behind Sex Differences* (Icon Books, 2011)

p.120 *All decisions by bodies acting in a public capacity have to pay due regard to promoting equality of opportunity* – https://www.gov.uk/government/groups/review-of-public-sector-equality-duty-steering-group

p.120   *The full diversity of British people* – http://www.bankofengland.
         co.uk/publications/Pages/news/2013/093.aspx

p.121   *Churchill had implied her work was trivial because her novels explored*
         women's lives rather than the Napoleonic Wars or the French
         Revolution – Claudia L. Johnson, *Jane Austen's Cults and Cultures*
         (University of Chicago Press, 2012)

p.122   *They were spoken by Mary Beard in an interview with the* New
         York Times – http://www.nytimes.com/2013/02/16/world/
         europe/mary-beard-classics-professor-battles-internet-attacks.
         html

p.126   *A large proportion of the injuries were in the face and neck area* –
         Margie Orford, 'Power and Print: Misrepresenting Women in
         the Media, Onslaught and Fightback', lecture, Edinburgh, 31
         July 2014

p.126   *Those girls who interrupt do so more than twice as frequently when*
         they are in a group with only girls than when they are in a mixed group
         – http://www.slate.com/blogs/lexicon_valley/2014/08/14/
         child_interruption_study_boys_learn_to_interrupt_girls_as_
         young_as_4_ years.html

3. Leading Like a Woman

p.129   *One study in Egypt has shown that up to 86% of Egyptian women*
         had been sexually harassed – http://www.peacewomen.org/
         news_article. php?id=6229&type=news

p.129   *In the words of Mona Hussein Wasef* – http://www.
         theguardian.com/world/2013/mar/31/egypt-cairo-women-
         rights-revolution

p.129   *With the police doing nothing to refrain or hold them in check* –
         https://www.opendemocracy.net/5050/mariz-tadros/women%
         E2%80%99s-human-security-rights-in-arab-world-on-
         nobodys-agenda

p.129   *One woman who filed a complaint against two police officers for rape*
         was charged with public indecency – http://www.dailystar.com.lb

p.131   *Another woman has been stoned to death in Raqqa, this time for adul-*
         tery – http://www.huffingtonpost.co.uk/2014/08/09/women-
         stoned-to-death_n_5664759.html

p.131   *At which point they will be married off to jihadist husbands* – http://
         www.independent.co.uk/news/world/middle-east/iraq-crisis-
         isis-militants-plan-to-marry-captured-yazidi-women-9674922.
         html

p.132   *Even if they captured and killed us, we'd prefer to be dead than to stay*

– http://www.bbc.co.uk/news/world-middle-east-29333327?
ocid=socialflow_twitter

p.132 *In the UK, Kurdish women chained themselves to the railings outside*
Parliament to protest – https://twitter.com/asinayic/status/
514374306999324673

p.132 *But one of our women is worth a hundred of their men* –
http://www.bbc. co.uk/news/world-middle-east-29085242

p.132 *The man tells her, 'You have to pay attention by covering up. God*
loves women who are covered,' before driving off – http://www.
huffingtonpost.co.uk/2014/09/25/islamic-state-video_n_
5880060.html

p.133 *Dalia Ziada told the* Christian Science Monitor *in October 2012*
– http://www.csmonitor.com/World/Global-News/2012/
1005/Egypts-leading-female-voice-for-change-warns-that-
revolution-is-backsliding

p.134 *Atrocities committed against women are either too human to fit the*
notion of female or too female to fit the notion of human – Catharine
MacKinnon, 'Rape, Genocide, and Women's Human Rights',
Harvard Women's Law Journal, vol. 17, no. 5 (1994), pp. 5–16

p.135 *'The only position for women' in the Student Nonviolent Coordinating*
Committee was, in the words of Stokely Carmichael, a prominent civil
rights activist, 'prone' – http://www.newyorker.com/reporting/
2013/04/15/130415fa_fact_faludi?currentPage=all

p.135 *The men in charge dismissed Firestone as a 'little girl' (one of them*
literally patted her on the head) and told her they had 'more important
issues to talk about' – http://www.newyorker.com/reporting/
2013/04/15/130415fa_fact_faludi?currentPage=all

p.135 *Marilyn Webb and Firestone's speeches were both drowned out by rape*
threats from the crowd – http://www.newyorker.com/reporting/
2013/04/15/130415fa_fact_faludi?currentPage=all

p.135 *Fuck off, left. You can examine your navel by yourself from now on.*
We're starting our own movement – http://www.newyorker.com/
reporting/2013/04/15/130415fa_fact_faludi?currentPage=all

p.136 *Surely, she reasoned* – http://www.newstatesman.com/blogs/
laurie-penny/2012/02/women-white-miller-woman-young-2

p.136 *Even in 2014, the UK sent an all-male delegation to a 2014 NATO*
summit – http://www.bbc.co.uk/news/uk-wales-29080411

p.138 *In her BBC documentary* Women of the Arab Spring – http://
www.bbc.co.uk/programmes/p0207qrw

p.140 *In September 2013, Paula Escobar Chavarría wrote that Chile was 'un*
país engañso', a deceptive country, when it came to matters of gender

– http://voces.huffingtonpost.com/paula-escobar-chavarria/chile-camila-vallejo_b_3550561.html

p.141   *By 2012, the* Economist *reported that Chile's economy was growing by 6% a year, wages were rising, and unemployment was virtually nil* – http:// www.economist.com/node/21552566

p.141   *Chile's income distribution was still the most unequal in the OECD, with the wealthiest 5% earning 257 times more than the poorest 5%* – http://www.theguardian.com/commentisfree/2013/nov/18/chile-election-young-vote-for-radical-change

p.141   *In the OECD, the average amount of spending on higher education from public funds is 70%; in Chile it is only 16%* – http://www.bbc.co.uk/news/world-latin-america-15431829

p.141   *Only in Peru were school students more divided by socio-economic background* – http://browse.oecdbookshop.org/oecd/pdfs/free/9810071e.pdf http://www.bbc.co.uk/news/world-latin-america-14487555

p.141–142 *They routinely exploit loopholes that enable them to sell services such as housing to students at inflated prices* – http://www.elmostrador.cl/pais/2011/06/17/el-lucro-la-gran-piedra-en-el-zapato-de-lavin/

p.142   *Eight universities had sidestepped the laws that prevent them from turning a profit by outsourcing services to companies under the same private ownership* – http://www.americasquarterly.org/for-profit-education-in-chile-the-debate-within-the-debate

p.142   *Enter stage right 'Comandante Camila'* – http://www.bbc.co.uk/news/world-latin-america-15431829

p.144   *'the World's Most Glamorous Revolutionary'* – http://www.nytimes.com/2012/04/08/magazine/camila-vallejo-the-worlds-most-glamorous-revolutionary.html

p.144   *'Us women still suffer all kinds of discrimination, when we look for work, in healthcare plans, in wages, even when we participate in politics,' Camila says* – http://www.argentinaindependent.com/socialissues/first-ladies-fighting-for-equality-in-latin-america/

p.144   *'I don't know how others might have responded, watching the session live,' she told Francisca Miranda for the daily newspaper* La Tercera – http://www.latercera.com/noticia/politica/2014/08/674-592672-9-camila-vallejo-he-estado-dispuesta-a-las-criticas-y-malos-ratos-porque-creo-en.shtml

p.145   *And it is because of that that I have been prepared to put up with all the criticism and all the bad times that I've had to go through, because I believe in the project* – http://www.latercera.com/noticia/

politica/2014/08/674-592672-9-camila-vallejo-he-estado-dispuesta-a-las-criticas-y-malos-ratos-porque-creo-en.shtml

p.146   *The study found that early childhood education could 'mediate and even prevent the skill gaps for children from disadvantaged families'* – Kijong Kim and Rania Antonopoulos, 'Unpaid and Paid Care: The Effects of Child Care and Elder Care on the Standard of Living', working paper 691, Levy Economics Institute of Bard College (October 2011)

p.150   *A US study from 2011 by the Geena Davis Institute* – http://seejane.org/wp-content/uploads/key-findings-gender-roles-2013.pdf

p.150   *Another Geena Davis Institute study* – http://seejane.org/wp-content/uploads/GDIGM_Gender_Stereotypes.pdf

p.150   *When women hit 33%, men think women are in the majority* – http://www.npr.org/templates/transcript/transcript.php?storyId=197390707

p.151   *A later study taking in children's films and television between September 2006 and September 2007* – http://seejane.org/wp-content/uploads/ key-findings-gender-roles-2013.pdf

p.152   *One Canadian study* – http://www.psych.uw.edu.pl/jasia/davies.pdf

p.152   *The impact of sexist adverts on female students who were 'invested in doing well in maths'* – Cordelia Fine, *Delusions of Gender: The Real Science Behind Sex Differences* (Icon Books, 2011)

p.154   *In the United States in 2013, women earned 43.1% of undergraduate degrees in maths* – but only made up 25% of the workforce – http://www.ngcproject.org/statistics

p.154   *In 1986 the percentage of maths degrees earned by women was 46.5%, so it's not simply a case of waiting for the numbers to trickle through* – http://www.aauw.org/files/2013/02/Why-So-Few-Women-in-Science-Technology-Engineering-and-Mathematics.pdf

p.154   *Sara's experience chimes with the findings of a 2008 report from the Center for Work-Life Policy* – http://documents.library.nsf.gov/edocs/HD6060-.A84-2008-PDF-Athena-factor-Reversing-the-brain-drain-in-science,-engineering,-and-technology.pdf

p.160   *Women in leadership roles were labelled 'pushy' twice as often as men* – http://www.huffingtonpost.com/2014/05/30/pushy-women-how-we-talk-about-female-leaders_n_5411131.html?utm_hp_ref= working-it

p.162   *More respectable, likable, committed, and promotion-worthy than a woman who made the exact same request* – http://www.elle.com/news/lifestyle/work-family-balance-study?src=spr_TWITTER

&spr_id=1448_82744921&linkId=9373169

p.165 *This is as true for robots as it has proven to be for predictive economic models, and for safety measures in the aviation and healthcare indus- tries – New Statesman* article from last edition of May on NHS aviation – http://www.newstatesman.com/2014/05/how- mistakes-can-save-lives

p.170 *The United Nations Food and Agriculture Organization estimates this figure at 80%* – http://www.actionaid.org/sites/files/actionaid/ the_blue_ print_for_women_farmers.pdf

p.170 *The negative impact climate change is having on agricultural yields is causing outbreaks of disease, as humans encroach on bat habitats in an effort to find alternative food sources* – https://news.vice.com/ article/climate-change-and-infected-bushmeat-threaten- women-on-frontlines-of- the-ebola-crisis

p.171 *up to 75% of those who have died are women* – http://www. foreignpolicy.com/articles/2014/08/20/why_are_so_many_wo men_dying_from_ebola

p.172 *In an interview for the BBC* – http://www.bbc.co.uk/iplayer/ episode/p01jq25v/The_Documentary_Women_Farmers_A_D ay_in_the_Life_of_Polly_Apio/

p.175 *Were judged both by themselves and independent observers to have given better speeches* – Ioana M. Latu, Marianne Schmid Mast, Joris Lammers, Dario Bombari, 'Successful Female Leaders Empower Women's Behavior in Leadership Tasks, *Journal of Experimental Social Psychology*, vol. 49, no. 3 (May 2013), pp. 444– 448

4. Advocating Like a Woman

p.177 *Only a father could* – http://www.we-change.org/english/ spip.php?article41

p.177 *The amount of money a murderer or one who has inflicted grievous bodily harm pays the victim or their family* – http://www.we- change.org/ english/spip.php?article41

p.181 *In 2012 the figure was around 7.4 million* – http://www. theguardian.com/news/datablog/2013/jun/19/refugees-unhcr- statistics-data http://www.unhcr.org.uk/news-and-views/ news-list/news-detail/article/new-unhcr-report-says-global- forced-displacement-at-18-year-high.html

p.184–185 *Of the 'unsuitable stuff', the 'ugly things' that were done to her in this forest* – http://www.theguardian.com/lifeandstyle/2008/mar/ 14/women. theatre p.187   *At the end of 2013 there were 17,180 applicants, including dependants, who had applied since April 2006, and had not received an initial decision, 21% more than at the end of 2012* – http://www. asylumineurope.org/reports/country/united-kingdom/regular-procedure

p.187   *The appeals process can drag on for years* – http://www.nolo.com/ legal-encyclopedia/timing-the-affirmative-asylum-application-process. html

p.187   *Little is known about why people are detained and no official statistics on how many asylum seekers are detained or for how long exist* – https://www.google.co.uk/url?sa=t&rct=j&q=&esrc=s& source=web&cd=6&ved=0CFQQFjAF&url=http%3A%2F%2 Fwww.campbellcollaboration.org%2Flib%2Fdownload%2 F2462%2FFilges_Asylum_ Seekers_Title.pdf&ei=LPoWVKD 2AezA7AaX84C0DQ&usg=AFQjCNH6PBilwMn- GFCBOropZJc3uex1Ow&sig2=fbtp_czBfAOrh9RD6NzWeg &bvm=bv.75097201,d.ZWU

p.188   *An investigation was carried out by Asylum Aid specifically into the quality of decisions made by the Home Office on women asylum seekers* – http://www.asylumaid.org.uk/wp-content/uploads/2013/02 /unsustainableweb.pdf

p.188   *One case worker had never heard of the term 'female circumcision'* – http://www.asylumaid.org.uk/wp-content/uploads/2013/ 02/unsustainableweb.pdf

p.188   *Another decided on the basis of 'an article'* – http://www.asylumaid. org.uk/wp-content/uploads/2013/02/unsustainableweb.pdf

p.188   *A woman who was forced into an abusive marriage at the age of fourteen* – http://www.refugeewomen.com/images/refused.pdf

p.188   *A victim of sexual assault was asked if she had tried to stop a man from raping her* – http://www.asylumaid.org.uk/wp-content/ uploads/2013/02/unsustainableweb.pdf

p.189   *An Amnesty report found that photos of scars were not being accepted as evidence of torture* – http://www2.amnesty.org.uk/sites/default /files/a_question_of_ credibility_final_0.pdf

p.189   *One woman who feared 'honour' killing if she were returned to Iraq was refused asylum* – http://www.asylumaid.org.uk/wp-content/ uploads/2013/02/unsustainableweb.pdf

p.189   *These targets are backed up with the reward of shopping vouchers* – http://www.theguardian.com/uk-news/2014/jan/14/home-office-asylum-seekers-gift-vouchers

p.189   *The toy gorilla that is put on the desk of any UKBA official who allows a claim* – http://www.refugeewomen.co.uk/images/ Pdfs/asawoman. pdf

p.189   *As one female asylum seeker explains* – http://refugeewomen. com/wp-content/uploads/2014/01/WRWDetained.pdf

p.189   *The 1951 Convention relating to the Status of Refugees* – http:// www.unhcr.org/3b66c2aa10.html

p.190   *Her body is most likely to be used as a weapon of war* – http:// www.womenundersiegeproject.org/

p.190   *A Women for Refugee Women report* – http://www.refugeewomen. co.uk/images/refused.pdf

p.191   *In 2002, Rose Najjemba was raped by soldiers in Uganda* – http:// www.refugeewomen.com/images/refused.pdf

p.191   *These women need lawyers* – http://www.refugeewomen.co.uk/ images/Pdfs/asawoman.pdf

p.191   *As happens to 96% of women on the Fast Track system the first time round* – http://www.asylumaid.org.uk/wp-content/uploads/ 2013/02/unsustainableweb.pdf

p.192   *A woman who was raped by a police officer when she was imprisoned in Ethiopia tells Women for Refugee Women* – http://www. refugeewomen.co.uk/images/refused.pdf

p.192   *Another woman, who had been imprisoned and repeatedly raped by prison guards in Uganda, said* – http://refugeewomen.com/wp-content/uploads/2014/01/WRWDetained.pdf

p.192–193 *Part of a system where a victim of trafficking was expected to provide details of prostitution at her first interview* – http://www.asylumaid. org.uk/wp-content/uploads/2013/02/unsustainableweb.pdf

p.193   *In the face of research showing that 85% of female asylum seekers have been raped or tortured* – http://refugeewomen.com/wp-content/ uploads/2014/01/WRWDetained.pdf

p.193   *A 2012 Campbell Collaboration report* – https://www.google.co.uk/ url?sa=t&rct=j&q=&esrc=s&source=web&cd=6&ved=0CFQ QFjAF&url=http%3A%2F%2Fwww.campbellcollaboration.org %2Flib%2Fdownload%2F2462%2FFilges_Asylum_Seekers_Titl e.pdf&ei=LPoWVKD2AezA7AaX84CoDQ&usg=AFQjCNH 6PBilwMn-GFCBOropZJc3uex1Ow&sig2=fbtp_czBfAOrh9 RD6NzWeg&bvm=bv.75097201,d.ZWU

p.193   *Transferred without explanation and forced to wear prison jumpsuits* – http://www.cvt.org/sites/cvt.org/files/Report_TorturedAnd Detained_Nov2013.pdf

p.196   *Fawzia Koofi, a current member of the Afghan parliament, told the*

Guardian – http://www.theguardian.com/politics/2014/feb/
09/fawzia-koofi-afghanistan-mp-turn-off-microphones

p.196   *The Afghan parliament tried to pass a law that would have banned
victims of domestic violence from testifying against their abusers –*
http://www.theguardian.com/world/2014/feb/04/afghanistan
-law-victims-violence-women

p.196   *Hamid Karzai, the president, ordered 'changes' that, at the time of
writing, were unspecified –* http://www.theguardian.com/world/
2014/feb/17/hamid-karzai-law-afghan-women

p.198   *She said in an interview with the* Telegraph – http://www.
telegraph.co.uk/news/worldnews/asia/afghanistan/10235137/
Afghanistans-pioneering-female-MP-seeks-asylum-as-progress-
for-women-unravels.html

p.198   *If she were ever killed, her husband would not be prosecuted for
it –* http://www.amnesty.org.uk/blogs/campaigns/women-
afghanistan-sushmita-banerjee-killing

p.199   *To help her would 'open the doors to too many women' –* http://www.
telegraph.co.uk/news/worldnews/asia/afghanistan/10235137/
Afghanistans-pioneering-female-MP-seeks-asylum-as-progress-
for-women-unravels.html

p.199   *A climate where the justice minister denounced them as 'brothels'*
– http://www.tolonews.com/en/afghanistan/6661-justice-
minister-apologises-for-derogatory-remarks-on-women-
shelters

p.200   *The law that criminalised rape, child marriage, baad –* http://www.
telegraph.co.uk/news/worldnews/asia/afghanistan/10235137/
Afghanistans-pioneering-female-MP-seeks-asylum-as-progress-
for-women-unravels.html

p.200   *It was declared 'un-Islamic' –* http://www.telegraph.co.uk/news/
worldnews/asia/afghanistan/10235137/Afghanistans-
pioneering-female-MP-seeks-asylum-as-progress-for-women-
unravels.html

p.200   *The routine prosecution of rape victims and other abused women for
'moral crimes' –* http://www.theguardian.com/world/2014/
mar/07/hamid-karzai-afghanistan-women-eu-mellbin

p.203   *Karen had counted 100 women killed by men –* http://
kareningalasmith.com/counting-dead-women/2014-2/

p.205   *2008 Center for Work-Life Policy report –* http://documents.library.
nsf.gov/edocs/HD6060-.A84-2008-PDF-Athena-factor-
Reversing-the-brain-drain-in-science,-engineering,-and-
technology.pdf

p.209   *Evidence of escalating abuse towards [Natalie Esack] in the six months before her death and risk factors in [Ivan Esack's] behaviour* – http://www.bbc.co.uk/news/uk-england-kent-28328423

p.209   *For 2008 the figure is 72%, and for 2007 the figure is 70%* – https://www.gov.uk/government/uploads/system/uploads/attachment_data/file/116483/hosb0212.pdf

p.210   *In England and Wales the comparable conviction rate for rape is only 6.5%* – http://www.theguardian.com/commentisfree/2011/aug/21/open-door-fair-fact-rape?CMP=email

p.210   *The much higher figure of around 63%* – http://www.cps.gov.uk/news/latest_news/vawg_report_2013/

p.210   *A Ministry of Justice report* – https://www.gov.uk/government/uploads/system/uploads/attachment_data/file/214970/sexual-offending-overview-jan-2013.pdf

p.210   *In 2013 an internal investigation found that a number of police units in London were persuading women to drop their reports of rape* – http:// www.theguardian.com/uk/2013/feb/26/police-failed-investigate-sex-attacks

p.211   *In an article for* openDemocracy – https://www.opendemocracy.net/5050/lisa-longstaff/rape-victims-prosecuted-for-false-rape-allegations

p.211   *Making rape reports less likely to be false than any other crime* – http://www.cps.gov.uk/news/articles/speech_on_the_prosecution_of_rape_and_serious_sexual_offences_by_alison_saunders_chief_crown_prosecutor_for_london/index.html

p.211   *About half of the cases involved someone who 'had undoubtedly been the victim of some kind of offence', even if not the one which had been reported* – http://www.cps.gov.uk/publications/research/perverting_course_ of_justice_march_2013.pdf

p.211   *Only one in six rape cases makes it to court* – http://www.theguardian.com/commentisfree/2013/jun/12/jill-meagher-adrian-bayley-rape-murder

p.212   *An estimated 500,000 rapes take place every year, with someone being raped every 17 seconds* – http://www.independent.co.uk/news/world/africa/crisis-in-south-africa-the-shocking-practice-of-corrective-rape-aimed-at-curing-lesbians-9033224.html

p.212   *Rape Crisis South Africa reports a conviction rate of between 4 and 7%* – http://rapecrisis.org.za/rape-in-south-africa/

p.212   *The Rape, Abuse & Incest National Network (RAINN) estimates that a victim is raped every two minutes* – https://www.rainn.org/get-information/statistics/frequency-of-sexual-assault

p.212 *Only three perpetrators will spend any time at all in jail* – https://
www.rainn.org/get-information/statistics/reporting-rates

p.218 *A rate of 2.6%* – http://www.channel4.com/news/military-
investigations-fail-rape-victims

p.218 *The US Department of Defense estimates that there are about 19,000
sexual assaults in the military every year* – http://www.npr.org/
2013/03/21/174840895/sexual-violence-victims-say-military-
justice-system-is-broken

p.218 *It estimates a figure of 26,000 for 2012* – http://www.
washingtonpost.com/lifestyle/style/lawyer-leads-charge-
against-sexual-assault-in-military/2013/09/02/839f1668-130c-
11e3-b182-1b3bb2eb474c_ story.html

p.220 *They actually did charge me with adultery. I wasn't married. He was*
– Kirby Dick, *The Invisible War* (Chain Camera Pictures, 2012)

p.220 *In an interview with America's National Public Radio* – http://www.
npr.org/2013/03/21/174840895/sexual-violence-victims-say-
military-justice-system-is-broken

p.220 *There was no way that, you know, he wouldn't be convicted* – from
The Invisible War

p.221 *'But by making that choice, my reporting of it took over my life, ruined
my career and wound up, ultimately, getting me kicked out of the army,'*
she says – http://www.npr.org/2013/03/21/174840895/sexual-
violence-victims-say-military-justice-system-is-broken

p.221 *I was administratively discharged with no benefits after nine and a half
years of service* – from *The Invisible War*

p.222 *The only thing she knows how to do to help people, she told the*
Washington Post, *'is to sue'* – http://www.washingtonpost.com/
lifestyle/style/lawyer-leads-charge-against-sexual-assault-in-
military/2013/09/02/839f1668-130c-11e3-b182-1b3bb2eb474c
_story.html

p.222 *Systemic failure to stop rape and sexual assault* – http://burke-
pllc.com/files/2011/11/First-Amended-Complaint.pdf

p.223 *A banner at the bottom of her practice website* – http://burkepllc.
com/attorneys/susan-l-burke/

p.224 *At least 75% have been physically assaulted at the hands of the pimps
and punters* – http://www.avaproject.org.uk/our-resources/
statistics/prostitution.aspx

p.224 *Putting photographs of the women in residents' letter boxes* – http://
i3.cmsfiles.com/eaves/2013/06/Capital-Exploits-June-2013.
pdf–da8819.pdf

p.227   *Crimes against women selling sex in Merseyside are now treated as hate crimes* – http://appgprostitution.files.wordpress.com/2014/04/shifting-the-burden1.pdf

p.229   *49% of them had a criminal record directly relating to prostitution* – http://www.thetimes.co.uk/tto/opinion/columnists/article3999436.ece

p.229   *Sorry, what do you mean NO, this is what I paid for* – http://www.the-invisible-men.tumblr.com/

p.229   *Glumly obvious that my visit was just a chore* – http://www.the-invisible-men.tumblr.com/

p.229   *Gave the missus a good seeing to, so not a complete loss* – http://www.the-invisible-men.tumblr.com/

p.231   *With a further 9,600 considered to be 'vulnerable'* – http://i3.cmsfiles.com/eaves/2013/06/Capital-Exploits-June-2013.pdf-da8819.pdf

p.232   *The country had 'only one quarter of the trafficking cases of next-door Denmark', which decriminalised prostitution in the same year* – http://www.thetimes.co.uk/tto/opinion/columnists/article3999436.ece

p.233   *What Teju Cole has dubbed 'The White Savior Industrial-Complex'* – http://www.theatlantic.com/international/archive/2012/03/the-white-savior-industrial-complex/254843/

p.233   *The foundation hired an employee from the marketing company McKinsey* – http://hindunet.org/hvk/articles/0909/7.html

p.244   *The August 2014 edition of* Red Light Dispatch – http://apneaap.org/wp-content/uploads/2012/11/RLD_August-2014.pdf

p.244   *She comes from the Perna caste – which practises intergenerational prostitution* – http://www.psmag.com/culture/india-perna-caste-new-delhi-prostitution-rape-womens-rights-58957/

5. Choosing Like a Woman

p.248   *And so she set about building a school for her community, in a country where female literacy stands at about 40%* – http://www.tradingeconomics.com/pakistan/literacy-rate-adult-female-percent-of-females-ages-15-and-above-wb-data.html

p.248   *Two-thirds of those who aren't enrolled in school are female* – http://www.europarl.europa.eu/RegData/bibliotheque/briefing/2013/130677/LDM_BRI(2013)130677_REV1_EN.pdf

p.249   *'Just the opposite,' she told an NPR journalist* – http://www.npr.org/2013/01/06/168565152/after-fighting-to-go-to-school-apakistani-woman-builds-her-own

p.251 *50% and 24% respectively* – http://www.europarl.europa.eu/
RegData/bibliotheque/briefing/2013/130677/LDM_BRI
(2013)130677_REV1_EN.pdf

p.252 *This disparity in entrance requirements is, according to a 2012* New
York Times *report, a 'growing trend' in China* – http://www.
nytimes.com/2012/10/08/world/asia/08iht-educledeo8.html?
pagewanted=all&_r=2&

p.252 *With some courses, such as tunnel engineering and navigation, being
closed to women altogether* – http://www.huffingtonpost.co.uk/
2013/10/17/china-female-discrimination-jobs_n_4114473.
html

p.252 *Unequal female–male enrolment rates are not allowed in institutions of
higher education* – http://ouleft.sp-mesolite.tilted.net/?p=1674

p.253 China Daily *reports that the Ministry of Education 'did not respond
directly'* – http://ouleft.sp-mesolite.tilted.net/?p=1674

p.254 *A 0.01% increase in the sex ratio led to a 5–6% rise in violent crime*
– http://d-nb.info/987548689/34

p.254 *An MIT study found that China's increased sex ratio correlated with
increased bride abduction, trafficking of women, rape, and prostitution*
– http://www.mitpressjournals.org/doi/abs/10.1162/REST_
a_00356?journalCode=rest#.VCLGCStdW6w

p.254 *A CNN report linked the steep rise in the trafficking of women in
China to an over-abundance of men* – http://edition.cnn.com/
2012/11/14/opinion/china-challenges-one-child-brooks

p.255 *Since 2007, state media outlets have been reporting on the phenomenon
of* sheng nu – http://www.bbc.co.uk/news/magazine-21320560

p.255 *The gender pay gap has also been widening* – http://www.
chinadaily.com.cn/china/2013-05/16/content_16502360.htm

p.255 *All the while singing, 'I am as strong as you are, and I am putting all
I have into chasing my dream'* – http://abcnews.go.com/blogs/
headlines/2012/10/bald-chinese-women-protest-gender-
discrimination/

p.256 *Requested an explanation from the Ministry of Education on the
enrollment practices of these universities* – http://www.
womenofchina.cn/womenofchina/html1/features/rights/16/
9109-1.htm

p.256 *In a bid to eliminate gender discrimination in college recruiting* –
http://www.womenofchina.cn/womenofchina/html1/news/
china/17/5691-1.htm

p.261   *A standstill* – http://www.un.org/millenniumgoals/pdf/Goal_2_fs.pdf

p.261–262 *In 2014, the* Guardian *quoted a UNESCO report* – http://www.theguardian.com/world/2014/sep/25/michelle-obama-challenges-world-emulate-girls-courage-education

p.262   *Women with a primary school education are less likely to contract HIV/AIDS* – https://www.dosomething.org/facts/11-facts-about-education-around-world

p.262   *The best cure for the child bride epidemic is education* – https://tavaana.org/en/content/age-10-and-divorced-nujood-ali-and-fight-against-child-brides-yemen

p.262–263 *A total of 52.1% of brides in Yemen are still children at the time of marriage* – http://womensenews.org/story/journalist-the-month/100716/minoui-reveals-saga-yemen-divorce-at-age-10?page=0,0#.U6gy1Y1dX7Q

p.263   *Girls of this age are twice as likely to die in labour as a woman over twenty* – http://www.plan-uk.org/because-i-am-a-girl/about-because-i-am-a-girl/violence-against-girls/early-and-forced-marriage#sthash.Jq4uJaIr.dpuf

p.263   *It is against Yemeni law for a marriage to be consummated before the bride reaches puberty* – http://www.theguardian.com/world/2013/mar/12/child-bride-father-cash-spend

p.264   *According to a 2013 BBC report, 1,500 acid attacks are recorded globally every year* – http://www.bbc.co.uk/news/magazine-23631395

p.265   *In 2013, seven acid attacks were reported in Italy alone* – http://www.trust.org/item/20131220133749-wcpfj/?source=spotlight

p.265   *The Institute for Legal Medicine estimates that over 900 acid attacks have been carried out* – http://fusion.net/story/5260/colombia-has-more-than-900-victims-of-acid-attacks/

p.268   *In an article on radical feminism and women-only spaces* – http://notazerosumgame.blogspot.co.uk/2014/09/radfem-panic-when-demands-for.html

p.268   *Nearly half of all abortions worldwide are unsafe* – http://www.guttmacher.org/pubs/fb_IAW.html#1

p.269   *A notable exception being Ireland, where recently a rape victim who had been prevented from having an abortion had a forced Caesarean* – http://www.newstatesman.com/politics/2014/08/violation-after-violation-why-did-ireland-force-woman-hunger-strike-bear-her

p.269   *Or if there was a serious health risk to the mother or foetus* – http://

www.telegraph.co.uk/news/worldnews/europe/spain/
10531811/Spain-approves-new-restrictive-abortion-law.html

p.269–270 *Polls showed that up to 80% of Spain's population opposed the
move* – http://www.telegraph.co.uk/women/womens-life/
10680077/Spains-astonishing-abortion-bill-do-you-even-
know-about-it.html

p.270 *I was 16 years old, and I didn't want to be alive,' she told Eleanor
Klibanoff* – http://pulitzercenter.org/reporting/south-america-
el-salvador-nicaragua-abortion-law-politics-government-illegal
-pregnancy-rape

p.271 *Four days later, reports Nina Lakhani for the BBC, she was charged
with aggravated murder* – http://www.bbc.co.uk/news/magazine-
24532694

p.272 *It is estimated that thousands of abortions take place every year
in private hospitals* – http://www.bbc.co.uk/news/magazine-
24532694

p.272 *when her miscarriage was found to be the result of an infection* –
http://jhppl.dukejournals.org/content/38/2/299.full.pdf+html
?sid=b0811f36-d4e4-4b51-a830-e175e6eee40c%20%20For%20
those%20cases%20that%20are%20not%20mentioned%20in%20t
he%20article%20-what%20do%20you%20need?

p.274 *There is also a theme where women considering abortions are murdered
or commit suicide* – http://www.ansirh.org/_documents/research
/abortion-onscreen/abortion-onscreen-infographic.html

p.275 *Over half of its thirty-one states have a law stating that legally protected
life begins at the moment of conception* – http://www.thenation.
com/article/165436/mexicos-anti-abortion-backlash?page=0,0

p.280 *A 2012 US study found that two-thirds of eighteen-to-twenty-four-
year-old women regularly go through the expensive and painful
procedure of waxing their pubic hair* – http://www.independent.
co.uk/life-style/fashion/features/the-politics-of-pubic-hair-
why-is-a-generation-choosing-to-go-bare-down-there-
8539673.html

p.280 *In the UK in 2013, women made up 90.5% of all cosmetic-surgery
patients* – http://www.theguardian.com/news/datablog/2014/
feb/03/uk-plastic-surgery-2013-most-popular

p.280 *In the United States in the same year, women made up 91%* – http://
www.surgery.org/sites/default/files/Stats2013_4.pdf

p.280 *She wasn't wearing a headscarf – so she can't have been raped* –
http://www.womenundersiegeproject.org/blog/entry/the-
myth-of-how-the-hijab-protects-women-against-sexual-assault

p.280   *Full of blossoms* – http://www.bbc.co.uk/programmes/poi zn978

p.281   *A hostage in the hands of the Iranian government* – https://soundcloud.com/frl-journalist/masih-alinejad-on-bbc-my-hair-was-like-a-hostage-to-the-government

p.281   *I don't want to go to heaven forcibly* – https://www.facebook.com/StealthyFreedom

p.284   *In an interview with US political blog* Think Progress – http://thinkprogress.org/alyssa/2013/09/20/2658481/wadjda-haifaa-mansour/

p.284   *In the video she made that launched her as the 'villain back in my home country, and the hero outside'* – http://www.independent.co.uk/news/people/profiles/manal-alsharif-they-just-messed-with-the-wrong-woman-7778800.html

p.285   *At a Women in the World event* – http://www.huffingtonpost.com/2014/03/15/manal-al-sharif-tina-brown_n_4967493.html

p.286   *Manal wrote in an article for the political Islam analysis website* Islamist Gate – http://www.islamistgate.com/566#.UoUkl7bE inA.twitter%5D

Index